CRUEL SCHOOL

The 40-year history of golf's European Tour Q School

Ross Biddiscombe

First published in Great Britain in December 2015 by Constant Sports Publishing, a division of Constant Publishing of London, England.

© Ross Biddiscombe

For further details of the author and his books, go to www.golfontheedge.co.uk or www.rydercuprevealed.com

eBook ISBN 978-0-9562850-3-4

Paperback ISBN 978-0-9562850-4-1

Typesetting & copy design: Dolman Scott.
Cover background photo: Richard Kendal.
Cover design: Bill Hazlegrove at Hazlegrove Agency, Roanoke, Virginia, USA.
eBook publishing partner: Dolman Scott of Thatcham, West Berkshire, England.

Constant Publishing
is an imprint of
Dolman Scott Ltd
www.dolmanscott.com

What the golfing press says about Ross Biddiscombe's Q School books:

"**Recommended**" - *The Guardian*

"**Superb…heartily recommended…5 stars**" - *Golf Monthly*

"**A superb book…Ross paints an absorbing picture**" - *Sky Sports*

"**A fascinating insight…refreshing**" - *Today's Golfer*

"**The unique nature of Q School is well captured**" - *BBC Sport*

"**Does for Q School what** *Four Iron In The Soul* **did for caddies…a must**" - *Golf Punk*

"**Kept me enthralled**" - *Golfmagic.com*

"**Fascinating**" - *National Club Golfer*

"**Incisive…I found it difficult to put down**" - *Tee Times*

"**A unique insight**" - *Golfing Magazine*

"**If you only buy one golf book this year, make sure it's this one…a riveting read. An enthralling read**" - *Fairway To Green*

"**Ross's writing is eloquent, and his research effort very thorough**" - *The Golf Space*

"**Compulsive reading**" - *Liverpool Daily Post*

Also available by Ross Biddiscombe in print & eBook formats:

Ryder Cup Revealed: Tales of the Unexpected
(Constant Sports, ISBN 978-0-9562850-1-0 & 978-0-9562850-2-7)

Contents

Introduction

Starting in late 2005, the European Tour Qualifying School took over my life. I was searching for a topic appropriate for my first golf book and I remembered reading a fascinating feature about the Q School in a long-forgotten issue of *The Observer* sports magazine. However, I could neither find the issue nor much of anything else about this end-of-season tournament where the fringe players from the Tour meet up with the new young pretenders. I remembered that they all fight for a few invitations at the end of each season to the following year's European Tour where reputations are earned and much money is harvested.

With only curiosity to guide me, I attended a First Stage Q School event at The Oxfordshire Golf Club the following September. There I found no pressroom or even a single other journalist, just a tournament director in charge of a handful of volunteers and virtually no spectators. And yet, here was a tournament overflowing with human drama: almost every one of the 50 or more players had an emotionally-charged story to tell. There was the Australian player who had borrowed thousands of Aussie dollars from his in-laws to make the 13,000-mile trip; the nephew of Seve Ballesteros trying to emulate his famous uncle; a bunch of cocky twentysomethings who saw only glory and none of the inevitable sadness of failure; the fortysomethings giving themselves one last chance to "do a Tom Lehman" and become a golfing great in later life; those returning from injury or illness or just a long period of re-engineering their swings "à la Faldo". I was hooked, particularly (although, perhaps, rather ghoulishly) by the tailspin disasters suffered by so many players who had little more than blind hope of ever reaching the top of the sport. At times, Q School seemed much like watching a car crash – you couldn't take your eyes off it.

So, over the next 10 years, I wrote news reports, features, columns, blogs, tweets and books all about this torture chamber of a sporting event that had seen the likes of Westwood, Clarke, Olazabal, Lyle, Montgomerie, Woosnam, Goosen, Harrington, Poulter, Rose, Jimenez and many more pass through.

This book is my third that captures the raw human emotion running through this tournament. Material from my two previous books on the subject – *Golf On The Edge: Triumphs & Tragedies of Q School* and *Q School Complete* – forms the basis of this volume, but previous stories have been revisioned and plenty of new information and interviews have been added to make the misery and the magic even more compelling.

In truth, the power of the book rests in the poignant words spoken by the indomitable players who visit the School each year, sometimes it seems to me, in direct contradiction to their well-being.

These golfers became friends, men who I cared about and hoped would succeed. They allowed me to question them in-depth about their feelings and emotions as much as their golf. It is an odd juxtaposition for a man to be rated in the top 500 golfers in the entire world (remember, that means he's ahead of many millions of others) and yet feel that he is nowhere near good enough because he exists on the fringes of the sport, among the regulars at Q School. Visiting the School regularly often brings that situation to a head: you may have been a golf champion at some early stage of your career, but taking the final step onto the most prestigious stage is beyond you.

However, there are also few more heart-warming stories than a successful journey through Q School. It is a glorious accomplishment that can change someone's life, both personally and professionally.

But basically, Q School is about struggle: men trying to avoid failure and put food on the family table; it's their battle for self esteem, the search for enough courage to keep believing when the odds are stacked against them. Sports psychologists can make a lot of money out of Q School.

It is the words of the players themselves that speak most powerfully. One of the most memorable conversations I had was with Sandy Lyle, a Masters and Open champion who reached the absolute heights of the sport, but who began like so many others as a humble Q Schooler with just a bag full of potential.

I spoke to Sandy at The Belfry in 2007 and, although he may not always be the most eloquent of interviewees, the subject of the Q School made him very animated. His memories of his one-and-only visit were clear, even after almost 30 years, and his quote summed up the pain that so many players felt both back then and still today.

"Q School is gut-wrenching. It's not a nice week and once you're through it, you want to make sure it's the last time you see it. If you get into your mind what (Q School) means then you'd never make a backswing," he said and, with that, I understood.

After reading this book, I hope you understand too.

Ross Biddiscombe
November 2015

How It All Began

The European Tour Q School grew out of a time when professional tournament golfers were different to those we know today. It came about because of developments in the early 60s in America where, the modern-day great triumvirate of Arnold Palmer, Jack Nicklaus and Gary Player was bringing crowds to golf tournaments like never before. Even more crucially, there was a growing television audience and many pros in America were earning good money via a flourishing national golf tour.

Then in 1968, the few hundred regular American tournament pros decided it was time to distinguish themselves from the club professionals. The tournament pros began organising their own golf tour, known as the PGA Tour, that for the first time operated separately from the PGA of America, the organisation originally set up in 1916 to look after every pro golfer, especially the tens of thousands of club pros from all 50 states of the Union. However, the two different types of golf pro had grown apart and tournament golfers in America created their own structure in which to thrive. That structure included a season-long money list to rank the top pros and also an end-of-season tournament to position the fringe players and those wishing to join the tour the following year.

Not surprisingly, British golfers saw what was happening and wanted the same. Since their own professional golfers association was formed in 1901, traditional club pros had been happy with life in their shop, giving lessons, selling gear and playing in pro-ams. But by the late 1960s, there was a band of highly competitive pros who had dreams of earning a living playing tournaments not from a golf club shop and retainer.

The problem was that event prize money for the best British and European pro golfers was scarce at this time and forced almost every player to live both lives, that of the club pro *and* the tournament pro. Men like Neil

Coles, Peter Alliss, Bernard Hunt, Dave Thomas, Christy O'Connor Snr and a young Tony Jacklin all took club jobs at least at the start of their careers because there was not a living wage in prize money alone.

There were simply too few top quality tournaments in Britain and Europe and they were scattered randomly throughout the spring and summer. Few Europeans played in UK-based tournaments and the reverse was true about British golfers playing on continental Europe even though events like the French Open (first played in 1906) and the Italian Open (which dates back to 1925) had marvelous heritages.

In addition, each event in every country was organised individually by different people usually with the host club secretary or club pro as tournament director and that meant almost no consistency or co-ordination. British and European golfers needed a strong, single, international calendar of events if they were to match the Americans and also take advantage of golf's growing popularity with TV and sponsors.

The same split between the two types of golf pros that had happened in America started on the other side of the Atlantic in October 1971 when the highly respected John Jacobs was made Tournament Director General of a new division of the PGA that was to look after the tournament pros alone.

Jacobs got started in time to plan the 1972 season and added some continental European events for the first season of the Tournament Players Division (now the European Tour). By 1975, he had reorganised the Order of Merit structure that ranked players on the tour, basing it on prize money instead of a previously-used points system and, a year later, there were more much-needed improvements: Sunday finishes were introduced in selected tournaments to help develop more TV coverage and increase attendances at the events; and pre-tournament pro-ams were played to involve and encourage big-name sponsors. But there was another change that needed to happen, just like it had in America.

The system for entering tournaments had been one of the main gripes for newly-minted tournament pros in the 60s and 70s. The process had become unwieldy, impractical and expensive for the players who were becoming bored (and even bankrupt) by what was known as Monday Qualifying.

A typical tour week consisted of: Monday – qualifying; Tuesday – practice day; Wednesday – start of the tournament; Thursday – hope you make the cut; Friday – either leave the tournament because you missed the cut or play round three and get yourself into a money-making position; and Saturday – play round four, receive a cheque and travel home. Then Sunday was either a rest day or a day to travel to the next event. It was a punishing schedule in the days before the full development of fast motorway routes and multiple cheap flight options to destinations far away.

Also, the system for pros to enter into tournaments was completely different than it is today: the top 60 players from the previous season's money list were the core of the Tour and they qualified to play in every event on Tour (today, that core number of pros qualifying on the basis of the previous season's money list is 110).

After the top 60, then the next players on the qualified list were those who made the cut the previous week; this category rewarded players on form and also meant that when they finished the tournament on Saturday, they were not faced with the prospect of trying to qualify for the next event on the following Monday, two days later.

The next qualifiers would be a number of local pros performing well on the regional order of merit (tournament directors thought these players would attract more spectators from the area). For continental European tournaments this local number of qualifiers would often be larger than for UK-based tournaments (it was a way that the tour organisers could help the development players from across Europe). Finally, there would be some sponsor's invites and, once all those players had been allocated spots in the tournament, then the number of places left for Monday qualifiers could be calculated. It was often less than a dozen.

Of course, the more successful the tour became in attracting prize money, so the number of Monday qualifiers would increase. It could mean a player traveling to an event in time to play 18 or 36 holes of qualifying golf on Monday for perhaps only a handful of starting spots and, if he failed, then he went home without any income. He would try again at the next Monday Qualifying in seven days time, but even if he got one of the tournament starting spots, then he still had to make the two-round cut in order to earn any money to live on. This system had become increasingly clunky and too expensive (in both time and money) for many pros wishing to break through. You would have to be a masochist to continue that life for more than a year or two, so something had to be done – that something was Qualifying School, introduced at the end of the 1976 season.

The plan was for Q School (sometimes also known as Tour School) to help create a fully-exempt tour, a formula by which pros were ranked in a sophisticated ladder at the start of each season using categories that rewarded success. Rather than try to turn the pro's world upside down in one fell swoop, the first Q School was staged with something more simple in mind: to create a membership. The tour wanted to control the numbers of players entering tournaments and develop levels or rankings; it wanted a system that was aspirational. The idea of the first Q School was that only if you were successful, could you become a member of the Tour. Without Tour membership, a player did not have access to the growing number of tournaments and the increasing prize money. To be on the European Tour, therefore, was to be at the top level of professional tournament golf.

"We could see ourselves being swamped by entries into Monday Qualifying by pros who just weren't good enough, but fancied turning up. That was not ideal, so we wanted a system where only players with Tour membership could enter the pre-qualifying," says John Paramor, now the Tour's chief referee, but then a key member of the tournament staging staff.

The practical benefit of the Q School's pecking order system for entry is that it allows players both at the top and bottom of the pro golf ladder to know what events are available to them before the start of their tournament year; it allows them to plan their playing calendar; and it also gives them higher level tournaments to aspire to where the bigger prize money exist.

In 1976, the inaugural Q School event would be organised by senior tournament administrator Tony Gray along with Paramor. It was decided that the top 120 players and ties would become members of the Tour. This membership would allow entry to the Monday Qualifying tournament at all the events; it did not give players a single guaranteed start in any event, but it did separate them from the rest of the tournament pros and it did give them a unique opportunity to make money on what would be an increasingly lucrative Tour

Tournament entry for the season after the first Q School (1977) was as follows: the top 60 from the 1976 Order of Merit were allowed into each tournament; those who finished 61st to 120th were allowed into every Monday Qualifying event; the Q School Tour Card winners (better known then as 'membership' winners) were also allowed into every Monday qualifying event; and, finally, any player not in the top 60 Order of Merit category but who made the cut in the previous week's event automatically teed it up at the following week's tournament. In addition, each tournament could include local golfers from their region or country (eg the top 10 of a regional or national Order of Merit) and there were also players invited by the sponsor. This is how the make-up of a normal 156-man event would be constructed.

The bad news for those players who failed at Q School was that there were no changes during a season, no way to alter your category. So, if you missed out at the School in November one year, then you simply had no way onto the Tour for another 12 months; your tournament playing career was on hold. This was not quite the all-exempt tour that the administrators wanted, but it was a major step towards it.

The bulk of the European golfers were not yet putting pressure on the Tour chiefs to make changes to the rules of entry; many were still happy with the status quo. The traditional golf pro's life still functioned for even the younger pros of that era. For example, Ryder Cup captain-to-be Sam Torrance loved tournament prize money, yet still needed his wage as an assistant pro at

Sunningdale in Surrey and Howard Clark did the same at Moor Allerton in Yorkshire. Two income streams meant less risk. Certainly, the idea of giving up a pro's club job and simply relying on the Tour (a winner's cheque might be £5,000, but a finish outside the top 20 paid only a couple of hundred pounds) was a bit of a long shot. However, the die had been cast and there was no going back.

And so the European Tour Q School had been born. It was not fancy and there was almost no media coverage, but its invention was significant. As the popularity of European pro tournament golf increased, the Q School helped keep the sport under control: it sifted out the unwanted and the untalented, plus it began to build a history of stories that would add a whole new meaning to the torture or the triumph of being a golfer.

Q School Explained

To understand Q School, think of golf as a meritocracy. Just as a football teams move between leagues with end-of-season promotion and relegation, so professional tournament golfers need a system of rankings each season to ensure the best players will play in the best tournaments and lower-rated pros will take part in their own lower-rated events. You improve and you move up the professional ladder (promotion), you lose form and you tumble down (relegation). A Q School is part of the method that fixes the status of players on the professional ladder.

Pro golfers will usually begin their pro careers at regional PGA events or on the mini tours (such as the EuroPro Tour in England) where a high end-of-season finish will mean promotion to a more prestigious tour. Players can progress via this season-long method to the Challenge Tour and, by the same means, to the European Tour.

However, the European Tour Q School provides another, quicker, more dramatic way to the very top. There is no need for 12 months of slog on a tour, just turn up, play well enough and you receive a Tour Card, an invitation to some of the world's richest events.

No modern-day players, however, "just turn up". Generally, Q School entrants fit into three age-range groups: youngsters in their 20s and on the way up in the game; thirtysomethings who have been bouncing around the edges of the top level for a while; and veterans in their 40s trying to recapture a glorious past.

Players come from all over the world to what is now the oldest and most prestigious School since the PGA Tour version in America began sending its Q School entrants to the second-level Web.com Tour in 2013.

The European Tour version consists of 13 separate events in three different stages. The current cost of entry is €1,800 and, for those forced to start at the very beginning, it means 14 rounds of golf, while more senior players may only face the final six rounds.

Over 700 players start at one of the eight, 72-hole First Stage events that take place in September all around Europe. First Stage players will generally be either regular mini tour golfers, high ranking amateurs looking to turn pro or other fringe players who might be returning from an injury or a substantial loss of form.

About 25% of First Stagers (approximately 175 golfers) will progress to Second Stage which consists of four more 72-hole tournaments played in early November. About 300 players take part: the First Stage survivors, plus about 100 more accomplished players who have exemptions allowing them to go straight to Second Stage. Exemptions are handed out for various reasons, from being a previous Q School winner to achieving a high ranking on one of the smaller tours including the Challenge, Asian, EuroPro or ALPs Tours.

From Second Stage, there are approximately 80 who progress (about 20 from each tournament) who make up half the field at Final Stage that takes place towards the middle of November at PGA Catalunya near Girona.

The other half of the 156-man field are mostly players who have come to the end of a disappointing season, including those who will have finished just outside the top 110 in the recently-finished European Tour Race To Dubai. There are also other exempt players including former European Tour champions who have fallen down the rankings, very high-finishing Challenge Tour golfers, leaders of various mini tours and long-time pros still high in the career money list.

The field at Final Stage plays an opening 72 holes before there is a cut for the top 70 and ties. The survivors will then play a further 36 holes, after which the top 25 players and ties will be given Category 15 on the European Tour for the following season – aka a Tour Card. Any player making the 72-hole cut but failing to finish in the top 25 is compensated with an invitation to join the Challenge Tour for the following year.

The Tour Card provides the successful Q Schoolers with at least 20 starts. Some top events like the majors and World Golf Championship tournaments are still out of reach, but players have a reasonable chance of earning enough money to finish in the top 110 in the Race To Dubai and automatically retain their Card 12 months later. However, the competition is so intense that usually only a handful Q School graduates actually manage this feat. The vast majority return to the School the following year.

PART ONE

Seven Golfers On The Edge

"Golf is like a grindstone: whether it grinds you down or polishes you up, depends on what you are made of "– Anon.

When professional golfers talk about Q School, the most common word they use is "struggle". While pros may love their sport, a tournament like Q School threatens that feeling. There is so much anxiety involved that the joy of golf is often lost; this is one of the toughest events in the sporting calendar and you survive it rather than enjoy it.

Of course, a chosen few simply blast through the School without a problem, but it is the journeymen pros who make up the vast majority of every Q School entry list. They represent the heart and soul of the tournament. There are many who spend years trying to eke out a living on the fringes of golf's elite level; they battle normal life-issues – mortgages to pay; wives and children to care for; their own egos to combat – and many of them never achieve a regular place on the European Tour.

For these regular visitors to Q School, the event can become a magnificent obsession, an immensely dark place if failure is the norm.

The seven players featured here all dream of a permanent place at the pinnacle of professional golf, yet they have suffered at the School many times. Their journeys are physically, mentally and financially tough with a potential prize so fabulous (the jet-set lifestyle of a top pro golfer) that it can freeze their brains.

The level of expectation at Q School coupled with the real possibility of another embarrassing failure creates a type of tension that makes the event one of sport's most gut-churning. A single moment of brilliance can guarantee a Tour Card and a bright future, but an unlucky plugged lie in a bunker or a yipped three foot putt can ruin an entire year of practice and preparation, even an entire career.

Only the top 3% of players who enter the Q School marathon receive a Tour Card each year (usually around 25 to 30) and that means 97% (almost 1,000 players) are failures. Yet despite such long odds, the possible rewards are enormous enough to keep players returning year after year.

Many of the great and the good of world golf originally trod this path: European stars like Colin Montgomerie and Ian Poulter; international major winners such as Retief Goosen and Vijay Singh; and even modern-day champions like young Englishman Matt Fitzpatrick. However, not everyone sailed through the examination first time. For example, Monty did, but Poulter did not; the English Ryder Cup talisman was a four-time visitor before he secured a Card.

The bottom line is that succeeding at Q School is a rite of passage. In terms of nerves and tension, getting a par on the last hole at the School to win a Tour Card is right up there with winning one of the world's top tournaments. When your very livelihood is on the line, there are few more stressful moments.

This story focuses on 12 months in the lives of seven golfers between the Q School of 2006 and the subsequent event a year later. The seven are all at a crossroads in their careers and they know Q School intimately. They have different backgrounds and different ranges of ability, yet they have one thing in common: the dream of a Tour Card. All they have to do for that is play up to 14 rounds of golf – 252 holes or around 980 individual shots – on as many as three different courses and almost always in par or better.

For all seven, it would be glorious to succeed, but oh-so-painful to fail. It is a cruel school, indeed.

The Cast of Characters

Sion Bebb – The son of a Wales rugby union star.

Playing prospects @ December 2006 – European Tour rookie after gaining first Tour Card.

Built like a flank forward, Sion (his Christian name is pronounced 'Shawn') almost retired from tournament golf at one point during 2006 because the struggle to achieve his ultimate dream of a regular place on Tour was becoming too onerous, both for financial and domestic reasons. But at the end of that season, he won a Tour Card for the very first time after 20 years as a pro. But now he about to understand that reaching this summit was actually only a chance to try for another – could he earn the necessary €200,000 in the 2007 season to hold onto that Card? Sion, with his self- effacing nature and dry sense of humour, will soon find out just how good he really is in the cut-throat world of professional tournament golf.

James Conteh – trying to emulate his world champion father.

Playing prospects @ December 2006 – Playing EuroPro & Jamega minor tours.

When your father was a world champion boxer, you have a lot of sporting heritage to live up to. But there is no glamour in being the son of someone famous you are playing for a few hundred pounds of prize money and your mum is your caddie. For sure, James is a dedicated and accomplished player compared to many of his peers, but he is battling his own demons: he is a young golf pro with a dream of his own that is often shadowed by the achievements of his father, John. If James remains stuck on the mini tours for too long, a nightmare scenario will unfold that he has reached his career ceiling.

Phil Golding – former French Open champion & Q School veteran.

Playing prospects @ December 2006 – Relying on Main Tour invitations and Challenge Tour events.

No British golfer has been to Q School more often than Phil; his 17 visits are a record, although one that he is not particularly proud of. Yet his recurring Q School nightmare seemed over in 2003 when he won the French Open, his first European Tour title. The victory shattered talk of an unfulfilled career and there was even talk of him being ready for a Ryder Cup spot. However, three years later in 2006, he found himself back at Q School and failed once again to gain a Card. Now in his forties, Phil is wondering if he can rekindle his moment of glory or if failure at the next Q School at the end of 2007 will effectively mean the end of his career.

Euan Little – one-time Scottish golfing protégé.

Playing prospects @ December 2006 – Sunshine Tour and Challenge Tour events only.

Euan is a charming, unassuming Scot uniformly liked by his fellow pros, but he is still waiting for the glorious golf career that was predicted for him as a teenager by his famous coach Bob Torrance. He has yo-yo'd around the edge of the Tour for several years and in November 2006 suffered one of the most painful Q School heartbreaks, missing an 8ft sliding putt on the very last green at the Final Stage tournament to leave him one shot short of a Tour Card. Euan vows to improve in the next 12 months so that his immense promise will finally be fulfilled.

Andy Raitt – returning from an unlikely injury.

Playing prospects @ December 2006 – Full European Tour member after gaining Tour Card.

A freak injury to his left hand over a decade ago meant Andy has already lost his career once as well as his first wife, virtually all his money and the original hope of a glorious golfing future. In the last few seasons he has spent almost as much time in an operating theatre or a re-hab facility as on the golf course. Yet, somehow, he has also found the courage to fight his way back, and his Tour Card win in November 2006 was one of the great celebratory stories of recent Q Schools. But his battle with the injury is not over and Andy must now find out if his re-constituted golf game will stand up amidst the heat of the fiercest competition. Or is this season the last, isolated bright spark in a tragically shortened career.

Martyn Thompson – the club professional with a dream.

Playing prospects @ December 2006 – PGA regional events and pro-ams along with full-time job at Parkstone GC in Dorset.

Martyn is a solid family man, he's very successful as a traditional club pro, and life has been good to him. But there is still a stone in his golf shoe – deep down inside his soul, he believes that, at the age of 37 and without ever having gone particularly close before, he can yet break onto the European Tour for the first time. It would be one of the most romantic stories in golf if it happened – the long-time club pro who becomes a member of golf's elite. Martyn is not the only club pro sitting in his shop fantasising about the glory of life on Tour, but he is one of the few who is prepared to risk his quiet life at home to chase the dream.

Guy Woodman – searching for the real-life Big Break.

Playing prospects @ December 2006 – EuroPro Tour and other selected events.

Guy's dream since he was 12 has been to become a top tournament golfer, but his struggle has been almost overwhelming at times. His life changed when the American TV network The Golf Channel made him a star of their reality show *The Big Break* in 2005. Suddenly Guy was a minor celebrity and could almost taste the big time. This is a young player who has given up so much to be the best he can be, but will his TV appearance be the high-point of his career or can he use that unique experience to create something else – a life on the PGA European Tour.

Chapter 1 – December 2006

Another New Beginning

"For a lot of golfers, there is more pressure in Q School than trying to win on Tour…second most pressure is a putt to make the cut and everything else falls in after that" – Robert Lee, five times a Q School graduate from seven attempts and now a Sky Sports golf presenter.

Modern-day sport can be very confusing. It might say December 2006 on a normal person's calendar, the last month of the year, but this is actually month No 2 in the 2007 PGA European Tour golf season. At the very end of October, the 2006 schedule ended with the European Tour's grand final, the Volvo Masters (won by Jeev Milka Singh of India) and less than a fortnight later, into the first week of November, the 2007 season began in China with the champions-only Sheshan International (Y E Yang of South Korea was the winner). In fact, a second European Tour tournament of the 2007 season (the UBS Hong Kong Open) finished the following week before the last putt was sunk at the 2006 Q School. So, while Q Schoolers heads were still spinning, some lucky golfers were already earning money towards their playing rights in 2007. It hardly seems fair, but it is an indication of how fast the sporting world moves.

The successful Q Schoolers from the 2006 tournament faced with an immediate dilemma – should they chase 2007 season cash straight away and enter the very next couple of regular tournaments in Australia and New Zealand, also still in November or should they recuperate and wait until the South African events in December.

Only the very brave (or some would say, very foolish) left Q School immediately and headed Down Under. Andy Raitt was one of them, but he missed the cut in Australia and finished tied 49th in New Zealand, earning him a grand total of €2,106 that would not even cover his costs for the trip. Meanwhile, the majority of newly qualified Tour players like Sion Bebb returned home exhausted from Final Stage and waited until this month to start their next campaign.

So as December 2006 dawns, Sion is one of 34 graduates from Q School wondering what lies ahead in the next 12 months. The Welshman is exultant. He had very nearly given up on his dream last year, but finally gained his Tour Card a month ago for the first time after two decades of playing professional golf. Now at age 38, he sits among the elite of tournament golf – his next challenge is to keep the much-prized Card and that means winning lots of money as quickly as possible to consolidate his position, just like newly-promoted football teams who want early-season points to avoid immediate relegation.

The 20-year wait for a Tour Card will put extra pressure on Sion, but he hopes that he is both old enough and wise enough to handle it. He is the definition of the self-effacing pro golfer who has paid his dues during a steady rise up the pro ranks. Sion's feet will always be firmly attached to the floor, he is untouched by any pretentiousness that can overwhelm some sportsmen when they reach the heights of their profession. There is no outrageous ego here. Call his mobile on a non-tournament day and he is likely to be found washing his car in the driveway of his home in South Wales or spending time with his two young daughters. You could not imagine him meeting his accountant to discuss high-interest stock investments or complaining that his complimentary car at the next tournament is a hard-top and not a convertible. His Q School achievement has not changed any of his behaviour. He is calm and courteous and has a sharp sense of humour. He is a regular, family man who just happens to be a very good golfer.

Three weeks after he woke up as a European Tour player, his first tournament comes around, almost before he can take stock of his new situation. There has been a small celebration with his family, some sessions with coach Terry Hanson and he is suddenly in South Africa hunting for prize money.

Perhaps not surprisingly, Sion is nervous at the Alfred Dunhill Championship, which is held at the Leopard Creek Golf Club, a spectacular venue next to Kruger National Park in the northern part of South Africa. He has just left chilly 5° centigrade temperatures in South Wales for a southern hemisphere summer where the thermometer shows a body-sapping 40°.

Sion hits the very first ball of the tournament at 6.15am on 7 December, a landmark day in his career. In the end, only the date proves memorable. It is a poor opening drive and he is soon taking a penalty drop. This sets a tone that results in a disappointing 76. His second round is little better (74), but he crashes out of his first tournament of the season; the proverbial hero-to-zero in back-to-back tournaments.

To make matters worse, the winner at Leopard Creek is Alvaro Quiros of Spain, a man who had finished 20 places behind Sion at Q School. While the Welshman does not earn a bean, the Spaniard's win means full exemption for the rest of the 2007 season and the two seasons that follow. Of course, Sion could see Quiros's triumph as proof that any Q School graduate can win on Tour, but there is also an element of "why not me?" in the back of his mind.

Sion's disappointing pattern continues the following week at the South African Airways Open. He finishes the opening round with a nervy 78 and, although a second round 68 provides a glimmer of hope, he misses the cut again.

Sion's 68 is closer to the form that he showed to win his Card, but one good round is not enough because the standards on Tour rise every year. He is finding out very quickly that retaining a Tour Card is even tougher than anticipated.

Despite 10 previously unsuccessful visits to the Q School before 2006, Sion always had the technical skills to play regularly on Tour. Yet simply possessing that ability isn't enough – to be a regular Tour player over a number of seasons takes something else, some kind of X factor. The occasional start in a European Tour event – often either by invitation or because the majority of the top stars are absent for some events allowing spots for the lower-ranked players – is never enough to sate the desires of pros like Sion. Yet this level of desire is a recent development. The Sion Bebb who became a young assistant professional was not filled with dreams of the European Tour.

"I never thought about playing on any Tour in my early days. No one ever told me I was good enough; no one praised me really – just mum and dad, I suppose," he remembers.

Actually, the Bebb family knows a lot about ascending to the top of a sporting tree. Sion's father, Dewi Bebb, was one of Wales's leading rugby union players and twice a British Lion in the 1960s. He was also well known for his extensive work as an analyst on Harlech TV. It is never easy for a son to emerge from under the shadow of a celebrity parent, but Sion made it easier on himself by choosing a different sport from that of his father.

Sion began to love golf at the age of 11. Of course, he had already played some rugby at school having both watched and admired his Dewi's talent, but as a pre-teen, the young Bebb was sneaking onto the fairways and greens of Llantrisant Pontyclun Golf Club in mid-Glamorgan, a course that bordered the Bebb family's garden.

Following in his father's footsteps was still a possibility for the teenager who grew to over six feet tall and weighed a healthy 13 stones, but the professional revolution in Wales's national sport had yet to take place in the mid-1980s, and both father and son knew that there was little money in rugby union at that time to guarantee a healthy living. There was, however, a vacancy for an assistant pro at Radyr Golf Club in nearby Cardiff. It was the obvious choice as Sion's older brother already had a job there. Anyway, the only other alternatives were the police force, the fire service or working in a bank and Sion Bebb fancied none of these options.

Working at the golf club meant 12-hour days – 8am to 8pm – mostly in the pro shop where he would sort out members' golfing problems and answer their questions; take a few green fees; and sell as many Mars bars as possible. But there was always time for the 17-year-old to hit some golf balls.

In South Wales at this time, golf was not the big business it is today. True, Welshman Ian Woosnam had won the Masters at Augusta and even become No 1 player in the world, but the overall effect of this success did not translate into a tsunami of new golfers in Wales. Sion was one of a few hopeful kids hitting balls on the range. For him and many other young Welsh players, golf was a way of leaving school early and earning a weekly wage. There were no thoughts of playing on the Tour.

And so the story of Sion's life could easily have been a rather prosaic one, culminating when he passed the PGA exams to become a fully qualified pro.

In fact, he took a head pro's job at Mountain Lakes in Caerphilly and, at age 25, met a local girl, Rita, ("she worked as a tax inspector – that didn't go down very well when she told me," Sion recalls) who he settled down with. His relationship with his wife-to-be was the start of a profound change. Sion began to grow up.

"For about 10 years I'd been playing no more than just regional golf and some pro-ams. I thought the entry fee and the expenses were too high, even on the smaller tours. You had to finish [in the] top five just to win some money. The day-to-day pro-ams were very little money up front, so I stuck to them. I was about 24 or 25 when I realised I was getting better; these days they say that at 15 or 16. I just never practiced. But when I met my wife, I knuckled down and started to see a coach. It just took me a while to realise I could play to a higher level, I suppose."

Sion went to Q School for the first time in 1994 aged almost 26 and then returned almost every year after that. He showed plenty of determination, yet he never got really close to gaining his Card. However, the dream just became more tantalising. "My friends were playing on things like the Hippo Tour (today's EuroPro Tour equivalent) and they were doing well. I thought if they could do it then so could I. I started getting good results there, playing three- or four-round tournaments. The first big event I did well in was the European Club Pros tournament in Hungary. Four of us from Wales, we were invited by the PGA. It sounded like fun; it was a week away, an adventure. It was about £700 in costs but I finished second. I just played the same as I always did and I showed some form. I won about £6,000 and thought 'I should play more of these' because that was a lot of money to win. I played in it in Sardinia the following year and was second again, then I won it the next year, 1999. I was the first Welshman to win it.

There was a £10,000 prize, a Peugeot car to use for the year and I qualified for the PGA Cup team to play in America. That was a turning point."

Finally, the young pro from a famous rugby family could foresee fame and fortune in golf. But there would have to be another turning point.

Sion had married Rita in 1996 (the year of his first Q School attempt) and by 2001, their first child, Alys, was born. The couple sat down to decide if Sion's ambitions of the full European Tour were worth pursuing. On the one hand, he needed a regular income to feed his young family, but Sion and Rita could see he was making progress in the more risky world of tournament golf. They decided Sion should give it four or five years. This decision resulted in Sion trekking around the world on the secondary Challenge Tour in 2002 where a top-15 finish at the end of the season would mean a full Tour Card. However, Challenge Tour prize money is notoriously low, often only 10% of even the smallest European Tour event. It is a system supposed to incentivise the players, to allow only the strongest to survive. Well, that is true, to an extent, but the reality is that it also allows those with plenty of sponsorship to survive and Sion was not one of those.

Despite his young family at home waiting for good news, Sion did not set the Challenge Tour ablaze. He would return home from most tournaments with a cheque, but it often only offset some of the weekly costs, the £800 he needed for travel and accommodation. Even though Sion eventually managed to secure a little support from sponsors, the Bebbs were keeping the European Tour dream alive at a loss rather than a profit.

However, there was some progress. Sion finished his first year on Challenge Tour in 53rd on the rankings and that was bettered in 2003 when he climbed to 18th. But neither finish delivered a European Tour Card. Seasons 2004 and 2005 were uninspiring, with Sion finishing 40th and 34th, while Q School visits were equally frustrating. Perhaps, the 2006 season would be Sion's last chance. The early prospects were not favourable, but golf is the strangest of sports and the Welshman was about to find out just how strange.

Sion had spent much of the winter before the 2006 season looking for work rather than practicing, so it was not surprising that his early form that year was ordinary. Then, in July, his second child was born. Luckily for her father, young Madeline was delivered into the world at 2am on a Tuesday. The timing was crucial because, for Sion, it was also the week of the North Wales Open and, if his daughter had appeared any later, he would have missed playing in one of his favourite tournaments.

"The wife came home on Wednesday afternoon and I looked after her for a while and then phoned up the tournament office to see if I could have a late start on Thursday; they said 'no problem,' so I drove up on Thursday morning. I walked six holes in preparation and was last off in the first round. If the tournament hadn't been in Wales, I wouldn't have played, and if I didn't do well there then I probably wouldn't have played any more Challenge Tour events. Of course, I went without a care in the world. No pressures or worries about how I was going to play, although I was very tired, I'd not had much sleep and then had to drive five hours to North Wales. I can't believe how it happened now. A sports psychologist would have a field day. I just relaxed, didn't really care if I hit good or bad shots; I was just happy with the family back home. And the course is in Nevis, a lovely place, great views. I concentrated on the views; it was like playing a friendly game with my mates."

Sion phoned home each night and the news kept getting better; by Sunday evening, he had won the tournament. "I can't remember if Rita was happy with me being there or not, but winning changed my life. The week after was another Challenge Tour event in Ireland but I'd already decided not to go. Instead, there was a regional event in St Pierre, the Welsh Masters. I drove home from Nevis on Sunday, stayed the night, said 'Hello, baby' and went to this local tournament and won again. That was £17,000 in two weeks; it kept me going through the year. You just never know when your good week's going to be."

After being on the point of giving up on the European Tour, Sion's plans were back on track. Another trip to Q School was inevitable; maybe his luck had changed. At 38, Sion would be one of the older competitors, yet now he had fresh impetus. His Challenge Tour ranking meant no First or Second Stage dramas; he went directly to San Roque, the venue for Final Stage and six rounds of the highest pressure golf. Only the top 30 and ties would secure a Tour Card.

Sion's 11th Q School visit started like many of the others with a poor opening round. In the worst of that day's weather at the southern Spanish resort, he shot a 74 and followed it with a 76. He was six over par and tied for 110th position, looking like he was heading home early. However, the next day, the "new father" Sion Bebb re-emerged; he shot a 67 (second best round of the day) and moved up to tied 44th.

A two under par 70 in round 4 lifted him to a tie for 29th. From a disastrous start, he was sitting in position for a Tour Card with two rounds to go. Somehow there were no nerves in round 5 when he shot a 68 and moved to joint 10th place.

The final day was beset by high winds and lashing rain that exaggerated even the usual sixth round dramas. Sion certainly felt the tension when he bogeyed four holes in a row from his 5th. Shortly afterwards, an enforced bad weather break gave him some time to re-focus. "The break happened at a good time for me. I had to rush back to the apartment to decide if I was still going to take a flight home that night or the next day. Once I decided to stay the night, I relaxed." Sion returned to the 13th hole and shot level par for the final six. His 74 in very tough conditions was enough for a 14th place finish and a Tour Card. His achievement was probably the best feel-good story of the whole week: 20 years a pro, winning a Card for the first time and all that after a horrid start. In fact, no one who eventually won a Tour Card in 2006 got off to a worse start.

Not an overtly emotional man, Sion's pride at finally achieving his lifelong ambition was tempered by the absence of the one man he wanted to share it with most: his father. Dewi Bebb had died of a brain tumour in 1996 at the age of 59. "Before he died, I was only playing in local competitions and not showing any of the form I have now. It's only since he died I've reached the level I'm now playing at. It would've been fantastic for him to see me play (at this level). My mother always mentions that Dad would've been proud. I did well up inside when I got home and I'm sure he's watching me. I think you have to keep on trying and believing in yourself. It was just perseverance that got me through Q School in 2006."

The achievement of another thirtysomething pro at San Roque in November 2006 also prompted lavish congratulations from his fellow pros. Andy Raitt's Tour Card was chiseled out of persistence and adversity, his backstory almost the stuff of Hollywood screenplays.

Andy is a solid professional, neither brash nor cocky and he looks a little like Nick Faldo's younger brother. His constant smiling face and easy laugh make him the kind of character you want as a best mate and he knows how to enjoy life, often stopping whatever he's doing when it's "beer o'clock". Andy is large in the shoulders and usually moves no faster than treacle on the golf course, the one place where he takes life seriously.

The main drama in Andy's life started in 1995. He was 25 years old and had just turned pro after shining brightly during four years on a golf scholarship at the University of Nevada. He was already being hailed as a new young hope for the future of English golf; he had been voted the number one US junior college golfer; and won four college titles over contemporaries including Phil Mickelson and Jim Furyk.

Then in his first year as a pro, he innocently arranged nine holes of golf with a friend at the Surrey club St. George's Hill. Andy took his Staffordshire bull terrier Nikki to the course with him, but left his friend in charge of the dog while he checked their tee time. On his return, he was horrified to see another dog, an Alsatian, fighting with Nikki and sinking its teeth into her neck. Andy tried to separate the two dogs. It was a decision that would cloud the rest of his life.

The Alsatian, named Zomba, removed his teeth from Nikki, and instead sunk them into the little finger of Andy's left hand. The top of the finger and the fleshy part of its front was almost totally bitten off; the damaged sections were left connected only by a few strands of skin. With blood spurting, Andy detached the damaged part of his finger, wrapped it in some toilet paper and sped to the nearest hospital where surgeons were luckily able to rebuild the digit. But that's where most of Andy's luck with the incident ran out.

Such an injury would be alarming for almost any sportsman. For Andy, there was an immediate uncertainty that he would ever play again, especially as the injured finger turned black, became swollen and was septic for weeks. But after several months of anxiety, a healing process began. The main problem was that his left hand little finger was now five millimetres shorter than before and all of its upper padding had been lost. In addition, there was severe scarring and numbness.

Andy could easily have given up professional golf at this stage, but he was set for a fabulous pro career, so he fought to overcome this painful obstacle despite no one knowing what the consequences of the injury would be. Although early indications were that the damage would repair over time, there was no precedent. Andy's golf future was totally uncertain.

Amazingly, he started playing again after three months and attended his first Q School in 1995. He failed to win a Tour Card, but he had enjoyed some success that season and looked forward to climbing the professional ladder.

However, secondary effects from Andy's injury slowly began to manifest themselves. As he played more often, a whole network of muscles and nerve endings in his left hand, arm, shoulder and even the left side of his body were activated in a new way.

The grip of the club is one of the most significant aspects of golf and top pro golfers hold each club with the lightest of grips; they use their fingers not the palms of their hands. Andy's grip on the golf club was now different and also increasingly painful.

Then Andy decided to sue Zomba's owner, a case that initially looked to be of the open-and-shut variety. After all, the owner had stood aside and let the two dogs fight, and no one argued that it was the Alsatian who bit Andy and was the cause of the damage to his finger. There was talk of £1 million or more in compensation.

The legal case continued in the background of Andy's life as he kept playing, all the time adjusting his game to the effects of his injury. He made further unsuccessful trips to the Q School in 1996 and 1997 before finally achieving his dream in 1998 at the School in Sotogrande. Still, the court case remained unsettled.

He then spent the next three seasons as a classic journeyman pro bouncing between Q School and the fringes of the Tour. He still shot some good rounds, but there had also been warning signs that all was not well.

In one instance, Andy was vying for the Scottish PGA title at Dalmahoy, but in the middle of two swings in the last few holes, he "lost" the club-head on his downswing and the ball shot miles off-line. The shots came out of the blue, Andy had no idea what was happening. For the top pro to "lose" his feel for the golf club is the ultimate nightmare; it is like a skater suddenly losing his balance for no reason. Pro golf is a game of control and Andy was now uncertain what his body could do on the course; for any pro golfer, doubt in the mind is deadly. Many experts voiced their concerns about his future career on the Tour.

Andy's injury case finally came to the High Court in December 2002 just one month after he had won his Tour Card for the third successive time. Andy's life, however, was in turmoil – he had suffered other injuries (particularly to his shoulder) and his marriage was under intense strain. His legal team provided expert testimony from a number of golf experts, including top coach Denis Pugh and one of Europe's finest-ever players Colin Montgomerie. They were unequivocal in saying the loss of the top part of a little finger would hamper any professional golfer.

However, at the last minute, the legal team defending Zomba's owner found a single expert witness of their own, a fellow Tour professional who said Andy should be able to cope with the injury. To Andy's amazement, the court took the defence's argument to heart and the anticipated £1 million in compensation dwindled to a meager £4,900, while Andy had to pay the costs of the entire case. It was a financial gut-punch and, not only that, the case had taken over six years to settle during which time Andy's golf game had spiraled downwards. In 2002, he earned less than £35,000 in prize money – far less than his expenses for the season. An appeal was set up, but to no avail, merely adding to the legal bill. In the ultimate indignity, Andy was forced to pay £250,000 in legal fees.

The result seemed ruinous, yet Andy's dream of becoming a top Tour pro had never died and, shortly before the court case concluded, there had been a possible change in his fortunes. At a pro-am event in 2001, Andy met an eminent Brazilian surgeon, Jose Luiz Pistelli who specialised in hand surgery. The physician could hardly believe Andy's story and agreed to try and help. The surgery would be costly, but at that time Andy still believed he would win damages to cover the expense. Pistelli performed two operations on Andy's left little finger and, although, the digit was still short in comparison to his other fingers, progress seemed to be made. However, another high-risk surgery would be required when Pistelli would attempt techniques he had never tried before. The revolutionary surgery would mean lengthening the finger by cutting it open and inserting a vice in which a couple of screws would be turned each day in order to stretch the bone. Andy was hesitant, but once the court ruled against him, he found another level of strength to fight for his golf career. The final operation took place in the summer of 2005.

"I could've gone off and done something else, but I had already lost almost everything and I thought 'Right, I'll give this guy a try'. I went to

Brazil, had the surgery and had two flesh grafts. I saw the surgeon every day for over 90 days; he put two screws and two bits of hip bone in the finger so that it's long enough to get some traction. Gripping anything like a door handle, a kettle, a saucepan or a gear stick was difficult [before the surgery]. At one time, I couldn't even hold onto a beer glass and I still struggle to hold something like that even now."

But despite the difficulties, Andy believed in Pistelli who said afterwards that it was the best surgical procedure he had performed in 40 years. The £35,000 of medical bills was a large amount of money for any Tour pro, but Andy had a renewed faith in his recovery. Post-operation, he became a slave to physiotherapy either performed by an expert or by Andy himself using simple exercises like squeezing plasticine or opening and closing a clothes peg. The training strengthened the muscles in the left side of his body in general and the finger muscles in particular.

So, by the time of the 2006 Q School in November of that year, Andy was well and truly on the comeback trail. His last full year on Tour had been in 2004 when he amassed €110,000 and finished 135th on the money list, while 2005 was mostly taken up with the final surgery. Being in the Q School locker room in Catalunya for Second Stage was like coming home. It was his first visit for three years, but the *craic* was just the same. His injury had allowed him First Stage exemption, so he put aside the fact that he had played almost no tournament golf in over 12 months and lined up in in good spirits.

For two rounds Andy performed well, but on day three he found himself in trouble. He was six over after 10 holes and he needed a find "go-to" swing to grind him through the rough patch, maybe not the prettiest swing, but something he could totally rely on. However, this was his first serious tournament since the final surgery and he was caught between his new way of playing – with his newly-lengthened finger – and his old, pre-injury method.

Before the surgery, Andy was basically a straight-hitter who held the club neutrally (with neither hand more in control than the other) and let the club rotate and release during his swing. He spent all his formative golfing years practicing and perfecting this method. It was in his subconscious. Now, his conscious mind was fighting the subconscious because his new method of swinging involved aiming right and pulling the ball to the target. This allowed him to use his right hand (the uninjured one) to grip the club more strongly.

Under pressure in Catalunya, there were too many swing thoughts going on in Andy's head, plus he was feeling pain in the whole of the left side of his body again. Somehow he found a way to avoid total disaster: he did what all quality pros do and used every ounce of skill and determination to grind out the best score possible and lived to fight another day. His 75 actually included a late-round birdie plus a string of pars; he was still in the hunt for a place in the top 20 and a trip to Final Stage.

In round four, Andy hit some early birdies, stayed patient and concentrated like a true veteran. "I figured anything under par would be good enough and I knew I had to use all my experience. I got off to a good start and then it was just about being patient. It was a good day," he remembers. He shot a 67 and finished tied for 15th place, one shot inside the mark – he was on his way to the final six rounds of Q School a week later.

The weather was awful in San Roque for Final Stage 2006; it caused two days of delays. However, this worked in Andy's favour, enabling him to rest the strained left side of his body. He had played in seven previous Q Schools and knew the value of staying calm, especially in poor conditions, but his play was average at best over the first four days and he was lucky to sneak through for the last 36 holes right on the cut mark, tied 69th.

The next two days were career defining. A day five score of 1 under par moved Andy to 45th place and into contention for a top-30 spot. As day six began, he reckoned a round of 3 or 4 under might deliver him a Tour Card, but on Q School's final day in horrid, windy conditions, this seemed highly unlikely, especially as he had shown no real form for the first five days.

However, Andy did have some luck: day six of Q School is always a two-tee start and he was drawn to be one of the early starters at the 10th hole. It meant he would play in the best of the deteriorating weather. The more the wind blew later in the day over the San Roque New Course, the more it would help him.

The gods would smile a second time on Andy that day. As the afternoon wore on, the driving rain was making the course unplayable and tension was growing throughout the field. There was a question over whether the tournament would actually finish before darkness descended. As Andy reached his 18th hole, he was on 3 under for the day, 1 under for the tournament and, because of the awful conditions, there was a good chance that this score would be good enough for a Tour Card. But the organisers were threatening to stop play and Andy's worst scenario was walking into the clubhouse with one crucial hole to play. Luckily for him, the hooter sounded to signal a rain delay just after he had hit his final tee shot. Andy and his two partners then had the option of finishing the hole or walking in – naturally, they played on, Andy needing no worse than a regulation par.

His tee shot landed in semi-rough leaving him a 4-iron approach shot from a slight downslope. For his pre-injury, straight-hitting swing, this would be a reasonable challenge. But for a man with an injured finger and an aching body who was still insecure about his new golf swing, it would be an immense task because there was a lake waiting to the left of the green. With Andy's current swing method pulling the ball right-to-left, the water was definitely in play. "For 10 years, I'd been fighting the ball going left and there was water down the left for my last approach. I knew a par four would be good enough and, thank God, I hit a good shot, two-putted and everyone else had to sit around and wait."

Andy carded a 3 under par 69, a score that would tie the best of the day. He was in the clubhouse, dry and definitely relieved while his nervous rivals had between one and eight holes to complete. "I was in 27th place when I went in after the round. I knew the weather conditions would not make the course any easier. There was nothing to do, so we just left for home. I knew I had my Card later because my phone went ballistic."

There is a smile of huge satisfaction on Andy's face when he talks of this achievement because there is nothing that a golf pro likes more than calling it and then doing it. Andy had secured his Card, despite not having played in a four-round tournament for two years.

"I'm almost surprised, I suppose," he said later. "It's a weird feeling. I can't quite believe it. I'm really proud because I only made one bogey (on the last day). Other people in my life are happier than me in a way because I've been through an awful lot. For me, it's nice to just go back to work. The surgeon said it would be a project and it could take three years or five years or ten years. I just needed to make the finger as strong as it could be. This is just the start of trying to get back to where I was. Now I want to go on and win so that I can prove to people that I wasn't trying to pull a fast one when I tried to get the compensation." The injury is still a highly emotional subject for Andy.

With his Tour Card won just days earlier, Andy loses no time in playing his first event of the 2007 season in November 2006 and travels 13,000 miles to play tournaments in Australia and New Zealand. In Melbourne, he misses the cut, but is in the top five after two rounds in Auckland only to drop over the weekend to a disappointing tied 49th.

He then goes on to South Africa and, at the Alfred Dunhill Championship, his injury returns to haunt him. A chilly early morning tee time means his hand "feels like a claw" and he hits four provisional shots in the first 11 holes such is his alarming inaccuracy. He misses the cut. Yet somehow, a week later at the South African Airways Open, Andy's game falls into place and he is tied 4th with one round to go. He is paired with Retief Goosen on the final day and finishes tied 5th. "The course wasn't one I'd seen before; I just felt better that week and took my chances. It's really encouraging. I didn't play fantastic, but it was solid with lots of good shots. The Tour felt the same, lots of the same faces." He receives €35,000 in South Africa which, with €2,000 from New Zealand, adds up to a decent start to his comeback season. The previous decade of turmoil that had drained Andy physically, emotionally and financially can now start to recede into the past. He is tired of re-telling the injury story that has been central to his life for so long; he puts aside the bills for legal costs that still arrive and the continuing negotiations to pay off the dog's owner; he removes the thoughts of his failed marriage from his mind. There seems to be no sign of complete closure yet, but Andy now finds solace on the golf course. He may no longer be the happy-go-lucky young pro *circa* 1995, the fresh-out-of-college kid with the golf world at his feet, however to his eternal credit, the dream of being a top class Tour pro has never faded.

True, he is still learning how to deal with his golf game post-surgery, but after years of achingly bad luck, Andy Raitt is feeling re-born and the 2007 season could actually be a memorable one for all the right reasons.

Chapter 2 – January 2007

Resolutions and Sabbaticals

"If you think about Q School at the start of the year then you are lost" – Thomas Levet, Tour winner, Ryder Cup player and six-time Q School attendee.

While a few fortunate golfers left the final green at Q School in November 2006 in a champagne mood, most of the players were not celebrating. It is the nature of every golf event – the vast majority leave thoroughly disappointed. However, there are some particularly sad faces each year: those who fall within sight of the finishing line. For a handful of players, success or failure comes down to the very last green, even the very last shot at the end of the six-round slog. Two months ago, Euan Little was one of that handful of unfortunates.

The thoughtful, softly-spoken Scot is no newcomer to Q School; 2006 was his 11th visit. He had won his Card a couple of times (2002 and 2003), but Euan never went on to consolidate his place on Tour the following season.

There was no sign of any form last season until September when he finished runner-up at Q School's First Stage at The Oxfordshire and then got through to San Roque after a brilliant last round of 69 at Second Stage. Once at Final Stage, Euan seemed in control of his game for five rounds and was just inside the prospective Tour Card mark going into the last 18 holes.

But the wind, rain and delays on that last day took their toll. Euan was holding on grimly when he came to the treacherous 18th hole on the San Roque New Course. He needed a par to sneak in for one of the last Cards available.

On a normal day, this would be relatively easy, but not on the last afternoon of Q School and with a 3-club wind gusting right into his face. A bold drive left Euan needing all his power to blast a long-iron onto the green where water threatened on the right and a nasty gully lay waiting on the left. He knew that left was better than right, so unsurprisingly his second shot landed in the gully almost pin-high; he was left with a tricky up and down for the par he so desperately needed.

Euan stalked the chip shot and faced the classic dilemma – get too fancy and he would stay in the gully; thin it and a lake waited on the other side of the green. His nerve held as he flipped a delicate shot to within 8ft – his job as a top-level tournament pro golfer for the next 12 months then depended on holing that sliding left-to-right putt. Normally a super-fast player, Euan again stalked the shot, taking a little longer than normal. He set himself and tapped it forward; the putt lipped out. Bogey. Ashen-faced, he walked to the scorer's tent where it was confirmed that the Tour Card that was a fingertip away had been snatched from him by his 8ft miss. There is no more cruel scenario at the School than this.

The disappointment cut deep because this is a man who took up golf at age five and was tipped to climb to the very top of the sport. Young Euan had a cut-off club in his hand before he was old enough for school and followed in the footsteps of both his parents who were golfers at their local Portpatrick club in south west Scotland. As a young boy, he was a passionate Celtic fan and played plenty of football, but his parents particularly enjoyed supporting their son's golfing ambitions.

At first, Euan's older brother was a better prospect, but by age 13, it was the younger Little who was playing in the Scottish Boys Matchplay, winning through two rounds despite being the youngest competitor. There would be no working on the family farm for this youngster; he was on the golf course, down to scratch at 15, already under the wing of a famous coach, Bob Torrance, father of Ryder Cup hero Sam.

Euan's mild manner belied his competitive spirit and Bob recognised a real prospect, an unpolished gem. Early on, Bob told Euan's parents that the young boy would one day become a golfing millionaire – those words proved both a blessing and a curse. On the one hand, hearing that prediction made Euan confident that he would succeed, but a devilish possibility also entered the young prospect's mind: now he might not have to work so hard because greatness was guaranteed. The dual impact of Bob's early words would take many years for Euan to understand.

By aged 20 and still an unsophisticated amateur player, Euan attended Q School for the first time. He missed the Final Stage four round cut, but decided to turn professional anyway. This was 1996 and a few years of clambering up golf's learning curve followed. Over the next six seasons, Euan would play a fair amount of Challenge Tour (he would eventually win there twice) and then each year try Q School. However, the door to the Tour usually slammed in his face.

"When you miss out at the Q School you live for next year; you gear up for 12 months time. Everything you do always has the School in the back of your mind."

Although he succeeded at the 2002 and 2003 Q School, Euan failed to retain his Card each time (he finished 162nd and 182nd respectively on the money list during those two Tour Card years). In 2004 he was unlucky to be hit by salmonella food poisoning at Final Stage of the School (he was lying tied 7th after two rounds).

Then the young Scot reached a career low-point during 2005: his illness had taken a long time to clear up and his faith in himself was ebbing away. Fortunately, his golfing father-figure Bob Torrance was not ready for the player to give up. The Bob Torrance philosophy is that no matter how well you think you have hit the last shot, you can always hit the next one better. For Bob, striving for perfection is like breathing and Euan finally realised that by adopting the same philosophy in total and not just in half measures, improvement would follow.

Says Bob: "Golf is the most difficult game man ever invented. Ben Hogan was 32 before he won his first tournament. Euan is a natural player and I've got great hope for him. I say to him that he just has to put his nose to the grindstone. Every day we're working on his swing and, when he gets that right, he'll be on the Tour no problem."

Despite Bob's continued support, Euan fell out of love with golf in 2005. "After I got sick at Q School, I didn't even want to be on a golf course. For a while it felt like golf was a job, like I *had* to be there rather than wanted to be there. But now the feeling is totally different, I do want to be playing." It took months for Euan to turn things around. "It was as simple as waking up one day and wanting to do this. It happened after Bob said to me that his greatest fear for me was that I'd be 45 and watching the Tour on TV with my kids and them not believing that I once played in those tournaments. It really hit home. It was a case of telling myself I was good enough; I need to play without fear."

After a disappointing 2005 season, Euan put a great deal of store in 2006. He finally felt ready to pass the Q School test again and move permanently into golf's upper echelon. He had just turned 30 and – with Bob's help – he had resolved to swap the fun and games of the tour pro's life for a more dedicated outlook. Then the last hole nightmare happened two months ago and it hit Euan hard. "I can't describe the feeling I had. I went back to my room and I lay on the bed, called my parents to let them know and basically broke down."

But, this time, failure only spurs him on. Euan will be putting extra effort into his golf this season and the philosophy of hard proves successful on his regular winter trip to South Africa. With many top players still resting, he finishes tied 25th in the pre-Christmas Alfred Dunhill Championship and then tied 19th in the Joburg Open this month. His winnings total over €20,000, one of his brightest starts ever to a pro season.

With each new chunk of prize money in his bank account, the lipped-out putt at San Roque fades further in his memory and his determination to be a European Tour regular is re-affirmed. Euan is more convinced than ever that 2007 will be his break-through year; it is time for something special to happen.

Martyn Thompson did not suffer the same level of drama at the 2006 Q School as Euan Little, but his quest for a Tour Card is just as compelling. Martyn represents the thousands of golf club professionals who sit in their pro shops and fantasise about being a full-time tournament star.

Some club pros have the ability and not the desire for the Tour; others really want a European Tour career, but are simply not good enough. Martyn falls into another category: he has always had the desire, but just never had the chance to prove his ability. For inspiration, Martyn sees men like Ian Poulter (a struggling young assistant pro before making a Q School breakthrough) or Robert Rock (who was working at the delightfully named Swingers Golf Centre in Lichfield just before he made it full-time on Tour). Now, at 37 (although a little older than the likes of Poulter and Rock) with his life and family in tact, it is Martyn-time. This is the year to find out if he is a European Tour pro or not.

Martyn enjoys his PGA professional's job at Parkstone GC in Dorset with his wife Sally, three children and a home on the delightful south coast of England. He has been a full-time PGA pro for 15 years and chose this path at age 22, when he faced the kind of dilemma that millions of young sportsmen and women will understand – follow the dream or play it safe. He already had a family to look after because Sally (then still his girlfriend) had two children by a previous marriage, so why put this future at risk? Martyn opted for safety; he studied hard for his PGA final exams and took the club pro option. It was a no-brainer, a decision that most professional golfers would understand.

Now he is respected by the club members and his fellow pros in the Southern Region, plus he makes a good living. But sometimes 'good' feels a little underwhelming. Last year, while suffering from some kind of early mid-life crisis, Martyn got the Q School bug again, he was suddenly prepared to risk his comfortable existence for a chance of glory. His entry was an experiment, only his third Q School attempt ever and his first in well over a decade, yet he won through First Stage relatively easily. "I was driving the ball past lads 15 years younger than me and didn't play with anyone who I thought was better."

Martyn actually arrived 48 hours early in Spain for the start of Second Stage. But while others were pounding the driving range or tied to the putting green in preparation, the man from Dorset was relaxing. One hour's chipping and a quick session with the flatstick, these were all the fine-tuning that Martyn would undertake before one of the most important tournaments in his life. It was his normal routine.

In his first round, he was cautious yet confident and played 17 holes to near perfection. Martyn had hit all-but-one green in regulation and was 3 under par, a very creditable position until the 18th green when he missed a simple 4ft putt. There was a huge surge of disappointment; putting had always been his most obvious flaw and it had come back to haunt him once more. He should have been sitting in one of the 20 qualifying places, but instead he was back in the pack. At this level of golf, one shot per round is often the difference between a pay cheque and an early trip home.

The next day Martyn felt "jittery" for no reason and seemed rushed throughout his round. A bogey on his first hole and two more on his 5th and 6th left him a self-confessed "jibbering wreck". A 77 was the end result and his chances of reaching Final Stage fizzled out over the next two days. Maybe his lack of top tournament play was letting him down or perhaps a level of intensity was missing.

Over those four rounds at Catalunya, Martyn would hit 60 out of 72 greens in regulation, the kind of ball striking that should have guaranteed qualification to Final Stage for the first time. It was putting that let him down. It was a short time later that an old friend, Carl Watts, offered him a painful truth. "Carl told me I was a crap putter when he first knew me 15 years ago and I was still a crap putter. Then he asked me what I was going to do about it." That challenge was enough to maintain Martyn's Q School aspirations for 2007. All he needed to do was work on his main weakness.

For most amateur golfers, the challenge of working on a weakness is ever-present yet rarely acknowledged; we know our faults, but do little to eradicate them. By contrast, the most dedicated tournament pros sweat blood on the practice range looking for improvement in all parts of their game. They might work on a higher ball flight from their mid-irons one day, eliminating a kink in their back swing the next. They chip and putt almost endlessly so that their technique will hold up and their muscle memory will kick in when a title is on the line.

However, the average club pro has far less time to practice and also, crucially, less need to. Sure, they want to perform well when playing with members on their home course or if they take part in a regional PGA tournament or pro-am, but most of their days are spent teaching or operating their business, doing the basic tasks in the pro shop that earn them their living. Occasional prize money golf is a bonus. In January 2007, this situation is not good enough for Martyn. "With more preparation and a different mental attitude, I could've walked it to Final Stage at San Roque last November," he says.

The comment about his putting was "just what I needed because I had proved to myself at 2006 Q School that I could compete. I told Carl I'd done nothing to improve my putting in 15 years and he said 'Well, you got what you deserved'. And I knew he was absolutely right." So his 2007 New Year's resolutions are to practice more (especially putting), to get fitter and to commit to all-round better preparation.

Martyn pledges himself to a level of commitment more akin to that of a full-time Tour pro and certainly above anything he has previously attempted. "I called Carl and said I wanted to work with him. I'm someone who's never had a coach or a manager or a psychologist before. I've been self-taught, never practiced, I got by just on raw talent. People say you only get out of golf what you put in, but I've got 20 times more out of it than I've put in because I've never actually put much in."

Martyn's epiphany has been a mental one, he has finally realised that his minimum effort strategy at tournaments is a ready-made excuse for failure – if he didn't really try then how could he really fail? Any self-respecting mind guru would see the error of that attitude.

So this year, Martyn resolves to really try, not just pretend. He admits that a Tour Card is of vital importance to his final career CV, to his self-esteem, to himself as a pro. In doing so, he prepares to put other things at risk and realises that deep down inside him, not ever getting through Q School could be devastating. "It's like I've had an excuse already lined up before I even start."

In 2007, there will be no more excuses and the change will go beyond working on Martyn's golf game. For so many club pros, it is Martyn's everyday lifestyle – family, mortgage, money issues and the like – that blocks his way. He has spent his adult life tackling these things first. Martyn's first session with Carl is revealing.

"Carl comes down and spends the day with me and it's all about sorting the rest of my life out rather than my golf: how I run my business, the people around me, my diary. When he tells me what I need to do, I think 'Christ, he's right'. We should sort out all the things that were blocking my mind from playing. Then at the very end of the day, we walk onto the putting green and he watches me hit a few putts."

Martyn's preparation for Q School 2007 will be an all-year affair, not a last-minute stab at glory. "Previously, I'd gone there (Q School) just to learn, just hoping. Being a Tour pro is something in me that is trying to get out. Other people – even my wife – probably don't understand it. But I've got more enthusiasm for it now than I did 10 years ago. Maybe it's because time is running out. This is me trying to turn my life around. Perhaps I can still fulfil my life-long dream."

Martyn's new-found resolve has as much to do with his non-golf life as his golf one. "I've had financial problems in the past with my pro shop and some local rental properties as well as a building project. Even when I was at Second Stage in November last year, just before one of the practice rounds, I was on the phone to my solicitor sorting out something, so I was hardly focused on what I was doing. But after talking to Carl, I've scaled everything back and sold some of the rentals. I'm spending money on my golf instead. I'm building a 16ft x 12ft putting green in my shop so that I can close the door at the end of the day and have an hour's practice. In the past, I've not used my free time for *me*. Before, I'd've gone to the bar for an hour and had a drink with the members."

This is a man who has seen the very best at close quarters. Martyn beat David Duval during his amateur days and twice qualified for the Open Championship in the 1990s, one time making the cut after playing a practice round with Colin Montgomerie. He even caddied for his friend Lee James – then the British Amateur champion – when he played in The Masters alongside Tiger Woods in 1995. These would be career highlights for many club pros, but now they are not enough for Martyn.

"Golf has come naturally to me. It's like walking and talking. I achieved at every level, I played well without putting any effort in. The Q School 2006 was really the first time I'd failed at golf. I won at boys level, county and national level and because I've never had to put any effort in to get better, the work ethic isn't there. Now I've finally got to a point where I would need to put that work in. I'm not lazy, but because golf has come easy, the idea of practicing is foreign to me."

And Martyn believes that even in his mid-thirties, there is still hope. "Golf is not about age. I hit the ball as long and as straight as any of the young kids coming through now. Look at Tom Lehman who came back into tournament golf late and then won an Open Championship at 38. And there are endless stories like this, players who win big on the Seniors Tour because they've been journeyman pros or club pros for years. It's not a 100-metre sprint race. You can win on Tour in your 40s and I've just been too stubborn with my golf in the past. There is a part of my game – putting – that has let me down, but now I realise I have to change it. I need to change my whole technique and if in a year's time it hasn't made a difference, then I probably will say that it's not meant to be. For me at my age, I need to find out."

The New Year with its chance for resolutions means Q School regulars can practice their version of one of the sport's great maxims. For many of them like Phil Golding it's not so much 'forget your last shot and focus on your next one' but 'erase the memory of your terrible Q School last November and wish for something better really soon'.

This should not be happening to Phil. He won a remarkable French Open title in 2003, finally fulfilling his potential and creating a buzz about him maybe pushing on to make the Ryder Cup. But three seasons later, he lost his Tour Card again after a season of poor results. He qualified straight into Q School Final Stage 2006 because of his victory in France, but started off tentatively with a 76 in difficult conditions. Using all his experience, he clawed his way back into contention and was one shot inside the four-round cut mark when he pushed his drive on the 13th hole. His ball hit the cart path, flew out of bounds and a triple bogey crushed his chances. One stroke of bad luck and he was staring at the tournament scoreboard in utter disbelief – he was out of the Q School again. He could not even make the last two rounds.

His troubles last year had begun when his long-time coach Nick Bradley emigrated to America to work more closely with young English star Justin Rose. As the missed cuts piled high, Phil kept looking for a replacement, while also trying different caddies and even visiting a putting guru. Eventually, he found a hungry young coach from Surrey, but Jason Banting came on board too late to halt Phil's season-long slide. "I missed the cut by a couple of shots all year. I wasn't going to go to Q School at first, but my wife said 'What else are you going to do?'". Last November's School was Phil's 16th visit (only one other player, Jesus Maria Arruti of Spain, has been more often) and 11 have been unsuccessful, but none were as bad as this.

So, in the first month of 2007, Phil has no real idea what lies ahead. His tournament ranking is so low that he can expect entry into only a tiny number of Tour events plus an invitation or two. Even though his expectations are much higher, his results don't lie. Now 44-years-old, Phil knows his days on Tour could be over. "It's a bit of a shock, to be honest. I was a bit numb when I came back from the School. A couple of mates said that they didn't know what to say and were treading on eggshells with me."

Uncertain what his management company or some of his sponsors will do to help him, Phil is facing an enforced sabbatical, a year out of action. He could be twiddling his thumbs until Final Stage 2007 almost 11 months away. For a man so used to the life of a tournament pro, it will take some getting used to being at home, practicing alone, playing a few pro-ams or just making more trips to the gym. This state of the unknown is exactly what tournament pros hate; they thrive on the rigours of a playing schedule mapped out in advance. One of the huge advantages of a Tour Card is the ability for the players to plot their 25 or so tournaments for the year, avoiding courses they do not like and allocating time for rest before the bigger events.

As he sits in his home in Hertfordshire in January 2007, Phil is at a loss. "I don't quite know what I'm going to do. I haven't been in this position for a while. Maybe I'll do some company days, but these aren't what I want to do. I badly want to be on Tour again."

Phil's handful of top tournaments this year (like his invitation to the French Open as a past champion) are unlikely to prove fruitful because they are so sporadic. But the negative effects of dropping off the regular Tour are more subtle than just prize money. Phil is already missing the fellowship of the Tour, the feeling of glamour and excitement of a high-profile tournament, the applause from the large galleries of fans. Playing at on the European Tour feeds a player's ego.

Phil's sense of pride and his self-esteem are at stake here. After his French Open success, he enjoyed an elevated status, teeing off in the middle of the day with the featured players during the TV coverage. He had served his time with the lesser lights, starting his rounds at the crack of dawn every week or finishing as dusk fell. The truth is that Phil is embarrassed not to have his Card; this tumble down the rankings has punctured his self-image.

Yet, in order to climb back up to the Tour, Phil has to continue to be the epitome of a modern golf pro. He is strikingly handsome, with a mop of fine, blonde hair; he is respected by his fellow pros; and he is liked by the press – he cannot afford to lose the swagger that he has achieved over all these years and he will not.

So another year begins with Phil's belief as unshakeable as ever that he is good enough to be on Tour. He will work hard with his new coach and trust that wisdom – not the scrapyard – comes with age. This is not a delusion, it is pure self-belief and what professional tournament golfer wouldn't want a more of that?

Chapter 3 – February 2007

The Long Wait

"Q School is gut-wrenching. It's not a nice week and once you're through it, you want to make sure it's the last time you see it. If you get into your mind what (Q School) means then you'd never make a backswing"– Sandy Lyle, double major champion and Q School winner.

For tournament pro golfers below the elite levels, winters last far too long. The few who are fully eligible on the European Tour, for example, can play events all year round by heading to warmer climes in Asia, Africa, Australia or even America, but the majority of players who contest tournaments on Europe's mini tours have no such option. Their tours operate mostly in the summer months and golfing in the shoulder months before or after is usually restricted by the weather conditions. At best, a mini tour pro might find a few days of golfing sunshine abroad in the winter, perhaps combining practice with a holiday, but even that option is not open to everyone. The pros at the lower end of the tournament ladder are more likely to don an extra sweater and head for the covered section of the bitterly cold driving range. If this is the best you can do, then you have to do it; there is only so much indoor putting any man can endure.

So the winter months are a time of planning. By February, the opening mini pro tour event is still a couple of months away, but First Stage of Q School takes place in September and that is a scary thought for James Conteh. His next chance of a Tour Card will begin again in just six months, that might not be enough time to find the kind of form he needs.

The problem is that James is behind schedule. He will be 30-years-old in August and that's seven years older than his father John was when he became World Light Heavyweight boxing champion. The name 'Conteh' brings John to mind among many British sports fans of a certain age. James has yet to achieve anything close to his father's world title. Although his father's fame gives James some of his strength of spirit, it also fuels his own – perhaps unrealistic – expectations.

James was not even born when John Conteh reached the pinnacle of boxing as a 23- year-old back in 1974. Born in Liverpool to an Irish mother and a father from Sierra Leone, John took more than his fair share of hard knocks and promised himself that his children would be given a more protected childhood. So James – born in 1977 –avoided the tough backstreets of Merseyside and was brought up in the refined English home counties. Although he grew to be a taller (6ft 4ins) imitation of his father's light heavyweight frame, James rejected becoming a boxer after a few trips to the boxing gym at aged 6; being hit with boxing gloves was not his idea of fun. Father and son were both happy with that decision and also when golf became James's favoured sport in his teenage years. By his early 20s, James was showing considerable promise: he was a member of the winning squad in the English Club Team Championship and later became an assistant pro at the prestigious Moor Park Golf Club in Hertfordshire. But James did not want to stop there. His father had a world title and so he wanted to be a champion on golf's European Tour.

Unfortunately, an ex-boxer can do little to help a pro golfer. Certainly, John could talk about how passion and determination helped him reach the highest levels in the ring, but a boxer's unleashed rage and brutality are a far cry from a golfer's need for smooth body motions and a calm mind. A golfer's biggest fight is often with himself: allowing his body to do what his mind knows it should. So James largely works alone on his golf game while John, who took up golf later in life and plays off a competitive 12 handicap, finds it difficult to even walk the fairways with his son; his inability to help leaves John frustrated. The father only feels a connection when he puts his son's disappointments into perspective with a touch of Scouse humour.

"I feel emotional for James," says John. "I feel compassion for him and sorry when things don't work out, but he's just got to do his best; golf's the same as boxing when it comes to doing your best."

So James plies his pro golf trade on the mini tours; he is a regular on the third level EuroPro Tour and has even enjoyed a few outings on the two-year-old, Jamega Tour that operates even lower-key, two-round events in the UK.

The younger Conteh is thankful to have his family's financial support to allow him to make golf his profession, but James lives in that twilight world between making a real living out of his chosen sport and having to continually supplement his income with whatever paid work he can get. Sometimes he receives a little sponsorship, but generally he lives a hand-to-mouth life.

Winters are particularly long for him. James no longer works as an assistant pro, so when Q School and the mini tours end each autumn, there is little to do except practice in the chilly English weather until the spring.

When not on the range, he will be training barmen in a company operated by his aunt or work with a friend who is a tiler. He does these jobs only because he needs the cash.

"It's hard work as a golf pro and pretty stressful, but I still want to reach the European Tour a lot more than I want to quit," he says. At his age and if he had a solid chance of making it to the big time, James should at least have achieved a place on the Challenge Tour, one rung below the European Tour. Although he looks and sounds the part, even this level seems a long way away. If honesty prevailed, he would know that his odds for a Q School Tour Card this year are extremely long and a more realistic target for 2007 would be just to progress for the first time to the Final Stage of Q School. However, stark realities are not what most Q Schoolers want to hear. Believe in the dream and it will come – that is a much more common strategy.

Last autumn, James attended First Stage at The Oxfordshire and played with another young man with a famous sporting surname: Raul Ballesteros, nephew of Seve, who was taking his first steps on his own journey as a pro golfer. James, Raul and their fellow First Stagers understand that they are golf's equivalent of lower league, semi-pro football teams starting an FA Cup run. If Monty and Sergio are Man Utd and Arsenal then mini tour players are Sutton United and Stalybridge Celtic. The opening Q School event is like the FA Cup 1st Round, it is a breakout opportunity; progress from here and you will eventually play with the big boys. Every FA Cup has a fairytale team that reaches the later rounds, so why should James not be this year's Q School equivalent?

That particular fairytale would end with James on the European Tour and, to the untutored eye, that seems reasonably possible because, compared with normal golfer's standards, James looks every inch a very decent player. Like many of his counterparts at First Stage Q School, he hits the ball with precision and control; he can (and does) pull off some amazing chip shots; he hits near-impossible approaches with long irons; and he smashes drives over 300 yards. It's just that there is something missing from the golf game of so many First Stagers. Most likely it is mental fortitude or the ability to develop supreme concentration at the vital moments, but it could also be that they are still learning to fully understand their swing or develop a solid putting stroke. Still, the dream of fame and fortune drives them on.

Despite two well-known surnames in James's threeball, there is only his mum Veronica following them along with the girlfriend of the third player in the group Steve Parry from Lancashire. Spectators at this level of golf are a rarity. In fact, Veronica Conteh is not just watching her son for fun, she also acts as his caddie. First Stage of Q School is hardly a glamorous affair.

"I come when I'm allowed," says James's mother who is really caddie-cum-cheerleader-cum-nervous spectator. "I do love to watch him play," she admits. Her husband – now a regular on the after dinner circuit – thinks James should have a professional caddie, but that is an expensive option. Says John: "In boxing, you wouldn't want to come back to the corner at the end of the round and have a mate give you advice; you'd want a professional in your corner." John believes he would be too tense to perform the caddie duties himself, so his encouragement comes before or after a round. That system works for James as well because the son obviously wants to make his father proud, but both of them recognise that their relationship needs space. "They get on really well," Veronica says. "John just complains that he doesn't get any golf lessons from James."

At The Oxfordshire, Son doesn't speak much to Mum – Veronica plays only a little golf and would never think to offer advice – but the fact she is there in support means a lot to him. The fact that she drove him to the event after James totted up a few too many points on his license is also very much appreciated.

After four rounds, James finished right on the qualifying mark at 2 under after a steady, but unspectacular performance. Q School may be the only time each season that a mini tour pro like James will play four consecutive rounds of competition golf, so progress was quite an achievement.

Five weeks later at Second Stage in Emporda, Spain, the heat is turned up both in terms of temperature and rival talent. James's biggest problem is that between these two tournaments he does not play in a single pro event. It is the dilemma of the mini tour golfer – competition is thin on the ground at the sharp end of the season. It is also true that sometimes James simply cannot afford to enter a tournament, even a mini tour event. His life is often driven by available cash.

So, under the Spanish sun, James was stuck around par for each of his opening three rounds and stood at 1 over, well down the field, with 18 holes to play. There had been a glimmer of hope at the end of round two; he was 2 under after 17 holes (one under for the tournament), but he proceeded to triple bogey the last hole. "I hit the ball as well as anyone out there tee to green. But my putting was no good," he complained. His chance of Final Stage had disappeared once again and his life in sport's poverty trap had undermined his chances. However, in some ways, he is also happy with his progress after such limited tournament play – this was the first time in all his four Q School attempts that he had even made Second Stage.

Money is a still a problem as he plans his schedule for 2007– how much he earns in prize money as well as off the course determines how many tournaments he plays. In 2006 the cash did not match his aspirations and he played in just five proper pro events. To make the leap to Final Stage will probably need either a breakthrough in his game, heaps more preparation or bare-faced luck.

James says his desire is "100% there" and nothing will stop another Q School attempt in September 2007. He has already made his most comprehensive plan ever for a golf season including extra practice during the three months of winter inactivity. The hunt also begins for a sponsor with a friend putting a professional CV and sponsorship proposal together for him for the first time. He has plenty of time on his hands over winter, so why not use it wisely. His ultimate goal of a place on the European Tour remains. "I changed my coach two years ago and that really turned my game around, both my swing and my long game. It has made big improvements. But I could only practice in the lead-up to Q School. That's not enough. I know I'm capable of enough birdies, so now I need to cut out the bad play."

A mini tour pro like James spends too much time on the practice range and not enough in the heat of tournament battle. This year, more than ever, he is ready to play.

Another young man with an equal level of determination to succeed is Guy Woodman. For a journeyman golfer usually playing on the EuroPro Tour, Guy is remarkably famous. It's all thanks to an unexpected TV appearance. It was the kind of recognition that Guy had hoped for when he left behind thoughts of being a rugby player as a boy growing up in Berkshire. At aged just 9, his parents persuaded him to swap his rugby boots for golf shoes. Within three years, he was totally hooked and now admits that his dream to be a top golf pro is an obsession – it costs him money, a normal 9-to-5 job and plans for a long-term girlfriend. It even threatens his relationship with his parents. Wouldn't it be easier just to give up?

"A lot of people would. But from the age of 12, I knew that golf was what I wanted to do and it's always been that way. You get doubts about yourself, you ask yourself 'Do other things mean more to me?' And you get into a relationship and meet a woman and it's fantastic, but after a while you wonder what you're going to do about it. You see, I've always aspired to be a golfer."

Guy's introduction to golf came by chance when a game of rugby was cancelled. His parents were about to have a golf lesson themselves and persuaded their son to join them rather than sit at home doing nothing.

"I said to them at first: 'No, it's an old farts' sport, it's boring.' But I went along and I loved it, from the first time I picked up a club almost. I couldn't believe that I could actually not hit the ball when it wasn't moving. I thought I could just stand there and whack it. I immediately wanted to improve. I fell in love with the game and, anyway, I stopped growing enough for rugby so at weekends I turned to golf."

After some junior success and leaving the amateur ranks at 22, Guy turned pro, trying his hand on various tours including the Sunshine Tour in South Africa. But there were few highlights until a chance encounter with the makers of a new television programme on the American cable network The Golf Channel in 2005. The show was called *The Big Break* and had become a hit in the US, matching journeymen pros against each other in various skills-based games until one player walked away with invites to real tour events. *The Big Break* had become golf's favourite reality-style TV show with each golfer interviewed extensively about his performance, about his opponents and about life in general. There were insights into the minds of these men who all aspired to join golf's top rank. The fourth series of the show – *The Big Break IV* – centred on an ingenious new idea to pit some young European players against Americans in a kind of Ryder Cup-style event. Again, one golfer would eventually prevail and win a number of tour appearances. Although the producers wanted Guy, initially, he did not want the show.

"*The Big Break* is massive in America. But over here, not a lot of people have got The Golf Channel or at least not then. I'd seen it and it looked like a bunch of hackers. I saw the ad at the end of series three that said they were doing auditions for series four. I never thought anything about it. Then I get to my first EuroPro Tour event and there are posters up saying the *The Big Break* crew are here doing auditions. A roommate said he wanted to be on the programme and he couldn't wait. I said it was just some tuppenny-ha'penny show and I didn't want to be on it. But he said I should come with him. I thought it was going to be just filling in a form, but once I did that some woman said I needed to go down to the practice ground to hit some balls. I hadn't even done any stretching, but a guy on the range told me to hit all kinds of shots – a low one, a high one – then to get my driver out and stuff. It was all being filmed. Then they interviewed me on camera. I thought that went well because I made them laugh, but my mind was on the tournament and this was just a bit of fun. I never thought I'd get on. Two months later I got a phone call to say I'd been short-listed and was I available. By that time, I liked the idea and said I'd love to do it."

The show would be filmed during two weeks in June in Scotland, but the producers gave no further details even after Guy was provided with a plane ticket to fly to Edinburgh. "It was like being a secret agent; we weren't supposed to say anything to anyone, but word had got out that there would be three Englishmen and Warren Bladon (a former English amateur champion) would be one of them with me. There was a lot of apprehension: what was I getting into, what are the other guys going to be like, am I going to look like an idiot? In the end we couldn't have been treated better. I got to Edinburgh and Warren had been waiting about four hours before the next person turned up which was me. Then we were all put in our team bus and it was great. We all got on pretty well straight away. We were told it was a Ryder Cup format and we met the Americans the next day. They were a bit of a crazy bunch to say the least. They blanked us all at first because they wanted some antipathy between us all, but it didn't happen. They were actually great guys."

The Big Break IV was filmed at Carnoustie (scene of the following year's Open Championship) with no less than 35 cameras and a 70-man crew. It was a big ratings success for The Golf Channel and Guy was one of its stars. It gave him a taste of the high life, but also of the pressure of being the centre of massive attention. He finished runner-up in the competition and admits it was the biggest moment of his career to date.

"It taught me a lot. My first shot on the show was a three-iron off a tight lie straight into the wind. There were cameras around me, the crew and all your peers who haven't seen you hit a shot yet; you don't know how good they are or what they're thinking – I was absolutely crapping myself. It was alternate shot and my partner had just hit; I had the approach into the green. It wasn't a great shot; I was just glad to make contact. But you learn how to deal with pressure, especially the longer you go on in the show. I remember it was about my breathing and being in that moment. OK, there were three or four really good players there and you could say the standard wasn't great, but unless you've done it, you have no clue."

For Guy, it was an amazing journey in other ways as well. "The contacts I made were great. My girlfriend and I went on holiday to America afterwards, we wanted to visit The Golf Channel headquarters. They said I was going to be famous and I was even signing autographs at the airport, it was great. I met a commentator on the Nationwide Tour who said his son was my No 1 fan and invited us to stay with his family for the rest of the trip, to make ourselves at home." In the end, however, there were no US sponsors, no US tournament invites and Guy was left to use his TV experience at events like Q School.

Guy will be at First Stage again in September and is one of hundreds of young pros for whom Q School is the central point of their season, their potential pathway to glory. Pushing 30, though, it is getting to the point of now-or-never for him to make the European Tour. Last year, Guy failed at Second Stage despite his freshly-honed TV mentality, but he knows that every Q School produces a couple of surprise players, those who come right through from First Stage and win a Tour Card thanks to an unstoppable wave of good form. He is ever the optimist, so why could 2007 not be Guy Woodman's year?

In the past, Sion Bebb had been one of the tournament pros who sat around during the cold English winter waiting for action. But that is not his life now on the Main Tour; in fact, the winter is perhaps the most important part of his season because if he can get off to a good start, retaining his Tour Card will be much easier.

Sion's opening two tournaments in South Africa in December last year ended in missed cuts and it took him until tournament No 3 (the Joburg Open in January) before the first cheque was in the bank. It might only have been tied 73rd and €1,447, but it was a landmark achievement. In addition, Sion was learning that a regular Tour pro needs to adapt to different conditions at each event – in December's tournaments, it was the heat; in Johannesburg it was the altitude.

"It was progress to get some money on the board in Joburg especially with the unfamiliar conditions. If you start missing too many cuts then you start concentrating just on that and not on winning or getting a better position. I got that monkey off my back and needed to press on. I haven't played so well since I got my Card; I've played indifferent, really. You don't get many starts at the beginning of the year and the tournaments are in places where I've never played before. I was still on cloud nine for the first couple of events after San Roque although I had really wanted to rest until the spring; but I do like South Africa and wanted to go there. The main problem in the winter is it's one week playing, but then it's three weeks off; really, you want just to keep on playing to get in a rhythm. You have a month of hitting balls in the freezing cold at the driving range and then you turn up somewhere where its 100 degrees, 100% humidity and playing against guys who know the courses and understands the heat."

Sion has made a small change to his grip: his left hand was becoming too strong; normally a player should be able to see just two knuckles on his left hand on the grip, but Sion was seeing four. This slight alteration at the set-up is something that many amateur golfers think happens only at their level, but that is far from the truth. Pros are constantly studying their basic techniques in case they develop flaws; that's why they spend so much time on the driving range or on the practice green. But any fundamental changes can sometimes take weeks to bed down and it is far from ideal to attempt them during a season as important as this one. Yet Sion has no option; he needs to start earning some decent money and, anyway, it seems to have worked.

But if Sion felt reasonably content with his start to the season, imagine the feelings of Ariel Canete. The Argentinian could not even gain his Card at San Roque last November, yet he gets a slot in the Joburg event, shoots four rounds in the 60s and wins by two shots.

Canete was only able to play in the tournament because it is a co-sanctioned event (the European Tour has been joining forces with the Asian Tour, Australasian Tour and the Sunshine Tour since 1999 to stage events in the northern hemisphere winter) and the southern hemisphere summer allows larger fields of up to 200 players rather than the normal 156. Canete had originally planned to be at home on holiday, but decided to travel to

South Africa after a last minute change of mind. He expected nothing, yet he walked away a winner. He takes lots of congratulations, of course, but who could blame the recent successful Q Schoolers if they felt the pangs of jealousy too.

For the Indonesia Open this month, Sion needs to find some Canete-style form and fortune. However, there are extra difficulties to contend with. He has trouble adjusting to very grainy greens that are typical of this part of the world. Notwithstanding that, the flight – a buttock-numbing 29-hours via Dubai, Colombo and Singapore – caused an old back problem to reoccur. Then there was the heat.

"I'm not bad in the heat usually and I wear a slightly larger glove than normal when it gets really sweaty, but I couldn't even fit an extra large glove on my hand because it had swollen so much. I've never felt so hot in all my life. When I bent down to pick the ball up, I could feel the heat from the ground. I was seeing stars." Sion was feeling his back pain as well as being de-hydrated, so after an opening round of 80, he withdrew and caught an early flight home. "The heat just got to me even though I was drinking a bottle of water every hole, doing everything correct. I had slept to the right time zones and everything, but it was just too much. You never know unless you try, so I can't say it was a waste of time because you can't turn down any starts."

However, Sion now knows a lot more about what's in store this year. He has played four tournaments of the 10 to have taken place so far in the 2007 season and made only one cut; he is not fully fit because of his back and conditions have been against him; plus what luck he has had has all been bad. And things will only get harder: as the year unfolds, more of the top 100 players will contest the events and even making the cut may be a struggle.

Then there is the ever-present question of the bank balance. Because he has played in more winter tournaments than ever before, Sion has also spent a record amount of his own money on travel and accommodation. With one tiny prize money cheque to offset his outgoings, the reality of being a regular pro on the edge of the Tour is now fully understood. No one could blame Sion for wishing he had stayed at home for the last two months.

Chapter 4 – March 2007

Near & Far

"I didn't realise what Q School meant because I was playing well at the time. You can't think about the future (at Q School), that's what separates the journeymen from the good players" – Lee Westwood, former World & European No 1 and Q School graduate in 1993.

As March begins, the European Tour has already been operating for four months (since November last year) and staged 13 tournaments in a total of 10 different countries including China, Australia, South Africa, Dubai, Malaysia and the USA. This is a remarkable change from the European Tour of even a decade earlier.

The expansion into non-European countries with warm climates during the northern hemisphere winter began in 1999 with the Johnnie Walker Classic in Taiwan in November that year.

Once that event was judged a success, it was inevitable that more non-Europe-based tournaments would find their way onto the European Tour. Where once upon a time European pros believed the golf tournament season began in April and ended in October, this warm weather trend allowed pros to earn significant money between November and March as well. Co-sanctioned competitions with the Asian, Sunshine or Australian Tours became the norm.

In fact, by the 2007 season, there were a total of 13 non-European tournaments played before the start of March and another six in this month alone. Asian, African, Australian and American tournaments brought the total number of European Tour events for this season up to 52 compared to just 30 a decade ago. Although the co-sanctioned tournaments mean means half the field may be from the local Tour, the European pro can now play for money almost every week of the year.

Many new Q School graduates, including Andy Raitt, have been clocking up plenty of air miles already this season, starting with Australia and New Zealand last November, but jet lag is the least of Andy's worries. His troublesome left little finger injury is causing uncomfortable pain throughout his hand, arm and shoulder. It is an ever-present problem. After a winning a few thousand euros in November and December, Andy visits South Africa, Indonesia, China, Spain and Portugal before the end of this month, but does not make a single cut in any of the five tournaments. By the end of March, the 5th place finish at the South African Airways Open in December seems like a lifetime ago. "It's a nightmare right now. I've never missed five cuts in a row in my life; maybe two, but never five. It's weird. I'm in a transitional period, I suppose, trying to open the club up and actually hold my width on the back swing, but I didn't expect this. Plus there's a mental side to it, I just don't know where my bad shots are coming from. It's incredibly frustrating." Lack of form accentuates the journeyman golfer's normal anxiety to get some cash in his pocket. In addition, Andy is missing his daughter more than ever.

Despite the problems, Andy continually looks on the bright side; that is his nature. He knows the Tour is a grind and he must work on the technical side of his swing, so why not just get on with it. "I've got to be patient and get physically stronger. I need to stabilise my left shoulder and balance my body. It still feels good to be back on Tour because, if you have one bad week, then at least you know you can have a better one soon." The difference, though, between Andy in the past and now is stark. When he first played a full Tour season in 1999, Andy made 15 cuts out of 24 events and he proved himself to be a consistent performer. It was the same story until 2004 when he decided to have the finger surgery. Now, after missing two seasons, he is almost back to square one. "You don't have to do much to miss the cut on the European Tour because they're all good players." At least the necessary hard work is not something that Andy has ever been afraid of.

He was introduced to the game by his Scottish father and showed enough raw talent to attain a four-year scholarship at Nevada University in the US. He returned home a better golfer and also with a degree in communications. Living abroad was good for Andy and after his American experience, where he learned to work on strength and consistency, he believed life as a tournament pro was his destiny. Initially, he was a hot prospect, but he never reckoned on a freak injury and, although he is working as hard as ever on the range, the pain in his body is not the only thing undermining him. His court case is still causing him financial problems.

"I owe £43,000 to the dog owner who took a portion of the sale of my former house; the rest of the profit went to my ex-wife. Now I've got a legal aid bill just come in for £26,500. I'm writing a few letters saying I'll give them whatever so they'll go away and leave me alone. It would be easy just to go bankrupt. Unfortunately, my earnings are public knowledge, so that doesn't help. I might earn a big cheque one week and nothing for ages. I've just had to give up worrying about money. The rest of life has got to get easier."

Andy's fragile state of mind needs a boost as he is entering a crucial part of his season. If the missed cuts continue much longer then his glorious Tour Card win back in November will have been for nothing and even his whole Tour career could be in jeopardy.

Sion Bebb is trying to make the most of every opportunity in this breakthrough season. He has teed it up at almost half of the 'winter' tournaments, but missed out playing in the lucrative three-week Middle East swing in January and February because of the reduced fields. Q School grads know that most of their 20 or so starts each year will not be in the majors or those high quality events places like Dubai and Qatar. It is just another barrier for them to jump to maintain their top-level status. While former champions are given a high Tour Card category so they can pick and choose their events, Q Schoolers receive a lower category and must often visit small prize money tournaments with unfavourable conditions. Each player has his to find own rhythm to the season and make the most of every opportunity.

Sion's ranking as the 14th best player out of Q School only gives him a Category 11b playing status (*Note: some of the categories referred to in this book have changed since 2007; for example, the Q School ranking in 2015 is Category 15 and the Challenge Tour ranking is Category 13*). By contrast, the winners of major championships or the other most prestigious tournaments are Category 1; Tour champions from the last two seasons are Category 3; the top 115 from the previous season are Category 7; and even the top 40 career earners over the history of the Tour, the top 20 finishers on the Challenge Tour plus local qualifiers and invitees receive better category status than Q Schoolers. The full list of eligible golfers is always greater than the 156 players who normally compete at each tournament and the Q Schooler is a poor relation, often waiting patiently for a last-minute drop-out to the original entry list.

So, although the 21st century European pro has more opportunities than ever to scoop his share of the millions of euros in available prize money, there are several obvious downsides: firstly, the fringe players like Sion fly many more hours than ever before in the cheapest seats on the plane (not in first class or by private jet) chasing relatively small amounts of prize money; secondly, even the low cost fairs and budget motels seem expensive when your budget is tight; and, thirdly, they always leaves their families behind. It is not a life that everyone enjoys.

Success in San Roque last November has come at a price. "It changed my life because I've got less money now," he jokes after his first four months of regular play on the Tour. He has put in the extra work but has yet to gain extra reward and he is spending considerably more money than he is winning.

Every start has become increasingly crucial and Sion is on the reserve list for Singapore this month as the Monday morning of the tournament week dawns. Then he gets 'The Call' – there has been a late withdrawl and he is in the tournament starting line-up. But this only underlines the dilemma of the journeyman player – do you make the costly, last-minute effort to play on a course you have never seen before and arrive there barely in time to either practice or acclimatise? Or do you stay home and wait for a better opportunity?

For Sion, there is no question: he rushes from south Wales via the M4 motorway to Heathrow for a 15-hour flight. By the time he arrives, it is 8pm on Tuesday evening and that leaves only one day to loosen up and practice. That leaves him with another problem: this is a two-course event at Laguna Golf and Country Club and it is too exhausting to play all 36 practice holes in a single day. He settles for 18 on the course he will play on the opening day and hopes for the best on the unseen course on day two. Again, fate is being unkind to the Welshman.

In his first round of the tournament, Sion shoots a one under par 71, but playing the tighter, second course blind the next day produces too many missed fairways. His 76 means another missed cut and it is a very long flight home with nothing to show for it.

The stop-start nature of the Welshman's season is giving him little chance to build confidence, but there are two events in Europe at the end of this month. It is just what he needs – shorter flights, one-hour time differences and no extreme heat.

In Madeira, however, it is the wind that is evil. Shooting an opening 76 means Sion is chasing again and his 4 over total for two rounds is well short of the cut. There is further annoying news because the tournament is won by a fellow 2006 Q School Card graduate, Daniel Vancsik. Another Argentinian has achieved what all Q Schoolers dream about: he has left his Category 11b behind and is now ranked in Category 3 as a Tour winner. The victory means no last-minute entries (like Sion had in Singapore) and no worrying about playing in enough big money tournaments – Vancsik's playing status will mean participation in everything except the four majors and the World Golf Championship events.

For Sion, he plays in Portugal a week later, still with lots of wind. He is not holing any putts and misses this cut by two shots. "You can't let yourself get too worried. You try to do everything cheaply, flights and hotel and stuff. But once you're out there, you can't let that bother you or there's no point; you have to concentrate on the golf. It's only once you've failed that you look back and think 'Oh, God what have I done.' One of the other downsides is not being with Rita and the girls and when I go away it's very easy to think of the family back home, but you just have to put it out of your mind."

It is, of course, not unusual for new players on Tour to struggle early on. Justin Rose is a great example. The Englishman missed his first 17 cuts on the European Tour, but is now regarded as a superstar. However, Rose was just a teenager when he turned pro and was the exception, not the rule. For Sion, it is now four months on Tour, seven tournaments played, one cut made and just €1,447 in prize money. Sitting next to Roger '007' Moore in a departure lounge in Dubai on his way back from Indonesia this month was not the kind of highlight Sion had hoped for by this stage of the season.

Although his spirits are relatively high, he has already slipped behind many fellow Q Schoolers in the crucial season-long money list. He put aside some savings to fund the early part of his year, but how many more costly trips and missed cuts can he afford? He hopes that this is not a question he will have to ask either himself or his wife Rita.

For lots of reasons, James Conteh would love to have the problems of Sion Bebb and Andy Raitt. Instead of travelling the world and testing himself as an international tournament golfer, the young Englishman has been stuck in Hertfordshire struggling to even practice in the dull, damp weather.

James's playing plans revolve around the EuroPro and Jamega Tours that stage events almost exclusively in the UK. It means car journeys not airplane flights and staying either with other golf pro friends in one house or in a cheap motel, but it also means no events until April. Friends from his Moor Park club help with money to give James a chance to plan his own schedule, albeit that it bears no comparison with the jet-setting of those on the Main Tour.

The life of the mini tour pro has some similarities, though, with those in the higher echelons. James and his contemporaries will often sit around and talk about the game, its anguishes and its triumphs. There is a camaraderie that is part of the joy of being a tournament pro and, right now, it is what James is looking forward to.

"The game is a big puzzle really, it's just so difficult, so we do tend to help each other on the tours. I might ask someone to look at my putting stroke and it's not a faux pas to do that, you might even see something in your own technique when you're helping another player. It's feedback we all need and it's kind of strange in a way, I suppose, but some of us share the same coach and we know what we're working on. It's good to have friends at these events. However, in an ideal world in any tournament, I want to finish first and all my mates to finish second, third and fourth. But if it's them who have the great scores then I'm really pleased for them."

In addition, whether it is mini tour or Main Tour, the pros are forever working on the mental side of their game. Pro golfers seem able to remember almost every shot of every round they have ever played, especially the significant ones. For James, he sees his off-season job as recalling those good rounds, the best memories – like his course record at Stoke Park – and filing away nightmares like the triple bogey on the 18th at Emporda last November in his opening round at Second Stage. He is also thinking about how he would spend a few extra pounds. "I think the more you play in competition, the better you become, but I seem to have a longer off-season than on-season and I've never had a full winter of golf. Ideally, if I had some money, I'd go down to the Sunshine Tour in Southern Africa. It's harder to motivate yourself on a cold English day, but if the option is doing nothing, then you still go out and practice. I work on technical aspects of my swing rather than just playing. The problem would be that if I started playing really well, then there is no tournament to take part in."

When practice is postponed by weather, there is always some cash to be earned such as working with his friend the tiler. James admits that doing other work helps take his mind off his golfing dreams and makes him hungrier to return to the sport. After all, this is only his fourth year as a pro, so he still has plenty to learn about himself and how to survive even on the third level of pro tournaments.

"Mentally, it is better for me to work than just hang around waiting for a tournament. I don't get pressure from my girlfriend or my parents or at least they never express it to me. How long do I give myself, being a golf pro like this? I don't think about it that often, but I want to do it for as long as I think my goals are achievable and I know the guys around me – even those I played against at Second Stage – are no better than me. So I know I can be on Main Tour. I'm getting mentally stronger, I'm a bit more focused during a round and my technique is improving. I just need to play more."

So until there is a tournament to play in, James will have to wait to prove his theories are true.

Euan Little's theory of how to put his 2006 Q School disappointment behind him is to ply his trade on the Sunshine Tour. Euan knows South Africa very well; he has summered down there for the past five years and even had an Afrikaans girlfriend for a while. Yet until this year, he had never committed to a long run on this Tour. It is a mistake that he was only now beginning to realise.

"It was laziness really (not playing Sunshine Tour before). For me it's like a re-dedication or maybe a dedication for the first time." Words of encouragement from his coach Bob Torrance have hit home, but there was also a moment closer to home that helped spark the change. It happened in July last year and was not one of Euan's proudest moments.

"I can remember the day it happened. I had a terrible falling out with my mother. I was going to leave for a tournament that day but got in late the night before. I had slept in and, probably because I'd been misbehaving, I had a row with her. She ended up in tears and I ended up in tears and I jumped into the car and drove straight to the tournament. I felt like it was probably the lowest point in my life; I thought, how am I going to get through this?"

The Littles are a close-knit group and Euan is particularly close to his mother. This is a Scottish farming family dating back several generations with many traditional values and morals. Being a young, single man in such an atmosphere is bound to cause tensions.

"I had had a late night, a lot of alcohol, but when I saw my mother crying because of the hurt that I'd caused her, I realised I had to give myself a shake. I stayed away for two weeks and hardly spoke to her. The only way I was going to get myself out of trouble with her was to raise my golf game and that's what happened. I finished second and then second the following week as well. Then I thought this is the mindset and mentality that I have to have every week and that was the turnaround in my career. I now believe that I have to keep that feeling and there's nothing that I can't achieve."

The family row had shaken Euan to the core. A player who thought he would make a golfing before he was 30 had reached that age without fulfilling his potential. Instead, there was just heartache. Finally, he was taking responsibility.

"I've always been a mother's boy, going to her when things go wrong. I was feeling sorry for myself, ashamed of the hurt I caused when I got to that first tournament. I've never tried as hard in all my life. I had to prove something to myself and to her. I had got into a rut. Now I really believe that good things can come out of bad things."

Euan's reluctance to commit himself to the game of golf had its roots when he was 13 and visited Bob Torrance for the first time for a lesson. "I will always remember a statement Bob made to my parents. I was playing with ladies clubs and he wanted me to go to Ben Sayers in North Berwick to sort out some proper golf clubs. My parents picked me up that day and, as we drove off, I told them I had to get these new clubs. Bob was going to speak to the boss and sort it out. My mother told my father to stop the car and turn back; she didn't believe it. By the time we got back, Bob was in the bar and he said: 'Don't worry about your son, he'll be a millionaire by the time he's 30.' There was I, a young boy all wide-eyed, and I thought that life was going to come very easy. Here I am now talking about failing at Q School at 30-years-old and I'm still not a millionaire. But I've never forgotten what Bob said."

The truth is that those words probably ended up doing more harm than good. The Euan of today admits that for many years after that incident he never worked hard enough on his golf game. And, while Euan indulged in the good life rather than the rigours of the driving range, thousands of young pros following behind him entered the sport with a more dedicated attitude and stole a march on him. "Golf hasn't come easy like I thought it was going to. But when I turned pro in 1996, it was a different ball game altogether, the guys were still partying at nights and I fitted right in there. Now I think about winning tournaments and I've never felt like that before. Ten years ago

I'd be going to Madrid for a tournament, for example, and thinking that it's a big party. This is how I started when I turned pro; it was a totally different lifestyle and mindset at tournaments back then. So much had been expected of me and it was coming easy. It's a terrible attitude to have and it's why I'm in the situation I am now. I'm 30-years-old and done very little with my career. Now I see that it's a privilege not a job. Now kids are coming to the gym after a round. If you'd've said to someone in 1996 that you were going to the gym after a round they'd have looked at you like you were crazy. It was the bar then. Now it's even me who's going to the gym. I hate the phrase, but 'last chance saloon' slips into my mind. It's about finding desire and this is the first time I've had it; I'm going to bust my arse to get where I want to be."

The proof of this particular pudding is in the bare facts – Euan is making cuts and making money in South Africa with ease. The two co-sanctioned events with the European Tour and Sunshine Tour landed him €20,000 by the end of January and since then he has maintained good form. In the subsequent weeks, he has two top five finishes in other Sunshine Tour events and has found himself in contention for titles. Now he is back Scotland for more coaching from Torrance; Euan is itching for another chance on the Main Tour. His opportunity comes at Madeira this month, the European Tour's first event of the year on 'home' soil.

A cautious opening 73 is understandable, but Euan follows that with a 66 to put him in tied 8th position and a third round 69 brings him up to tied 4th place on 8 under. The only problem is that this is the tournament where Argentinian Daniel Vancsik is playing like a god and Euan's fight is for a top 10 finish to guarantee another start the following week. His last day is relatively uneventful, but he does hang on to 4th and earns another €29,000. "I was a little bit tight on the greens, there was no freedom in my putting stroke. But you have to find out why and learn from it; it could be because I haven't been in that position enough. I had two birdies and only one bogey; my game was good."

Euan has another impressive finish in Portugal seven days later: tied 25th for another €11,000. Astonishingly, he has achieved his highest ever world ranking (407th) while the money he has made will take the pressure off the rest of his season even though more opportunities on the Main Tour will be scarce.

"What I do know is that since the run-in with my mother, I've tried my hardest on the golf course. I'm now playing to the best of my ability and if it's not enough each week, then that's it. I think the penny's finally dropped for me."

For some golfers, the hundreds of rounds, the thousands of golf swings and the millions of air miles are not going to improve their game. Instead, just one row with a loved one will do the trick.

Martyn Thompson understands the importance of a happy family. While the vast majority of his future Q School rivals will be travelling near and far for competition, the club pro from Parkstone is staying close to home. His normal week includes playing the occasional round with a member, giving lots of lessons, managing the pro shop and simply being around the place as much as possible because a sociable pro is an asset to any club.

Life is good. Martyn's 'office' is a delicious parkland golf course with large groups of tall fir trees and gently rolling hills. He is a pro golfer who tries to be a pro father too; he provides a good life for his family with his club job, but also dabbles in a few seaside apartment deals. His wife, Sally, enjoys working four days a week in the health care industry and, while his two eldest children have flown the nest, his eight-year-old son provides joy in the home. Who would ever want to leave all this for the suitcase-style life of a European Tour pro? Well Martyn does.

His happiness at home is actually part of the career conundrum that Martyn is still working out in his head; sometimes it seems he would rather be fixing up a beach hut or worrying about the next family holiday than practicing his much-maligned putting stroke. Back in January, he committed to a stronger golfing work ethic – certainly one of the keys to his Tour dream – yet it is springtime and there is little sign of any actual renewed effort. Strangely, Martyn is the first to admit his failing. "Rather than doing the extra work I'm finding other things to do. It's like I'm afraid of failure, so I create my excuse for when I don't succeed at Q School – I just didn't have enough time to practice. It's a lie really."

Martyn's dream is buried under a mountain of activities away from the practice ground. One of his problems is that he is the consummate club pro – he is trained to help others play the game better rather train himself. So that is what he does instead of listening to this voice in his head that says: "I want to follow my dream to play on the Tour!"

So despite the money he spent on a new indoor putting green, Martyn is always constantly else, undermining his New Year's resolution to bring his golf game up to Tour standards. When he is away from Q School, he cannot focus on how much the tournament means to him. Yet Martyn represents so many club pros when he thinks of what might be. Catch him in that mood and it is clear that success at Q School is still a burning desire. But, what will it take for Q School to come to the very top of his list of life priorities? It is not a complex psychological question, but if Martyn Thompson, exemplary club pro, is ever to become Martyn Thompson, famous European Tour golfer, then it is a question that he needs to address immediately.

Chapter 5 – April 2007

A Question of Cash

"I remember being absolutely devastated (when I failed at Q School) because it's your year's work done. A few of the guys get drunk, a few cry and then, after a few days, you have to think 'Well, how am I going to pay the mortgage?'. You have to re-group. It's our living after all" – Barry Lane, multiple Tour winner and Q School graduate four out of seven attempts.

Like most major sports around the globe, golf has become a multi-billion dollar business. The main reason has been the spectacular growth in television rights fees delivering more prize money and sponsorship. Rights fees soared in the early 1990s as digital television channels – including the sports-only networks – emerged. Almost at the same time, there was the Tiger Woods effect: the perfect player for the new generation, someone who intrigued the whole world of sports.

The change for the players has been stark. In 1985, for instance, Scotland's Sandy Lyle won the PGA European Tour Order of Merit with what seemed then like a very large amount of money – almost £140,000. Yet 10 years later in 1995, Colin Montgomerie was European No 1 with £835,051, more than six times Lyle's figure. By 2000, Lee Westwood's Order of Merit-winning total was over £2 million (€3.1 million) and, by the end of last season (2006), Padraig Harrington's earnings as Europe's No. 1 was almost £2.5 million (€4 million). So, the £140,000 that Sandy Lyle won more than 20 years ago would now only just be enough for the Scot to creep into the top 115 on the money list and save his Tour Card.

And the largesse does not end with prize money. For the very best players there is also tens of thousands of pounds or dollars in appearance fees and personal sponsorships. In 2006 Tiger Woods earned nearly $12m in prize money and a further $87m in endorsements, according to figures from Golf Digest magazine, while his huge appearance fees were not even usually paid into his own bank account, but into his charitable foundation's.

The world's best players are like film stars spending their fortunes in ever more lavish ways – a string of magnificent houses (second and third homes in tax havens like Monaco, Switzerland and Dubai are common nowadays); high performance sports cars or vintage automobiles (Miguel Angel Jimenez and Darren Clarke have many); top class racehorses (Gary Player breeds his own thoroughbreds); fabulous paintings (Luke Donald is an avid collector); and spectacular vineyards (the Nick Faldo Shiraz 2001 is particularly fine or you can visit Ernie Els's huge winery in South Africa). Such highest amounts of cash and prizes are for the very best players, but they are desired by everyone.

Yet while the superstars are the exception, even the 100th best player on the European or US Tour will enjoy a healthy living. His prize money will exceed £150,000 and he will be treated like a king at the top tournaments: there is a sponsor's car for the week, a range of gifts for himself (not just golf clothing and equipment, but watches or electrical gadgets like iPods or GameBoys) and maybe even his wife (free access to the hotel spa, perhaps). Then there is more money like bonuses from equipment manufacturers or from personal appearances, corporate days and some smaller, non-Tiger-sized sponsors wishing to pay for at least a touch of European Tour stardust.

However, the money does not trickle all the way down to the journeymen players. Talk to them and they will tell you that for every tournament pro with a fat wallet, a garage full of flashy motors and no mortgage repayments on his three uniquely-designed homes, there are hundreds of other players teaching a few lessons to high-paid executives during the off-season and worrying how to pay their next credit card bill.

Phil Golding is one of the luckier ones. He has won on Tour, he has earned well over £1 million (€1.5 million) over a 17-year tournament career and he has invested sensibly. But his earnings are certainly not in the superstar stratosphere and his near-record number of visits to Q School proves there have been plenty of fallow years. In fact, without his wife's income in the early days, Phil would have been really struggling. Now, with no Tour Card, the Hertfordshire pro must wonder if his days of struggle are about to return.

Last year Phil's season was a financial disaster as he finished 185th on the Order of Merit. He played a staggering 29 events – definitely at the upper end of a Tour pro's normal number – and his €51,000 in winnings (the Tour now uses the euro as its main prize money indicator) was a paltry return; no one played as many tournaments in 2006 for so little prize money. The point is that the more he played, the more he spent and the worse his results. With tournament expenses running at an average of around €3,000 per event, then last season Phil spent about 50% more money than he won. In Phil's golden year of 2003, he captured the French Open title and pocketed almost €650,000 for the season, while the next two seasons were also reasonable (in

2005 alone he finished 77th in the money list with €300,000). So 2006 was a major shock as well as a huge disappointment.

"I bought a new car after I won in France, although it took me two years to pay for it, but I remember my accountant saying we should buy property. At that time we didn't actually do that although we did make some reasonable investments like long-term savings plans," he says. Phil's sudden dip in fortunes has caused some changes to his lifestyle: he has cashed in some of his investments and cut down on expenses at tournaments. "Don't get me wrong, I'm not pleading poverty and liquidating the savings plans is OK because, I suppose that's what rainy days are for. But now I'm much more aware of the money. Before, I'd spend a couple of thousand pounds a tournament and not be conscious of it. Now I am."

It is easy for a Tour pro to spend £2,000 (€3,000) every time he tees it up for an event. There are flights and airport transfers; accommodation for up to six nights (two days of practice plus four playing days providing you make the cut) and a professional Tour caddie who will charge as much as £850 for the week and take a percentage (usually between 5% and 10%) of any winnings. Add in regular payments to your swing coach, perhaps even a personal trainer and a mind coach and there you have it – thank goodness the food in the players' lounge is free.

Adding to Phil's 2007 season problems is that he will often only be able to enter the events with the smaller purses. He has already played in two low prize money tournaments – in Indonesia and Portugal – and missed both cuts; it is too early to panic, but he cannot help thinking that he will again earn less in prize money than he spends.

"For 25 events a year, that can mean £40-50,000 a year in expenses. You hear about some players almost going bankrupt, some re-mortgaging their homes just to keep going. I know a couple of players who have had to sell their houses and downsize. It's dangerous ground to do that. Fortunately, I don't have a mortgage and I've my Taylor Made/adidas sponsorship this year of about £8,000. They've been loyal to me this season and that's good. But I'm deliberately keeping down my outgoings; I'm trying not to spend very much."

Even though Phil is not among the lowest end of earners, there is an inevitable strain on the player and his family. "My wife Sally has been very supportive, but not all players get that; any wife could easily say 'OK, pack up; go and get a normal job'. Missing out at Q School feels like being made redundant. Luckily, Sally understands. She had a good job with EMI and reluctantly left with a pay-off. She'd been all go-go in a busy world, but now it's the best thing that's ever happened to her. She's said she'd go back to work if necessary, but I hope that doesn't have to happen. She has her own nest egg from the redundancy and if she didn't have that then we would really be in a tough situation."

Many pros on the European Tour have been winners during much of their career – as amateurs or in regional pro events and on mini-tours – and to suddenly find a time when the victories dry up is mentally difficult. For Phil, finding the words to explain his poor performances on the golf course leaves him slightly tongue-tied. The modern tournament golfer has been taught to find the positives even from the most negative situation. But although this might work easily within the sport itself, it is a different matter to the outside world. "I kept meeting this guy at my son's tennis academy on weekends and he'd say 'So you missed the cut again?'. I began to resent him saying that and even the word 'cut' was difficult for me to hear. When I'm not playing well, the way I speak about myself is subconsciously positive. I have to make myself speak this way. I've seen Tiger (Woods) interviewed after a bad round and he says: 'Well, actually, I'm hitting the ball quite good.' Yet I've just seen him knock it all over the place. It's also important not being around other negative players and sometimes you have to disassociate yourself from them."

Much of Phil's uncomfortable feelings are about his bruised pride. The missed cuts, the subsequent lack of money, the need to explain himself – the tournament pro in the doldrums is not a happy person to be around.

"You do bottle your emotions a lot on Tour. Sally used to say how she'd be treading on eggshells with me when I came home after missing a cut in case she upset me for the next week. I wasn't easy to live with. Since my son Lucas came along, I'm much better than I was. Before him, I was miserable and sulky and Sally would say I shouldn't get so low because I needed to get back up for the next tournament. Also, pros can be selfish and self-absorbed. I might go practicing or to the gym to do what I have to do for my golf; maybe I'd say I'd go out for an hour and four hours later I'd still be hitting balls. I'd come back late and get bollocked for that. Tour pros need a very understanding partner."

Phil dreams of returning to the Tour for two reasons other than money and to repair his ego. Firstly, he has a need to be the provider for his family. For most of his pro career, his wife Sally brought home the steady salary and he pursued his golfing ambitions come what may, but more recently Phil has taken over the role as the major breadwinner and it is a role he is happy to play.

"We all like nice things – cars, holidays and stuff – but it's not about the money now. There are players who have to make a career decision forced on them – either your family or the Tour. You either stay home or your marriage is finished – that happens. But, for me, everyone knows that Sally had a very good job and she paid the mortgage for years while I kept on playing. When she packed up, I wanted to be the provider. It's pride for me. It's my turn now and I did it in '03, '04 and '05. Last year was a blip. It's taken a year to find the coach that I wanted and now I need to compete again."

The second reason for Phil's continued burning desire is his son. "What is keeping me going is to do it for Lucas. It's a vision for me to win again and have Lucas come out on the green like Ian Poulter's daughter Amy did when he won a couple of years ago. It's not about the money. Lucas is the drive for me; I want him to be there when I win again. The other day he said to someone 'Do you know my dad's a professional golfer?' He's so aware of things now. It's so sweet; you can't buy that sort of stuff."

There are many tournament pros who have never reached the heights of Phil Golding's career and live each season from hand to mouth, taking jobs in the winter or asking parents, partners and local sponsors to help tide them over until they make the grade.

Guy Woodman is such a case. The golf bug bit him from around the age of 12, it was then that he started wanting to emulate his heroes, the likes of Nick Faldo, Greg Norman and Bernhard Langer. But it wasn't going to be easy. He was reasonably talented, but there was no brilliant amateur career to alert sponsors and no rich parents to pay his way. With only a little help from family and friends, Guy has been funding his own dream for over a decade.

"I've always had extra jobs since I left school, just so I could keep playing, both as an amateur and a pro. The deal with my parents after I left school was that if I wanted to play full-time amateur golf and pursue a career in it, I had to get a job. I started in Little Chefs and Harvesters washing up in the evenings, anything I could do; I was 17. I'd play all summer as an amateur and work all winter. And that's pretty much been the case ever since. I've done all sorts – landscape gardening, security guard, stacked boxes in warehouses, whatever's needed to save some money and play a little. I might go out once a month or once every other week if I'm lucky and if I do go out I don't drink. I can't afford to do it; it's as simple as that; anything to keep the costs down. Basically every penny I earn now goes into my golf."

And Guy's costs are not just a bit of travel, accommodation and equipment. "I have to see my chiropractor – £50 a pop – once a month; there's a masseuse once every other week – that's £50 as well; and I regularly drive up to Middlesbrough to see my coach Andrew Nicholson. I've been working with him for two years and he's a fantastic coach for me."

In 2005 to help kick start his career, Guy offered 300 £1,000 shares in himself to friends, business contacts and members of Stoke Park GC where he works. It is a fairly common alternative to normal sponsorship and Guy sold 10 shares in year one, six in year two and another 10 at the start of this year. But this is not money to live on; it simply feeds the dream.

"You aspire to be in the Rolls Royce class, but you start off as a Skoda. Each EuroPro Tour event costs £275 to enter and then another couple of hundred in add-on costs, so it's effectively £500 each time you peg it up.

Even then, you still need to get off to a good start and earn some prize money or you have to ask your parents or someone for some help. People think all golf pros travel the world and have a great lifestyle, but it's not like that at all for lots of us. The public don't know the amount of hard work it takes to get there. People only see the top guys and that's what they presume you are. When they know a bit more, they say 'Well, you're not a professional then, you're like a semi-pro.' And I tell them I *am* a pro and I'm working my nuts off to get to the top."

Like many sportspeople – especially those in solo sports like tennis or athletics – there is often a certain selfishness that golfers show as part of their characters; they push others aside and shun a quiet, 9-to-5 life; they want their dream and they want it on their own terms. The selfishness is not malicious or mean, but a product of the depth of their desire.

For Guy it means a wife and family are not even on his radar. "Before you get involved in any relationship, you have to tell the woman that golf is your thing. And they start off saying they're fine with it. They have this idea you're going to be a rich guy in a couple of years time. Then after a while it hasn't happened and the relationship goes tits up. At the end of last year, my relationship was going awry. We lived two years together and we moved back in with my parents and that's where it all went wrong. My closest friends and family know my dream to play on the European Tour and understand it, but there does come a time when they ask what's going on.

"I know I'm one of the luckiest guys alive following my dream, not a lot of people can say that. They might have more money, a wife, a family, but they might not be the happiest at work. I'm doing something that I really love. To me it's not a sacrifice giving all that stuff up, but there comes a time when I have to make a living."

Having understanding parents is a blessing for Guy, but the strain of little money coming in is often just below the surface. "My mum and dad only have to ask a question in the wrong tone and it upsets me. You're on edge a lot of the time. I know I can be quite grumpy. If I get frustrated, I don't want to talk about it and we have our fall-outs but we know now when's the right time to say something. I shout and scream a bit and in past years we've had moments when my mum's picked every trophy up and thrown them in the bin; she's taken my clothes and thrown them out of the front door and told me not to come back. But a few days go by and everything gets talked over and you make up, so there are the times when you look back and wonder if it's worth it. Some people go through their lives and don't have the same kind of trouble, but these things make us stronger in the long run."

Guy's competitive life revolves around the EuroPro Tour, the third level tour for pros in Europe and, although it is healthy, three-round competition and the winner will take home £10,000, the rest of the prize money does not reflect the effort of the players. "It's a tough tour – 150 guys playing each week for first place. The winning cheque is good and fourth place can get £1,200, but it's costing £500 a week just to enter let alone all the other costs. You play your heart out, finish top 10 and even then you are probably playing for a loss. That's brutal. I am a PGA member, so I can play some pro-ams and I would aim to do half-and-half perhaps with the EuroPro this year."

Guy will room with a bunch of his pro friends at EuroPro events to keep his expenses down and he has almost no social life. He is also trying to become a fully qualified PGA professional, so when not practicing or playing a tournament, he is studying or spending many hours in the club shop at Stoke Park earning extra cash. He lives this strange, spartan existence chasing an almost impossible goal might seem obsessional to some, but not to him.

"I wouldn't give up my dream even if someone gave me money to stop. No chance. The dream is worth a lot. I wouldn't take a million to give up the dream. I'd rather earn it. I know if I was playing good golf then I'd earn that anyway. Not everyone is the same. A lot of guys are doing it just to feel fine. They're out there dreaming but they don't want to put the hard work in. They want to say that they're a tournament professional trying to get on Tour and if someone dangled a carrot of some money then they'd give up. And there are some who have loads of talent and don't have to work too hard. I'd rather earn through my dream, through my passion. Life would be a bit empty if I just had a million pounds from nothing."

This month, the EuroPro season starts and Guy has high hopes. He is inspired by former EuroPro players like Marc Warren and Ross Fisher winning on the Main Tour. His early season form is nothing to write home about, but if nothing else, Guy enjoys the tournament atmosphere. "On EuroPro events I room with a bunch of guys and there's lots of camaraderie, it's good *craic*. We all talk about golf. We're friends, but we're in it for ourselves ultimately. If you see one of your mates in the hunt then you want them to do well and encourage them. We want a positive atmosphere and we can feed off one another. If it's not yourself then you want one of your buddies to win and make money. If you're up against that person, you have to put friendship aside; we all know that. When it comes to the battle you never wish bad on any of your friends. You want to win with good golf, you want to test yourself and if you're better on the day then so be it, you move on. If you're not good enough then you congratulate them."

If Martyn Thompson ever rises to the heights of a place on the European Tour then his accountant will be the first to notice.

Every club pro will receive a retainer from the club itself (on average, around £2,000 per month) as well as income from lessons at £15-£25 a time and profits from sales of golf equipment, clothing and the rest of his stock in his pro shop. Most pros may not quite be in the six-figure income bracket, but they are usually financially comfortable. However, if the club pro were to succeed at Q School and acquire a Tour Card then he would have to give up the benefits of life as a club pro and risk going into debt. It is a risk that Martyn says he is prepared to take.

The reason is that 11 years ago, when Martyn went to Q School for the first time, he found out that he was good enough to live with the top players. Chasing the millions of pounds in prize money was suddenly an alternative to working in the pro shop for eight hours a day. That year (1996), he qualified for Final Stage and was actually joint leader after two rounds. "I psyched myself out of it; I'd studied the Q School for years and seen all these great players come through, but then got there and wondered why I was in the lead. I thought to myself I should be learning about the event, not winning it. I put myself back down where I thought I belonged at the time that was the middle of the pack. I think I missed a Tour Card by about four shots in the end."

He was even invited back to the Final Stage the following year via his high position in the PGA British Order of Merit for club pros, but decided he could not jeopardise his final club pro exams that took place the following week.

"I now realise such an invitation could be worth a fortune; I'd give my right arm for that invitation now. But I had an offer of a pro's job, so I could see me failing at Q School and not doing the preparation for the exams and failing that too. I could've been left with nothing. The right option for me at the time was not to go to Q School."

It took Martyn another 10 years before he felt his financial safety net was in place and allow his Tour Card dream to re-emerge. "I have probably got more enthusiasm for the idea now than I had when I went to Q School in 1996."

But although the rewards are bigger, so are the expenses and the potential losses. Martyn believes a Tour Card would generate local sponsors to cover his costs and news of his friends and contemporaries on the Tour provides further incentive. "Now when I see players on Tour doing well who are no better than me, it frustrates the hell out of me. They aren't more talented, they have just used their time better."

Yet despite talking the talk, Martyn is not walking the walk. His good intentions are falling apart and he is still not devoting enough time to practice. First Stage is just five months away and those around him are realists, they wonder if Martyn will actually be there at Q School in September. And even if he is, will he be ready?

Chapter 6 – May 2007

The Big Challenge

"I think Q School is a tougher test (than Challenge Tour), but if you've given it five or six attempts and still not getting your Card, then you might want to go and do something else" – Jamie Spence, Tour winner and six-time Q School attendee.

May is a big month for golf's mini Tours. In years past, golf in Europe only really began in the spring. April would provide a gentle start and then May was when the season would hit its stride; by early October, the pro golfer's tournament year was virtually over. Nowadays the European Tour has expanded into a worldwide, year-long travelling circus, but the mini tours have generally maintained the shorter seasons.

The Challenge Tour (owned and managed by the European Tour and able to push into a few warm weather countries over the winter) is something of an exception within Europe, but the third-level tours - including the EuroPro Tour (sanctioned by countries including France, Switzerland, Italy and Austria), the Tartan Tour (Scotland), the ALPs Tour (central Europe), the Nordic Golf League (Scandinavia) - are locked into this northern hemisphere continent. After that, there are some strong national PGA tours in countries such as Spain and the UK that also operate seasons of around seven months or less. But generally it's around a six-month season in Europe.

For some pros, these smaller tours are regular hunting grounds year after year, while for others they are starting points, the stepping stones to the higher levels of golf. Basically, this lower level of pro golf is rich with either young players cutting their competitive teeth or older pros licking their wounds, trying to climb the back up the golfing ladder.

The standard on the Challenge Tour is very high; it regularly delivers some of the best European pros: Thomas Bjorn, Henrik Stenson and Trevor Immelman are among the most successful recent graduates. The fields of players are multi-national, the courses are usually of a high quality and to win here requires four highly polished rounds of golf. Currently the top 20 players after the end-of-season Challenge Tour championship receive an 11a Category Tour Card, one level higher than those players who succeed at Q School. The Tour bigwigs want the Challenge Tour to be the No 1 pathway to the Main Tour.

The EuroPro Tour – supported by the Professional Golfers Association – is usually the third tier tour of choice for UK players whose contests are three-round events. Finish top five at the end of the EuroPro season and you win eligibility on the Challenge Tour next year.

If you cannot play any of the top three tour levels, then below that are PGA-organised tournaments in every region and pro-ams at clubs all over the UK and Europe where a few hundred pounds may go to the winner. Regional strokeplay events are mostly one-day affairs, maybe 36 holes and mostly for club pros like Martyn Thompson. However, the young assistants who dream of life on the European Tour can also cut their competitive teeth there.

In fact, the PGA is the organisation that launched professional tournament golf in the UK and eventually into Europe. The PGA was formed in 1901, but it was only in October 1971 that the leading tournament players of the day separated themselves from the club pros – the tournament players formed the European Tour and created their own big money schedule of events while the club pros remained in the original PGA and focused on life at their local golf clubs and their smaller regional events. Modern day PGA tournaments may be among the lower rungs of the pro golfing ladder, but many of the UK and Europe's greatest players have begun with a few rounds in a regional tournament in their own country.

Eventually, it comes down to money and whether there is enough prize money for pros to make a living. Even on the second tier, the Challenge Tour, only the top couple of dozen players make much of a living from their winnings alone. A Challenge Tour champion can receive £30,000 while a EuroPro champion will get £10,000. A PGA pro finishing first at a normal regional tournament may earn a couple of thousand pounds at best, but it is the minor prizes that are so contentious. Again, even on the Challenge Tour, players outside the top 10 receive little more than loose change. Fifteenth place on the Challenge Tour might be worth around £1,000 while on the EuroPro the pay out for the same finish is more like £100. Finishing 15th at a PGA event, particularly a pro-am, may mean no cash at all.

By contrast, on the Main Tour, 15th – even on some of the smaller events – is worth 10 times as much as on Challenge Tour (that is, £10,000) and, in the larger tournaments, 20 or 30 times more.

So, for most players with some Main Tour experience, it is often hard to find motivation at the lower levels. Euan Little is certainly one player who does not relish it. He played two Challenge Tour events this month, finishing 63rd place in Belgium (earning about £250) and missed the cut in Manchester where he was suffering from a heavy cold.

"The Challenge Tour does not inspire me in the same way as the Main Tour. I know I'm going to an inferior golf course 95% of the time and it is not set up as tough as a Main Tour course. The Challenge Tour standard is good and I am prepared to play there, but over the past 11 years, it has put me into financial problems. You need to finish 15th to break even for the week and I'm not prepared to put myself at that kind of risk. In the Main Tour, there are better monetary rewards. You see guys on Challenge Tour doing well and there are young kids who relish the opportunity, but I've been in that position. This will be my swansong on Challenge. It'll be Main Tour or another Tour for me from now on, but not Challenge, unless the prize funds increase, but more especially if the courses get tougher. At 31, I'm not prepared to stump up £750 to win a thousand."

For Euan, his Challenge Tour events are in danger of undermining the progress he has made with his renewed dedication. Just before his two disappointing results in Belgium and England, he missed the cut in Andalucia in a Main Tour event by a single shot. His season still looks relatively healthy considering his few opportunities to play, but the chances of avoiding Q School (he is eligible to go straight to Second Stage) look almost non-existent. And, although his on-course attitude on Challenge Tour disappoints him, at least he has moved on from his previous, less-than-professional off-course behaviour.

"In the past, on the Challenge Tour, we partied at the wrong time; we'd party on a Friday night sometimes. But now I'd rather focus on my golf during a tournament and wait for a week off. Partying is definitely still part of the culture of all the Tours, but it's getting less and less."

The Main Tour during the 70s and 80s boasted plenty of good-time-Charlies. From journeyman pros to champion golfers and Ryder Cup stars, the drinking culture involved almost everyone back then. Twenty or 30 years ago was a time when Tuesday was "the big night out" as the players often got together for a pre-tournament celebration. Then, if you missed the cut, drowning your sorrows alone was not an option. The bar not the gym was where most players were found at the end of each day.

In addition, a group of young sportsmen travelling the world living the lonely life between hotels always attracted the ladies. True, the music and film businesses definitely boast more groupies, but men's sport – yes, even golf – is not without its band of happy female followers and a couple of decades ago there was no media spotlight or kiss-and-tell consequences to worry about when it came to the players' off-course activities. The European Tour in particular has always been a place where players have socialised more openly; it is one of the most pleasant aspects of the Tour itself, but at times it went too far. By now, though, the party culture is fading into history. The era of the fitness coaches and mind gurus came largely with the new millennium.

But old habits for Euan die hard. "It is very difficult not to party sometimes, especially because at some tournaments, there is a social event every night for us. There are some guys who still like enjoy a drink, many of them are the ones who I grew up with on Tour. Now, though, the younger guys don't generally consume any alcohol at all; golf rules their lives." Just as Euan has re-dedicated himself, so have others who have enjoyed the benefits. Simon Dyson was a self-confessed party animal on Tour at one time, but nowadays he knuckles down to practice his golf in an evening of a tournament rather than take a trip to the hotel bar.

Simon is contrite when he talks about his good-time image. This year he even boasts of off-season fitness plans aimed that helped him get off to a flying start. "The drinking has been calmed down a hell of a lot. Last year I gave pretty much everything up; I was in the gym five or six times a week. I've felt the reward for that. When I let it slip for a couple of weeks, I start to feel it. I don't smoke much unless I go out on the lash and I don't have time for that. I've taken everything into moderation. I know how it felt now when I gave everything up and felt fit; I felt really good about myself."

The proof of Simon's new regime will come later this year at the US PGA Championship in Tulsa where final day temperatures reach 110° Fahrenheit. Simon will shoot a best-of-the-day 64 to finish tied 6th and best European. For him, progress is now a question of fitness. He knows Tiger Woods is the fittest player on any Tour and that is one huge reason why the world's No 1 can handle the end-of- tournament pressure.

Simon has risen from Q School failure via the Asian Tour to be a champion on the European Tour. He will do everything to prevent a drop into the lower levels or even to Q School; he knows the competition is incredibly fierce. Only the top 115 players (from almost 350 who will take part in at least one tournament every year and the hundreds of others who are waiting in the wings) are automatically invited back with a Tour Card to the European Tour after each season. So, for aspiring journeyman pros like Euan Little, the choice between push-ups and partying is a no-brainer.

Both Phil Golding and Sion Bebb have played plenty of Challenge Tour events and won on that tour, but they agree that once you have dined at the high table, it is not easy to return to a place below the salt. Sion began his pro tournament career with regional PGA events and moved on to the old third tier MasterCard Tour; he gained his place on the Challenge Tour from there, but it was not much of a living supported by some seed money that he had saved and a little sponsorship. He spent five years trying to make the next leap forward to the Main Tour.

"My first year on Challenge Tour (2002), I made a loss and in the second year I just about made a profit. It was always tough financially and my wife and I would go through each year and see how the finances were. It's risk and reward. I had a bit of sponsorship from the Ryder Cup of Wales; it's difficult to live without it."

In those days only the top 15 finishers on Challenge Tour money list at the end of the season earned a Tour Card for the following year, so when Sion finished 18th in 2003 and won just over €50,000, it kept him going for another couple of years. "[My performance that year] showed me I was capable of making the Main Tour. I had a 2nd and a 3rd, everything bar a win, but I still didn't make much money. We gave up holidays, we were still in the same house, still with no conservatory and we were driving the same old cars. Rita was fantastic with me being away and money being short. We had no kids at first, but then Alys turned up in 2001 and that was extra responsibility; it makes you want to play well for her sake, you're trying to win money to look after her. Rita could quite easily have said 'No more, I want you home'. Many wives would have. I've got a lot to thank her for."

Challenge Tour was teaching Sion how to be a top tournament pro, but after the 2005 season, he was not making enough progress or enough cash; it was almost time to think again. "I'd given it four or five years, but there were more financial difficulties and Rita was pregnant again. I couldn't keep leaving home with £800 and coming back with £500 even though I was doing relatively well. We made the decision that if things didn't turn around quickly then I wouldn't play the tours."

Sion started looking at alternative jobs during the winter of 2005 and 2006 even though in his heart of hearts he wanted one more year as a touring pro. "I wasn't looking forward to another type of job, but I had to do it and that was that. I went for an interview as a limousine driver one time; I would've done anything to get a few hundred quid to keep me going." As the 2006 season was about to start, Sion tried for a job in a South Wales factory as a car parts fitter, but the lure of the golf tours was too much; he and Rita decided that with his first tournament about to start, life on the shop floor could wait.

So during early 2006, Sion was on the edge of retiring from the Challenge Tour in particular and tournament golf in general. Then he made his fateful decision to play in the North Wales Ryder Cup Challenge at North Wales during the week of the arrival of his second child. That victory meant his dream was alive again.

Phil Golding is in very much the same situation. He will play a little Challenge Tour this year just to have some four-round practice and, although the competition tests him, the majority of players – lots of slim-hipped, hair-gelled twentysomethings – feel odd playing partners for a man in his mid-40s. Phil tees it up at the Oceânico Developments Pro-Am in Manchester at the end of this month (May) and, although he plays fairly solidly for level par after two rounds, he misses another cut. The fact is that – like Euan Little – Challenge Tour events do not mean enough to him.

"All the young kids hit it miles and there are good players here, but I don't know hardly anyone on Challenge Tour these days. I've been there and done it, but I suppose it's all about belonging and I wonder why I'm there nowadays." As a recent Main Tour winner, Phil is exempt from both First and Second Stages of Q School, so even a Challenge Tour win would make any difference, it would not improve his playing status change for the season. "Yes, I want to win and play good golf, it's just that most of the older ones among us, we don't believe we should be there." However, there are other fortysomethings who choose to think differently about Challenge Tour.

Peter Baker was a star of Europe's 1993 Ryder Cup team, the same year as he reached No 7 in the European Tour money list. But instead of his career taking flight, Baker slipped inexorably down the rankings. He had three wins on the Main Tour by the early 90s, but nothing afterwards. By the new millennium, Baker was failing to keep his Tour Card at each end of the season and was relying on the career money list rankings for his starts. Being in the top 40 earnings list for total Tour earnings provides a Category 9 playing status that compares well against Category 11 for successful Q Schoolers. However, after the 2006 season, Peter lost even his Category 9 safety net and faced the School, but before then he was an assistant captain to his good friend Ian Woosnam in the successful European Ryder Cup team in Ireland. Going from being involved with a winning Ryder Cup team to Q School was quite an extraordinary contrast and it failed to inspire Peter to win his Tour Card. Like Phil Golding, he faced a year of waiting for a few Main Tour invites plus as many Challenge Tour events as he could handle.

"I had a grandstand seat at the Ryder Cup and I was jubilant at winning and it was very inspiring, but then I had to get on with my own career. Sometimes, you just burn out and that had happened to me. When I failed Q School, it wasn't a difficult decision to try the Challenge Tour."

It took the 39-year-old from Wolverhampton a few tournaments to settle down, but by this month (May) he had adapted to the Challenge Tour rhythm and finished 6th in the Telenet Trophy in Belgium.

"I enjoy Challenge Tour," he says now. "I like the fact that you have to do everything yourself. You realise how spoiled you are on Main Tour with free food and courtesy cars and everything. Challenge Tour is similar to how Main Tour was 20 years ago; you even carry your own bag instead of having a caddie. It helped me prove I can compete again."

In June, Baker would go on to win his first Challenge Tour title and then repeat the feat in October to secure his Tour Card by finishing 12th on the Challenge Tour money list. But is Peter viewed as a fallen hero by his fellow pros? Euan Little doesn't think so. When talking of Peter's determination to succeed on a lower level Tour despite having once reached the immense heights of a Ryder Cup spot, Euan's thoughts on the matter are insightful: "Well, at least he's *played* in the Ryder Cup. Who wouldn't want to have done that just once?"

But there are not too many stories like Peter Baker's. Most pros who slip off the Main Tour for a few years are gone forever.

Guy Woodman is one player who is still taking his chances on the EuroPro Tour. May is, in fact, the month when the first full EuroPro tournament of this season takes place. However, his opening 82 at the Wensum Valley International Open in Norfolk is not the start he had dreamed of during his long winter lay-off. Just like pros on the Main Tour, Guy falls foul of tournament pressure; it's just that his pressure can be slightly more urgent – sometimes he just wants to earn at least enough to fill the petrol tank of his car for the journey home.

"Playing on the EuroPro, you're going to be on edge all the time, it's just normal. If you've got the finance behind you or if you've got support or if you're born into money, then it takes a bit of burden off you. But I've never had those things. My father was a policeman and now works as a warden at Windsor Castle and my mother is a secretary. My dad has a decent pension, but my parents couldn't support my golf. It was my job to find the cash. Most of my career, all my eggs have been in one basket: progressing via the tournaments I play in, that's how I've survived and that's why I'm tense so much of the time."

There are four EuroPro events this month and Guy can play in only two; he misses the cut in both. Despite the setbacks, he is thinking ahead to the Q School and each EuroPro tournament is at least practice for that challenge.

"You know Q School is coming up in a few months and you try to peak [for it]. You can miss every cut all year and peak at the time of Q School and that would be great. But if you're missing cuts on the EuroPro, your confidence suffers. I make sure I don't play too many events; I work with my coach instead and make sure I'm physically fit. I periodise my practice. There's a lot of golf to play in a year, so you make sure you're prepared in every way you can."

Preparation for players on tours like the EuroPro is only a little less intense than those at the higher levels; everyone is practicing hard and looking for consistency over several weeks or even months not just the occasional one or two rounds. It is consistency that will lead to progress up golf's professional ladder. For instance, a top five finish on the EuroPro Tour at the end of the season means exemption from First Stage of Q School and going straight to Second Stage.

"We do everything the very top players are doing just to get that edge. That's where I'm aiming – the very top. But things off the course are different for us." It is the lifestyle of many EuroPro players that is in stark contrast to the superstars of the game.

"I still live with my parents," says Guy, "and that's difficult. They've been incredibly supportive, but they're on at you if things don't go well. They'll say: 'If you don't get through, what are you going to do then? What are you going to do next year? You can't keep living here.' If there's very little money coming in, it puts a strain on a lot of areas of your life. You've got a lot of pressure on yourself." The third-tier tournament professional basically has a low-paid job with high-cost expenses; it is a classic formula for disaster as the players often are blinded by the prospect of potential rewards one day in the far distance on the Main Tour. Many thousands of aspiring EuroPro players over the years will never even tee it up at a single European Tour event, but there are always some who make the leap. Englishman Matthew Richardson is one of the most recent examples: he topped the EuroPro money list last year and then went on to win his Tour Card at Final Stage of Q School. Guy knows that this year it could be him.

However, Guy needs to stop worrying about the practical problems involved in his tournament life, especially the money. A EuroPro tournament costs £275 to enter (by comparison, no one pays to enter European and Challenge Tours events because there is so much sponsorship and TV money) and, if travel and accommodation is added, then even a few hundred pounds can take some finding. "The big money in golf doesn't leak down to us; it's just like football. On EuroPro, you've got to finish top 15 to win any prize money at all and every week there's 156 guys and they can all play a bit. You might be able to dismiss a third of the field; to be fair, they're wasting their time, but all the rest could win."

By contrast, if a player simply makes the cut on the European Tour then he can still pocket decent money. At a prestigious event like the BMW Championship played at the glamorous Wentworth Club in Surrey this month, 70th place picks up almost €8,000.

Players at the EuroPro level cannot look too often at events like the BMW or it might crush their hard-won self-belief. Their major concern has to be winning the next tournament within their current ability range and they can only worry about the next level if or when they arrive there.

The EuroPro player needs the same single-mindedness as any top tournament pro; he is prepared for sacrifices, but sometimes he also requires an alternative option for his life, a safety net. Guy is smart enough to be training to become a fully qualified PGA professional. It might lead him to become a club pro one day if his tour dream ends.

Both for money and for experience as a future club pro, Guy works regularly at Stoke Park Golf Club; any practice time for tournaments must come after his many hours in the pro shop. "I'm attached to Stoke Park, I pay a membership fee and they're very supportive to me. Members have been good, especially with sponsorships, but it's not the ideal option. They want to see results."

Guy works about 30 hours a week in the pro shop – usually all day Sunday and Monday and then a few shifts during weekdays – and also has to find time for studying for the PGA course. He understands intellectually that committing to a fallback situation as a club pro is a slight undermining of his dream, but it is a pragmatic step.

"I want to play on the Main Tour so much that, subconsciously, you can go into the tournaments carrying this big burden. Maybe training to be a PGA pro means I've dropped some of the burden, but I still have to sacrifice a lot, I still can't make plans. All I know is that I could be a club pro in three years earning a regular salary. Maybe it will come to that. Basically, I'm fed up of being broke."

Just avoiding being broke is a lot different from gathering in the riches on offer on the European Tour. But everyone has to start somewhere.

Chapter 7 – June 2007

Persistence & Pain

"Q School is a frightening experience, like a bright light panic. It's the kind of place where you want your mummy, but you can make some decent money if you get through and have five good years on Tour" – Richard Boxall, Tour winner and two-time Q School attendee.

By June each year, the European Tour has taken root again in its home continent; journeys to Asia, Africa and Australia are things of the past. This first month of Europe's summer marks the start of a huge run of big-money tournaments with the world's foremost golfers all involved. So, with these top dogs expecting to run off with most of the prize money this month, the journeyman pros are facing less opportunities to play in tournaments and also a higher level of competition than at any time during the season. This is crunch time: players will either fill their bank accounts or be pushed aside by the stiffer competition.

The first big pay day in June is the Wales Open at Celtic Manor near Newport, the venue of the Ryder Cup in 2010. While the actual Ryder Cup course itself is not quite ready for this year's event, a quality field turns up including almost all the current crop of top Welsh players. Sion Bebb is among the home hopefuls and his season is coming to a crossroads. Last month in Andalucia, he banked only his second cheque of the year after he scrambled into the weekend right on the bubble and finished tied 44th, worth just over €5,000.

In the previous month (April), there was also another painful reminder of how cruel the European Tour can be. In Madrid, heavy rain caused huge delays, meaning Sion started his first round a day late on Friday. He finished at 3pm that day (shooting a poor 77) and then had to be back on the tee for his second round 20 minutes later. Nevertheless, he recovered and, by the 14th hole of round two, was four under and one shot off the cut mark only for darkness to bring play to a halt. Spending a whole night worrying about his next four holes was poor preparation. At the crack of dawn on Saturday, he could not manage that single, crucial birdie despite good approach shots on all four remaining holes. However, there was still an outside chance that the rest of the field would under-perform and the cut would drift upwards, so Sion waited the whole rest of the day for the other 155 players to finish round two. There was a chilly wind and he still had a chance of making the cut as the final group reached the 18th - if one of this group shot bogey on the last hole then Sion was in. He watched, he waited and he was disappointed – no dropped shots, no prize money for the Welshman. The casual golf fan is often unaware of such small-scale dramas, yet they are the heartbreaking facts of life for a golfer in Sion's position.

The Welshman has missed eight cuts in his ten tournaments so far and lost more momentum because a re-ranking of the Q School and Challenge Tour graduates. At the start of the season, Challenge Tour graduates are given Category 11a status with Q Schoolers at 11b, but by May, the two groups of players are lumped into a single, new Category 11 based on their early season earnings. For Sion, the complicated system has not helped him at all – he was 14th in 11b Category behind 15 Challenge Tour players and now he is 29th in the newly aligned Category. He had a chance to move up the rankings and did not take it, but on the bright, even his bad run of missed cuts has not hindered him.

Sion needs to find positives wherever he can and it is no time to give up on his first full season on Tour. The Wales Open has always been circled in his calendar as a chance to shine; after all, he knows the hilly Celtic Manor course as well as anyone. Add in some excellent practice sessions, plus local support from family and friends and this could be his turning point. That is certainly how his story begins.

In fact, on day one it seems like all the Welsh players are inspired, including Sion who is among the early starters. Followed by a small, appreciative crowd, Sion is playing with authority; his cousin Huw takes a photo of the scoreboard after 12 holes because Sion is leading the tournament on 4 under.

However, Sion duffs his tee shot at the 13th, hits a reasonable recovery only to find it plugged in a greenside bunker; a double bogey 6 knocks the wind out of his sails. For a golfer who has missed so many cuts this season, it is a mini crisis. Sion loses a little concentration and does not account for the slowness of the greens after some heavy rain, but he recovers and scraps his way to a one under par 69 – one of his best rounds of the year. Afterwards there are TV, radio and print interviews and, with daughter Alys on his arm as the press circle him, Sion still looks confident.

However, for round two, he needs to improve because the whole field is enjoying a birdie-fest. Sion is among the later starters, so he will have a good idea of the cut during his round. He begins with some solid pars, but his putter is stone cold. Despite all his expectations, he shoots another 69 and finishes one shot off the mark. It is one of the most disappointing moments of Sion's recent career, especially as his season is now well past halfway and his chances of playing in the bigger tournaments are diminishing. He looks on disconsolately while his fellow countrymen are interviewed about their prospects for the weekend.

There is a small shaft of light when he travels to Austria the following week and plays all four rounds, finishing tied 33rd and earning over €10,000. But the cool facts of this small success cannot disguise that Sion is a long way off retaining his Card. After Austria, he is 230th in the money list with just €16,852 from 12 events, close to disastrous on his finances because he has spent over double that amount in travel, accommodation and other tournament-related expenses. Another small success in France the next week is also of little comfort. Sion ties for 26th place, his best finish of the year, but it is in the wrong tournament. The Open de St Omer takes place in Europe at the exact same time that the US Open is staged in America. The prize fund in France is tiny and a week of effort brings in only €4,600 to Sion's coffers, yet over in Oakmont Pennsylvania, tied 26th is worth €42,687. Even finishing place at the US Open (63rd place) is worth over €12,000.

Sion is fully aware of what is happening to his season. "When you get into a rut of not making cuts, you're not surprised when you miss them. You can't turn up at tournaments just thinking about not making the cut, it's a bad mindset. I've felt I've hit the ball well but not been able to putt. During a 20-tournament season there are usually a couple of times when it all gels together, but that hasn't happened yet. Of course, it's a bit worrying."

At least he has been relatively injury-free despite a small scare. Earlier in the year Sion had a slight back injury brought on from wearing six-year-old orthotics that were supposed to be solving a case of flat feet. After a trip to an osteopath and a new set of orthotics, he is in rude health. Strangely, if injury was behind the lack of form then Sion's situation might be easier to swallow. Right now, however, he has no excuses.

Injury is one of the tournament pro's greatest enemies, especially at this time of year with so much money to be won. Every player suffers from a twinge or two because the pro golf season is long and hard: lots of playing, practicing, travelling and constant tension, but anything more than an occasional ache is unwelcome. Guy Woodman is certainly aware of how injury can wreck the best laid plans.

Five years ago during a winter in South Africa on the Sunshine Tour, he was playing some impressive golf. One top ten finish won him an unexpected place in the prestigious South African Open at Erinvale and he also teed it up at the Dimension Data at Sun City as well as the Tour Championship. Life was good and he returned to the UK full of confidence. "I shot a course ırd in the first stage of the EuroPro Tour qualifying event in the spring ınd won it. I even finished sixth in my first tournament that year. The next week I flew to Portugal and that was when my back went."

Just like so many pros, Guy's back is his weak point. The golf swing is a very unnatural, repetitive motion; the turning motion causes stress and the back muscles takes plenty of the strain. Although he had never suffered a serious injury before, Guy had a real problem.

"We were playing practice rounds in Portugal and I felt a little niggle. Tiger Woods was on the golf scene by now and I was doing some heavy weights to bulk myself up because that's what he was doing. I just wasn't working on my flexibility. The weather was cold and it was raining. I felt a twinge in my back and took some Nurofen. By the end of my round I didn't know if I could play the next day. I rested well, but I got up in the morning and it was still really hurting. So I took lots of painkillers and played the first three holes and suddenly I could hardly walk. I thought I'd be alright in a week, but it was never the case."

Guy's decision to turn to tablets to regain his sense of invincibility rather than seek immediate advice would prove a long-term and costly mistake. "I had treatment for nine months seeing all these different people saying different things. One guy said I had to have my jaw broken and re-set. I had MRI scans that said I had two pro-lapsed discs. Someone put me in touch with a specialist in Harley Street who worked with lots of the players like Justin Rose and Retief Goosen. He was the first person to know what was going on. He gave me exercises. The way my pelvis was aligned with my vertebrae, they were opposing one another and putting pressure on my discs. So it was a lot of re-hab, re-alignment and icing to get rid of the swelling."

Guy's first attempt to return from the back problem failed and, in all, he missed two full summers of golf. During that time, he earned no prize money, yet the cost of being a tournament pro was still evident in all the medical bills.

Guy is by no means alone with his injury woes. Most serious injuries do not completely disappear from the bodies of sportsmen and women who will do almost anything to prevent the problem flaring up again: bandages, body supports, warm-ups and warm-downs, gym work and, of course, painkilling drugs. Injury stories on Tour are as common as golfers on the driving range. The question is: will an injury end Guy's dream this year?

Now in his 40s, Phil Golding knows that an injury is probably his biggest potential problem as he tries to extend his career on Tour. He has avoided serious problems and long absences from the Tour by a mixture of good luck and good judgement. This season's break is about bad form not a bad back and Phil's past seven months have actually been quite relaxing for his body and also his general well being. Although there is still some stress from not earning any prize money, he has been able to enjoy extra time with his six-year-old son Lucas and wife Sally while staying healthy and fit at the same time.

"Nowadays, I always eat well and I do plenty of gym work; I'll work out four or five times a week. I make sure my diet is good, I do a lot of stretching; even on holiday I'll go for a run for half an hour. I'm the same weight as I've been for years – about 180lbs (82 kilogrammes). It's about making an effort. I've even been to see a biomechanics expert who gave me a routine just for myself. When you look at what the body does to hit a golf ball and the amount of balls you hit, then you will get problems with wrists and shoulders. The problem is being forced to play to try to keep making the money. You have to sometimes limit the practice or at least do less dynamic work, more on your short game."

Phil's recent fitness improvements came after years of good luck avoiding injuries. "I get a bad back now and again, but I've learned how to stretch it out. I had tennis elbow a few years ago and had to take a bit of time off. It was hard not being able to play and I even tried playing with a strapped arm. I feel I played too much golf a few seasons ago; it happens, though, especially when you're chasing results. The top players only play 20-25 times a year."

One probable reason injury has stayed out of Phil's life is that he came from a sporting family and was an accomplished multi-sportsman in his teens. He originally wanted to be a cricketer, but golf got in the way. He became a top Middlesex golfing amateur before turning pro in 1981 and qualified as a full PGA Professional three years later. But £15 a week as an assistant pro selling chocolate bars and giving lessons to members was not Phil's dream; he wanted a life on the European Tour and went to Q School for the first time in 1983.

"People make a big deal out of me going to Q School so many times, but the first four or five years I should never have gone. I wasn't good enough, but club members paid for me to go, so I kept trying. There were 50 Tour Cards available in those days and I was one of the youngest players there." It would be 1993 at his 10th Q School visit when Phil secured his first Tour Card.

The prize funds on Tour at this time were still relatively modest by today's standards (the staggering upward spiral would only begin after a certain Mr T Woods came on the scene a couple of years later), but Phil was driven by money. He still remembers searching for golf balls to play with as a youngster and, as an assistant pro, he would clean the toilets or wash cars to earn extra cash and then spend it playing tournaments.

"I was conscious of money then (1993), not having any to spend. Now every tour golfer has plenty of golf balls and shoes and the like. You get blazé about it after a while, spending £1,500-£2,000 a week on Tour."

When money was tight and there were crises of confidence, Phil kept aiming for the top. "I could've given up the game many times, but it's an addiction, it's a drug. Even when I got married, I was dedicated to my golf. Sally believed in me all the way through, but if she had not supported me then I would've chosen golf. Nowadays, I think what else would I do? I'm qualified to do a club professional's job and I'd never say never. Getting a club job is not a bad life – teaching, a bit of playing, corporate stuff – but I wouldn't want to do it."

Despite being close to the seniors end of the pro game, Phil will play on the Main Tour for as long as he can or is injury-free. The desire still burns. "Deep down, I'm pretty tough. You have to be in this game. The older pros say how they wish they'd carried on playing. But sometimes it's also a money issue – can you afford *not* to keep playing?"

Having a cut-back schedule this year – Phil will probably only play a dozen tournaments before Q School – actually makes him appreciate each limited chance. But it is also draining him mentally. He made his first European Tour cut in Spain in May finishing tied 40th and this month had back-to-back four round tournaments in France and Germany, but his best showing was tied 33rd. In eight events, he has won only €24,000 and is 220th on the money list. He has high hopes for his French Open invitation next month (as a former champion, the tournament organiser rolls out the red carpet), but it might be his last event in 2007 before the School which is looming large already.

At this point in the season, the continuing story of Andy Raitt and his injury is the personification of pain and persistence. To put things into perspective, try to imagine a concert pianist who attempts to play the hardest concertos in the uncomfortable knowledge that his little finger might, at any moment, hit a wrong note seemingly of its own volition.

Andy's problems were summed up by then the great Ben Hogan many decades ago when he wrote this: "You can't make the (golf ball) move unless you have the proper hold on the club. It's like steering an automobile. You don't steer to the right all the time, you also steer to the left. That ability has to come from the grip, which is the transformer through which the juice flows." Gripping the club is central to Andy's lack of confidence in his swing and Hogan's words are the kind of testimony he needed a couple of years ago to win his court case.

By the time of the BMW International in Germany towards the end of this month, Andy has made only four cuts in 17 tournaments and is a lamentable 184th in the money list. Although he is putting a brave face on his season, there seems no light at the end of the tunnel.

The life of the golf pro can be a demoralising place – waiting around at airports, late night practice on the putting green, waking up alone in another hotel room in yet another country. There is often too much time for reflection, especially if you are missing cuts and flying home early every week. This is all true for Andy, but his torrid recent life delivers yet more potential problems: there is a threat of bankruptcy; his ex-mother-in-law still chases him for money; and his limited access to his young daughter is depressing. If all this was not enough, Andy's life revolves around trying to find a solution to an injury that just will not go away. He will sit at a dinner table talking of how stabilising his hand, his wrist and his shoulder will help his golf swing while all the time unconsciously clenching and unclenching his fist almost as if hoping that the pain will suddenly disappear. Andy's chances on Tour are being undermined by forces he cannot control.

"It's been the worst stretch of my career ever. No matter how bad I've played, I've never missed cuts like this. I knew it would be a tough year because I set out to go back to trying to release the club like I used to instead of playing steady crap. So my wild shots are really wild and I'm losing balls on a fairly regular basis." Andy's dilemma is that he can still play almost-decent golf by taking into account his injury, but he is determined to find a better way, a path to the golfer he once believed he would become. But the Tour has moved on since his brief heyday and the competition is brutal.

"When I first got on the tour I made 16 or 17 cuts and a top 10 early on, but now it's more difficult. It used to be the top 70 players who made the cut, but now it's only 65 and ties; I'm spending too much time just thinking about if I can make it to the weekend. You don't have to do much wrong to miss the cut now because they're all good players."

However, if Andy wants inspiration about what can be achieved despite injury, then he can relate to another Q School pro from a few years ago. Englishman Jeremy Robinson was diagnosed with arthritis at the base of his back in 1998, yet tried to play the School that year. "It was OK for the first couple of rounds," he remembers. "If it had been an ordinary tournament then I'd've pulled out. It just happened that I kept having reasonable rounds and giving myself a chance to get my Card, so I kept coming back the next day. I was only able to hit about five shots on the practice range each morning to loosen up a bit and was going to the physio for a massage each day. I was also on plenty of painkillers. The main problem was not tee shots, they were fine; it was when I had a shot from a bad lie or out of the rough and had to go after it a bit, that was the worst. The pain was so bad that I even yelled out a couple of times. My memory of the whole week is just being in pain."

Still in contention on day six of Final Stage, Jeremy played the San Roque New Course starting at the 10th. "It was painful all the way around. I ended up using a 3-iron as a walking stick to ease some of the pressure off my back plus my caddie was picking the ball out of the hole." The consequence of his injury was steadier golf. Jeremy turned down the power; hit shorter, straighter, more conservative tee shots; and his approaches always came from the fairway. Avoiding the rough that would tax his body was vital.

Jeremy came to the last hole on the last day needing a par for a Tour Card. He had a short pitch shot to the final green, but after six rounds of constant pain, he duffed it, leaving himself an unlikely 20ft putt. "By that stage, I'd had enough; I was really just thinking about getting finished and heading for home. Being bent over every putt was one of the more painful positions for me, so it was not easy to concentrate. I just tried to make sure I wasn't short of the hole."

Despite all that had happened, somehow Jeremy holed the putt and won his Card; it would be the very last one awarded that year. "I could hardly walk for days when I arrived home after the flight. Of course, because I got my Card, I can look back now and say it was the right decision to carry on." Jeremy did no permanent damage to his back at that Q School, but by 2002, four years later, his tournament career was over.

Nowadays, Jeremy Robinson runs both a corporate golf events management company and his own driving range near Worcester in the Midlands. He fought through pain at Q School because of what a Tour Card meant to him and it is a situation very similar to Andy Raitt's. However, Andy's fight is also with some dark thoughts.

"The only way I've learned to cope with it is not to give a shit," he says. "Otherwise, a lot of the time I look at my hand, my career and my financial situation and I think that if I got hit by a bus then it wouldn't be the end of the world. Seriously, I walk around the golf course thinking about it a lot. Yes, it's dark, but it's a pretty hard thing to live with. You spend all your life trying to get better at this game, but you get worse and worse; then you're going to get some compensation for it, but you end up losing everything you have."

Has he changed during all this suffering with his problem finger? "I think the injury has affected me more than anything else. I'm trying to become more positive, but it's really hard. I got divorced a month after the court case was over. I was probably a difficult bloke to live with because I was in constant pain. We'd had problems and huge financial difficulties and I'd been out for nine months with shoulder surgery. The idea was that we survive until the court case was over. We thought we'd walk out with a load of money – the amount was academic – but it didn't pan out that way. Then my wife said enough's enough. As it turned out, it helped losing the court case because if we'd walked out with four million quid then I can't imagine how difficult the divorce would've been. In fact, I walked out with a quarter of a million pound debt and it was still difficult to get rid of her."

Despite the flashes of darkness, Andy wants nothing more than to prove himself worthy of his place on Tour. At least these days he is surrounded by people who want to help – his girlfriend, Lindsay; a sponsor for the first time assisting him financially; and a good friend-cum-coach working on his swing. Andy has fought back so hard and with such determination that any golf fan would want him to succeed this year. But as summer reaches its height, Andy's place among the elite is starting to slip away.

Chapter 8 – July 2007

Winning & Worrying

"Winning is easier (than succeeding at Q School). If you're in with a chance to win then you know you're playing well, so you can let the pressure go a little. But if you're playing a six-round tournament you can't afford to have a couple of bad days, so I'd say Q School was more stressful when you come down the stretch than winning a tournament" – Miles Tunnicliff, two-time Tour winner and 12-time Q School attendee.

American comedian Jerry Seinfeld once quipped that the New York Marathon was a pointless event to take part in. "It's a race with one winner and 30,000 losers!" Well, to the uneducated fan, professional golf tournaments look the same: 156 players tee it up, but only one person wins. These are not good odds, yet every single player will hit that first tee shot either believing – or at least hoping – that it is their turn, that they catch lightning in a bottle. That's because they know that winning changes everything.

A pro win can be a fleeting moment, a single peak in a career or it may be one of many highlights during several seasons of success. Alternatively, that win may never happen at all and, of course, victories become harder as you climb golf's professional ladder

To win on a mini tour like the two-round Jamega Tour in the UK or the ALPs tour on continental Europe can certainly help launch a career, but it pales into insignificance compared to the consequences of capturing a trophy on the full European Tour. Such success brings heaps of prize money; lucrative endorsement deals; the admiration of your peers; and invites to lots more chances to win at even higher levels because European Tour champions receive either a one- or two-year tournament exemption. It is estimated that only about 2% of European Tour golfers actually win at this level, but there is still plenty of riches for those who miss out on the titles. Take Roger Chapman of England. In over 500 tournaments on the Main Tour between 1982 and 2006, he won only once (a relatively small event in Brazil in 2000 where few of the world's best players turned up) yet he is still in the top 80 all-time career earners at this time with over €3.3 million in prize money.

Often times, one win is not enough. Some newly-crowned champions fret about whether their first victory was just a fluke, a simple one-off. Are they worthy of the triumph? Perhaps they were lucky because other players dropped lots of shots or the field of players was weak. That is the perversity of golf and sport – winning can remove one pressure, but replace it with another.

Guy Woodman is still searching for that elusive first win after seven years as a pro. It is not that he lacks talent, it is just that winning as a pro is not easy. Guy was regarded as a gifted junior and won trophies as a teenage amateur. He recognised that there would be extra pressure in the professional ranks and he accepted the constant practice, the evening jobs to fund his tournaments, the stress from parents and girlfriends, the unrelenting improvement of his peers. For many young players, the tournament demands and lifestyle seem overwhelming, but for Guy, it was as necessary as breathing.

Yet acceptance does not automatically deliver competence. Even in this his eight season as a pro, Guy finds life tough on the mini tours. His opening few results have been mixed – a too many missed cuts and too few pounds in the bank. Then in the fifth EuroPro event at Collingtree Park in the Northamptonshire countryside of the English East Midlands, Guy makes a change to his normal tournament routine – he asks a friend to caddie for him.

Brian Keely had attended the Wales Open, but couldn't get a bag and so he works for Guy instead. "I said I'd pay for his digs," says Guy, "and give him 10% of my winnings. I thought the most I'd give away was a couple of hundred pounds. I'd missed the first two cuts by a shot this year and I wasn't in the best of form mentally. Brian knows a bit about the mental side of the game, so it was good. I thought just to make the cut and a top 15 would be progress." After two rounds, Guy is among a dozen players in the mix and will need something special to lift himself from the pack for the third and final round.

On the front 9 on the last day, Guy hits every green in regulation but two-putts each time; he feels that he has failed to make a significant putt all week. He turns to Brian for some advice. "I knew I was being over-analytical, but it was the same every week. I couldn't seem to make any putts. Brian told me to see the ball tracking into the hole, bring my eyes back to the ball and – still imagining it tracking in – hit the ball and see what happens." Guy tries the new technique with a 20ft uphill putt and holes it for a birdie. The next hole, a 30-footer also falls into the cup; and it happens again on the16th when he holes from 25 feet.

By now, Guy is within a shot of the leader. But he bogeys 17 and takes a peak at the leaderboard. He thinks his chance has gone – one more hole and two behind. But the par 5 18th at Collingtree is a fabulous finishing hole and offers a death-or-glory opportunity. Seeing the scoreboard loosens Guy up and he decides to risk everything by going for the green in two shots.

"I was very nervous; tough par five, water down the left, trees down the right and an island green. But Brian again got hold of me and said: 'This is what you practice for, this is what we want. Let's do this.'"

Guy rips his drive down the middle of the fairway and uses a rescue club for his tricky approach; it is 230 yards to the pin. "Deep down I didn't know if I had that shot in me. I'd looked up at the leaderboard and the leader had gone to 10 under; there was a logjam of people on 8 under with me. I thought I would go home with nothing if I didn't make it." In the end, the ball stops 25 feet from the pin and he rolls in another glorious putt that sends him into a playoff with Russell Claydon and Adam Frayne who also finish on 10 under.

Both Claydon and Frayne are more experienced (in fact, the roly-poly figure of Claydon was a regular on the European Tour a decade ago and even finished 20th in the 1997 Order of Merit), so Guy is not favourite, particularly because negative thoughts creep into his mind just moments after he feels the joy of his eagle putt on the final green.

"On that 18th, I felt incredible elation, but then – and this is me all over – I was scared. I'd never won and when Adam and Russell were still out there also on 10 under, I was hoping one of them would either birdie the 18th or they'd both bogey it. I thought that if I got in the playoff I'd embarrass myself." Such an admission may seem like a startling one for a committed pro golfer, but once again it is an indication of how the sport is a mental battle as much as a physical one. Guy is not the first pro to ever suffer from low self-esteem at a vital moment in his career and, certainly, millions of amateur golfers will recognise what is happening to the young pro. Luckily for Guy, this week he has chosen to employ an experienced caddie. "If I'd been on my own, I'd've been a wreck. Brian and I went to the range and practiced playing the playoff hole – the 18th – again, driver and then rescue club, picturing the shots each time. It was just what I needed."

When the three players meet on the tee for sudden death, Guy gets lucky again – he draws the No 1 tee position, so he can focus fully on his own shot. Winning a playoff is not about how many shots, but about shooting one fewer than your opponents.

"It was only after getting the No 1 driving position that I got the feeling of *The Big Break*; the people and the TV cameras, I felt at ease. I thought I'd got nothing to lose and hit driver." The TV programme had been Guy's first real exposure to high profile golf; he finished second in the series and during one round drained a 45ft putt to win a car for a year. Although there were no fans on-site at the TV show recordings, the thought of an audience of many millions watching in their armchairs at home was enough to infuse the whole event with a special kind of tension. Guy's understanding of that tension is now paying off.

The Big Break runner-up hits his driver straight and long; Adam and Russell take 3-woods and are 20 yards behind him. Adam is undecided about his second shot; he changes clubs to a 4-iron and this proves fatal as his ball falls short and into water. Russell makes the green in two, as does Guy, and they both record birdies. The three-man playoff is now down to two.

It's back to the 18th tee and Guy's drive finds the semi-rough. Russell, however, pulls his drive into the water hazard on the left. The door for a first professional tour win is now wide open for Guy, but he must still hit another perfect rescue club approach.

"I had a slightly smelly lie in the semi, so I still had to hit a good shot. I knew if I got on the green in two I would win. I stuck to the process, the same routine and made the swing." Guy's ball is safe and he grabs his victory with both hands. Strangely, though, there are no massive celebrations on the green.

"It was mixed emotions, actually. I had a one foot putt to tap in for the trophy. I knew then I was going to win and as I went to mark my ball I felt all these emotions welling up inside me; I thought I was going to cry. It suddenly hits you – you're going to win because of all this hard work you've put in over the years. And I know it's only the EuroPro Tour, but any level now you have to play well to win. When I knocked the ball in, it was weird; it was a huge relief to know that I could do it and beat some good players in a playoff. Now everyone could see that maybe I've got what it takes to move up to the next level. But, at the very end, it was like 'Is that it?'. I felt numb; there was nothing there."

Guy shakes his head when he remembers the feelings. All that worrying about winning for the first time and now he knows that one win is not enough. "That night I had to go to a wedding reception. I drove back home and my parents were in tears. Seven years just to win at this level – it's crazy really."

For every first-time-pro-winner like Guy who has paid his dues at scores of golf tournaments, there is a young star who bursts onto the scene and manages a victory almost before he has found his feet as a professional. Ross McGowan is just such a man in 2007 on the Challenge Tour. While Guy waited seven years to put his hands on his first professional trophy, Ross managed it in seven months.

Ross was only a very promising amateur at Q School's Final Stage last November. He found the experience rather tortuous and never really contended for a Tour Card, but he put the disappointment behind him, signed as a professional with Andrew 'Chubby' Chandler's ISM agency and was promptly sent off to the Sunshine Tour in Southern Africa to gain some experience.

Finding a little form, Ross made cuts, made money and made himself into a professional. He began to understand the constant travelling, the new courses each week and the higher level of competition. He even got to the top of the leaderboard a couple of times. Back in the UK by February, the 25-year-old was looking forward to a Challenge Tour season with maybe a couple of full European Tour events thrown in.

In fact, Ross showed some form on the Main Tour in Portugal in March with two opening rounds of 68 and was buzzing when he teed it up in Manchester for the Oceânico Developments Pro-Am Challenge, a strangely formatted event where amateurs play alongside the pros in the final two rounds of the tournament. A stunning second round 63 at the Worsley Park Hotel and Country Club course – including six consecutive birdies – could almost have been forecast and he eventually secured victory at the tournament after a playoff. Two months later, he racked up win No 2 to virtually guarantee a top 15 finish in the Challenge Tour rankings and, hence, a Tour Card next season without a visit to Q School.

By contrast, Guy Woodman's EuroPro trophy is not enough to avoid the School. However, the £10,000 winner's cheque is very welcome and there's a chance now of a top five finish in the end-of-season EuroPro order of merit that would mean a ticket directly to Final Stage. The problem for Guy is that even his first win is not enough to stop all the worrying.

For Phil Golding, winning is something of a distant memory. It is now five years since he grabbed the French Open trophy. Not long after, he asked himself: 'When is the next title coming?' Phil wishes he knew the answer to that question. The French victory in June 2003 happened just after he celebrated his 40th birthday and followed 16 trips to the Q School. It was his 201st European Tour event and proved to be a magical week.

Phil had won as a professional before – on the Challenge Tour in the early part of his career – but this was different. The French Open is one of the larger events on the European Tour with 1st place prize money of around £300,000. It attracts a very strong field each year and former champions include Colin Montgomerie, Nick Faldo, Retief Goosen, Seve Ballesteros, Greg Norman and Jose Maria Olazabal.

Many thousands of pros never win on the Main Tour, so a veteran like Phil taking this trophy was as welcome as it was unexpected. Plus the victory had come just a few months after even his remarkable tolerance of struggle had been stretched to the limit.

Phil's own resilience as a golf pro had begun to waiver towards the end of the previous season. Yet again he needed an outstanding result from the last tournament of the year; it would take a top 10 finish at the Italian Open to avoid Q School. He was out early in the last round, shot 63 and it seemed he had beaten the odds. As the leaders were finishing their own rounds, Phil seemed to have achieved his goal; he was even interviewed on Sky Sports about his gutsy performance. Everyone thought he had done enough to earn a Card at the very last minute, but sport is a wicked mistress sometimes. There was a burst of low-scoring very late in the day and Phil ended up 12th. It would be Q School again.

"I was gutted. I wanted to finish right then, give up altogether. But I spoke to a couple of players on the way home and they said that I simply had go to the School. I'd just shot a 63 and played well. Sally said I should do it. So I went there alone; carried my clubs in my lightweight, pencil bag; practiced on my own and then met a guy who wanted to caddie but who'd done only one other tournament. I trained him up in a day and we finished third."

From that moment, Phil had the kind of momentum that golfers dream about and the 2003 season was a huge improvement. He led a couple of tournaments over the next few months going into the final rounds and missed only four cuts in 16 events. Consistency is a much sought-after currency and Phil had some. Even so, he had no inkling that the French Open would be the tournament he would cherish for the rest of his life.

"I didn't think it was my week, I was quite tired, I'd been playing five or six weeks in a row, I'd had appalling practice, but found something on the range, something clicked. It was to do with my set up, about holding my right knee on the way back and firing it on the way through. I had fallen into a bad habit, I guess. Anyway, I hit the ball straight and shot 66 on the first day and was leading. All the papers said it wouldn't last. The guy from the Daily Mail wrote some naughty things about me, but I had a nice warm feeling that week. I was hitting the ball better and better. And I putted well and any player who's in contention for a pro tournament will have to putt well."

The first round 66 was one of his best ever on Tour, but although Thomas Bjorn and David Howell both came into contention during round two, Phil kept his cool and remained among the leaders. Another classy 68 in round three – including a birdie on the last hole – put him into a one-shot lead with 18 holes to play.

The stories coming out of the pressroom talked of the widespread sense of déjà vu because the previous year's champion, Malcolm McKenzie, had won at the age of 40 after 20 years of trying. Phil's story seemed like a potential carbon copy, as long as he could cross the finishing line in front.

On the Saturday night Phil slept fitfully but still felt ready in the morning. During the final round, his good form held, but he was struggling to keep his emotions in check. "It was tough out there. Every time I thought of my family I got a bit emotional on the course. I knew how they would react to every birdie and I had to bring myself back to the present and remind myself to concentrate on every shot. It was the longest day of my life."

Phil kept checking the scoreboard to make sure he did not miss his chance. "I saw David (Howell) had made a birdie on the 18th so I knew I needed a four to win." The par 5 18th at Le Golf National in Paris has plenty of frightening water, but Phil would not be denied. He hit the green in two, took his two putts and grabbed the trophy, much to the delight of himself and also his fellow pros.

The two decades of work as a pro and the 16 visits to the Q School were never far away from his thoughts both during and after the final round. He quipped in his winner's speech that his normal November routine was so well trodden that he might just have to go along to the next Q School to watch.

"After I won, I had to do a drug test; it's not normal on Tour, but French laws state you have to. I was so dehydrated I couldn't pass water for two or three hours and I missed my flight home. I got a later flight and then got picked up by a limo at City Airport and was finally back home at 10.30 at night. My whole family were outside the house banging on pots and pans; that was about the only celebration I had time for."

In fact, the joy of victory is often short-lived for professional golfers because as soon as they achieve one level of success there is another level waiting to be scaled.

"I did feel different the next week. But I actually felt more pressure. I felt like I had to do it again quickly. I put pressure on myself because the victory came almost out of the blue; you find yourself having to live up to your win."

The newly-discovered pressure destroyed Phil's post-French Open week. He spent the Monday after his victory talking to the press; flew to Dublin on Tuesday for the European Open where he enjoyed the congratulations of his peers; played in the pro-am on Wednesday (not part of his normal schedule because previous to his win, his status on the Tour was one of a journeyman); and so, by the time he teed it up on Thursday for the start of the tournament alongside Tour superstars Padraig Harrington and Thomas Bjorn, his head was in a total spin. His first round score was a 7 over par 79.

"All my time was taken up [in the week of the European Open]. I should never have played there, but I had never won on Tour before and I didn't know how important it was to take time out to enjoy the win. I had no time to practice in Ireland and in my first round, I was in the water two or three times. I was really embarrassed."

Other players knew how he felt. Colin Montgomerie tried to soften the embarrassment for Phil by telling him how he shot 80 the first time after winning. Phil's concentration was shocking that first day, but the real reason for his performance was that he did not feel he belonged with the other top players on Tour.

This month's French Open is perhaps Phil's best chance of avoiding another trip to Q School. Along with his fond memories, he brings coach Jason Banting with him to Paris and tries hard to play down the possibility of a repeat to all those who ask, even though it is what he wants most of all. He stays in the on-course hotel, is treated well as the past champion and plays the best he can. A 4 over par opening round is a huge disappointment and he misses the cut by two shots.

Phil's 18th trip to Q School is now inevitable. He knows there are bound to be 30 players at Final Stage in better form than him, so the odds are stacking up. In the summer of 2003, Phil was a European Tour champion with a two-year exemption and the golf world at his feet, but in July 2007, the former champ is in a golfing twilight zone; his top-flight career might be over. Yet the taste of victory remains. When he talks of the experience now, Phil looks into the far distance and can still picture the day of glory in his mind. "You don't eat very much on the last day, you don't sleep very much the night before, but you can remember the whole week from start to finish – the noises, the atmosphere, what people say to you. It's amazing."

At the end of the day, everyone remembers the winners, but in golf there are lots other excellent performances that mean a great deal to the players involved. James Conteh is still without a win in his four-year pro career, but a 7 under finish on a two-round Jamega Tour event this month for tied 6th is followed by an 8 under for tied 3rd a week later. These are his best showings of the year by far and give him some hope for First Stage of Q School that is now just over two months away.

July is also the month of the Open Championship and in 2007 it is staged at Carnoustie, one of the most feared courses on the major roster. James is among hundreds of pros from all over the world playing in the local qualifying rounds in the week before the tournament begins. Apart from gaining his Tour Card, to play in an Open Championship would be the next best thing for James and, in the two-round qualifier, he actually enjoys some of his best golf of the year, finding himself among the leaders. But he cannot beat the tiny odds for success. There are only three spots for the Open at his event in Scotland for 100 players. Eventually, James finishes 10th and misses out.

The casual observer might say that James is fooling himself to think he can qualify for a tournament as prestigious as the Open. However, professional golf is full of young men who are one round away from the greatest achievement in their lives. "The margins are so small," says James, "and it's hard to pinpoint why one player is doing better than another. Most often it's on the greens. You can play almost identical tee-to-green golf with someone and they knock in a couple of putts and you don't. That's all it takes for them to be 2nd and for you to be 40th."

If James needs an of indication that anything is possible in professional golf, then it comes at another Open qualifier this month. Steven Parry shoots 65 on the second day to finish joint top of his field; he is a most unlikely qualifier, an assistant pro from Lancashire. Yet this is the same Steven Parry who played with James in the first two rounds of First Stage of Q School last September at The Oxfordshire. Steven did not even make the three-round cut in that tournament, yet 10 months later he is playing in the Open and James is not.

As it turns out, the toughness of the Carnoustie links and the atmosphere of a major championship are too much for Steven and he returns home after 36 holes. However, he takes home nearly €4,000 for his trouble.

James and thousands of other mini tour pros wish they could have swapped places with Steven. For James, the fact that a mini-tour counterpart (whom he believes is no more talented than him) has played in the Open is yet more proof that his dream of a Tour Card is not so far-fetched as some people might make out.

Chapter 9 – August 2007

Seeing The Future Today

"Q School is horrible. I was very inexperienced in the early ones and, had I made my Card at the first stab, it would probably have been a mistake" – Ian Poulter, multiple Tour winner, Ryder Cup player and four-time Q Schooler.

While players at the top end of the European Tour are enjoying the climax of their seasons at big money tournaments, the journeymen are either praying for one final burst of cash-earning form or resigned to turning up at the First Stage of Q School next month.

Andy Raitt and Sion Bebb both had Tour Cards this year, but neither has prospered. In the three months between the Wales Open that welcomed in the month of June and the Johnnie Walker Championship at Gleneagles in Scotland that sees off August, both players teed it up at 10 tournaments. The courses and conditions were reassuringly European, but the pressure to perform against some of the best fields of the year has proved too much.

Of the two men, Andy has been the one suffering the most heartache – June was a fruitless disaster and two more tournaments in July also brought him no money. This month he travels to Sweden and Holland, but still no luck and by the time he comes to Gleneagles, Andy is despondent, his natural cheerfulness has deserted him and been replaced by intense exasperation. His fortunes are – as always – linked to his finger injury.

"The other guys on Tour are all bored with (the injury). I don't like talking about it and I never used to, but when I went to court they said 'Why don't we hear about this injury? Why don't you complain about it'. But if I had played well and went on talking about the injury then I'd've sounded like a prat. I guess I played this thing all wrong. It's funny because my ex-mother-in-law would send text messages about being so proud when I got through Q School and invite me over for dinner. The next thing she's threatening to sue me for money.

"I genuinely don't think anyone else would be playing on Tour if it had happened to them. If it happened to Monty or Darren (Clarke) or someone like that right now then they'd've just quit. Having been as good as they were, they'd never be that good again, ever; so they'd just stop. I don't consider my life like anyone else's on Tour because they're playing their own game and I'm playing whatever game I can salvage. So I'm on a mission now because I want to win a tournament to prove to the people who made it turn out this way that they can't do it to anyone else."

Andy is a work in progress, trying to recover the type of game he played before his injury. He wants his old swing back and, although his determination is strong, good results are slow in coming.

"My hand and shoulder and all the new muscles stiffen up when it gets cold. It's getting better – my arm is stronger and my body's getting better – but it's all about building up those new muscles. You can see that I struggle because I've got completely different calluses than everyone else on the Tour. They're on the lower third of my left little finger rather than the top of my palm. The hand does function better and I think in six months it will be better still. Before the surgery I could only play the one shot, basically a pull hook. I would aim right and pull it back to target and my misses were smaller than they are now. By trying to get back to how I used to play and have more than one choice of shot, I'm paying the price because my misses are a joke, so far right or left it's hard to comprehend. I used to be so straight and steady."

Thoughts of retiring from tournament golf or even leaving golf altogether are creeping into Andy's mind. "I never get away from my hand; my life is about trying to get my hand and arm and shoulder decent. If it doesn't feel alright at the end of this year then it's time to make a decision about whether I carry on or just quietly go away and do something else, not be a tournament pro. Part of me wants to leave golf alone altogether, but I'm not qualified to do anything else, it's what I do. Maybe I'd be stupid to walk away."

When a Tour player suffers a significant loss of form, his counterparts are never quite sure what to say or do. There is a family-feel on Tour, especially on practice days when players are in a hail-fellow-well-met kind of mood on the range. There are congratulations for last week's winners or good performers; family or friends to introduce; Tour gossip to mull over; and the press hangs around waiting for an interview. This pleasant buzz of activity does not usually include too many dark reflections because pros have been trained by their mind gurus to find positives in every situation. Out-of-form players keep their thoughts to themselves and the best pros focus on the promise of the future, not any effects of the past.

Andy does not want to become one of the Tour's whiners, so he has developed some new strategies to raise his spirits. "I want to enjoy the *craic* with the boys, so I've been driving a lot to tournaments this year. I went to Madrid and to Italy, then I drove home. I drove to Hamburg instead of flying. I stick on some music and get some alone-time, it's trying to get my head around it all. At the KLM Open in Holland this month I came within an inch of winning a BMW M6 convertible car with a hole in one. We were all saying 'This would be a good one to hole!' and I nearly did it. I saw all my debts disappearing in one shot. I wouldn't care if I kept the car or not, it'd just be nice to have some cash." Being the centre of that sort of attention among his Tour friends is more in keeping with the Andy of old.

There is also plenty of support from his family and girlfriend Lindsay. "She has been so fantastic. I don't know how I'd've managed this without her. I used to have a wife who did nothing but take, but now I have a girl who gives me her full support. My parents have been supportive too, even though my mum feels horribly guilty because she told me to take the dog for a walk that day the incident happened. They've been great and I don't think they'd like me to give up. They know I've wallowed a little bit in my head, but I try to make each week better."

At Gleneagles, despite help from his friend, coach and caddie Paul Thornley, Andy misses another cut and becomes resigned to going back to Q School; he will have to start at Second Stage.

"I really thought I was going to play better than this at the start of the season. I thought it would be the first year I'd have a chance to finish top 60 or 70, play steadily better rather than this. Some of it has got better; I've had more days at practice when I can put my hand up and say I'm striking it better, but I'm finding it difficult to take it onto the golf course. I'm more liable to have a good week, but I'm just not giving myself enough of a chance. Considering what I have been through, struggling out here doesn't phase me compared to walking out of a court room a quarter of million pounds in debt for having your finger bitten off."

Sion Bebb is also unhappy, but for different reasons. His first season as a regular Main Tour professional is somewhere between a disappointment and a disaster. As he tees up at the Johnnie Walker Championship at Gleneagles, Sion has made only six cuts and missed 15; he is 227th on the Order of Merit and has won just under £20,000. He is a worried man because he might be frozen out of tournaments for the rest of the season due to his ranking.

"Gleneagles could be my last tournament because there are shortened fields from now on. I'm 18th reserve for next week (European Masters) whereas normally I'd easily be in the field. I might have to play some Challenge Tour events. If I don't get in next week, then I'll play in the Welsh Pros which I won the last two years, so who knows. I could have a good week in Cardiff and few good Challenge Tour events and change my season around."

But although Sion speaks with sincerity, there is a lack of underlying confidence behind the words. His issue is his lack of a safety net of cash; he might not be able to even afford a trip to Q School.

"My money has almost run out and I am having serious thoughts about whether to go back to the School yet again – the cost, the potential disappointment, the upheaval for the family. Even if I got through, this year on the Tour has been so frustrating, so costly and with very little reward. It'd cost me three grand to go and we could do with that for my family through the winter rather than following the dream. I could have earned a lot of money just staying at home this year, but you have the opportunity and you have to give it a shot. Some players are not playing on the Main Tour because they are not earning any money. Guys who came through the Q School with me last November are concentrating on Challenge Tour. I could do the same and still maybe get into the top 45 there (which means a direct route to Final Stage). Right now, it looks like I'll go to Second Stage. Rita wants me to do it, but if I'm at home next month and we're struggling to get by, then we have to make the serious decision about whether I go through with it. We're dipping into savings; it's something we don't want to do. We have only so much left and when that goes through we don't know what happens next. I don't want Rita to go back to work. With what she was forking out on crèche fees for our first child, it wasn't worth it."

With a 20-event schedule on the Main Tour, a professional can easily get through up to £40,000 in expenses and with Sion's earnings being less than half of that, then it is easy to see how the pressure starts to build for players at the wrong end of the money list. The locker rooms are full of the ghosts of players past who had the briefest of lives on tour, losing a small fortune in the process. For some it is just not meant to be.

At Gleneagles, Sion has Rita with him and both his daughters. It is the family's first real holiday together of the year and it is doing Sion a power of good. Rita is in charge of the couple's two girls over the practice days, but Sion still finds time to ferry them from the range to their hotel and back. For six-year-old Alys, Daddy already has plenty of trophies at home so she doesn't mind what is happening to his career; she is just excited to be the centre of attention in the players' lounge and among the caddies. Her mood rubs off on Sion who is noticeably more relaxed, although his work situation never far away.

"We're talking with friends here who have done well and it's difficult, they're all excited about where they're playing next year and I've no idea what I'm doing. I might need to get another job to supplement my income again. It's just frustrating. I should have my Card in my back pocket by now, but I'm not playing well enough."

Sion's search for a change of form is endless. Like so many players, it is a matter of lining up all the best parts of his game at the same time. At the moment, his driving and approach shots are consistent, but his chipping around the greens and his putting are sub-standard. But knowing the problems is different than solving them. "This season, I've never put all of my gate together, the missing link's been one or the other that is quite worrying. You never know when you're going to play well and when your luck changes; you have to grind it out until that happens. It's a little bit of confidence that you need. I was looking for something in my swing this week that would click and, in the last six holes of practice, I felt it and I birdied 16, 17 and 18. I need a good start and something to hang on to rather than being a few over par in the opening round."

For once, Sion gets the good start he is looking for; perhaps it is a mixture of a course that he enjoys plus his family's close proximity. He opens with three birdies in his first seven holes and ends day one with a 2 under par 71. He goes on to make the cut easily and finishes tied 26th to pick up not only his biggest cheque of the season, but also the largest of his whole professional career – £12,880. It's a shot in the arm and lifts him to 209th in the money list. Then more great news comes after the tournament – Sion has actually gained entry into the European Masters in Switzerland the following week. Good form and good luck have come along together – is this the beginning of something?

Four days later, in early September, Sion gets to Crans Montana with renewed confidence and also a new caddie. Gary Marshall is normally the bagman for respected French pro and three-time Tour winner Jean-Francois Remesy, but he has a free week and the Scotsman teams up with the Welshman for the first time. Gary is an experienced caddie – something Sion has not always been able to afford – and knows the Swiss course very well.

Gary makes a difference from the very beginning. On the opening hole – a par 5 – the ideal landing spot for the tee shot is about 250 metres from the green and Sion normally hits his 3-wood. However, Gary is more aware of how a golf ball reacts on this mountain course with 5,000ft of elevation and advises a 5-wood instead. The result is a tee shot that lands in position 'A'. "Who knows where I would have ended up with the 3-wood," reports Sion afterwards. For the first time, Sion has a caddie he can rely on. Gary is working out the next shot while Sion is still concentrating on the current one. It sounds so obvious, but Sion is now piloting his game with an excellent navigator beside him. Despite a nervous start, Sion opens with a level par 71.

On day two, the new team finds some early birdies and shoots 3 under so Sion has made the cut by a good margin two weeks running. Not only that, he is handily placed for a change; although the leaders are at 11 under, Sion is teeing off his third round just six groups behind.

Then it happens, what Sion has been hoping for all season: his whole game – from driving to putting – sparkles. Three birdies on the front 9 are followed by three more plus an eagle on the back. Sion has just shot a bogey-free 8 under par 63, the best round of the week, and has soared into contention on 11 under for the tournament. Today, every fairway seemed enormous and the holes were buckets. It is the first time he has ever made such a mark on a European Tour event; he has broken 70 only seven times in 20 tournaments up to now in 2007.

Sion is playing his kind of game – plotting his way around a difficult course by hitting the middle of fairways and the centres of greens. He is also finally holing his share of putts and goes into the last day with a chance of winning a Main Tour event for the first time, playing in the penultimate threeball with Lee Westwood and Gonzalo Fernandez-Castaño.

Such heady heights can throw many pros, but Sion feels comfortable and grabs the challenge with both hands. His start is a little edgy with two birdies alternating with two bogeys in the opening for holes, but another two birdies have him 2 under for the round at the turn and he is still in contention with England's Philip Archer and Brett Rumford of Australia four shots ahead of him. On the back 9 (where Sion was 5 under par 24 hours ago), the Welshman needs to push for birdies if this is going to be a fairytale victory. But the tension of the final day leaderboard finally proves too much and five holes go by without him picking up a shot on the leaders. Archer and Rumford are now too far ahead, so Sion opts for absolute safety on the last three holes to gain as a high finish as possible rather than risk almost impossible birdies and an unlikely win.

The Welshman ends with a brave 4 under par 68 for fourth place and another record pay cheque (£67,000) that puts his bank account into the black. Plus, he wins an expensive Omega watch for the best round of the week and his top 10 finish means an unexpected place in the following week's British Masters at The Belfry. But Sion's under-stated sense of humour keeps things in perspective: his post-event quote reveals that he finally has some cash to fix his family's washing machine. He has moved up to 145th in the money list, but is still 30 places short of the Tour Card mark and will still have to attend Q School Second Stage if he cannot make another giant leap. It's far too early to break out the champagne.

Euan Little is not playing enough tournament golf. Since May, he has started only twice on the Main Tour, in Austria (tied 14th and €14,000) and France (the Open de Saint-Omer, a missed cut) plus one Challenge Tour event in Switzerland where he tied 14th and took home €2,000. His opportunities to tune up for Second Stage of Q School are running out fast. He plays in the Russian Open this month (August), but this tournament has one of the smallest prize funds on Tour and, although he manages another cut and finishes tied 44th, he earns just over €8,000. Then a Challenge Tour event in Scotland is a flop – he misses the cut. Finally, he travels to Gleneagles hoping to join Sion Bebb and Andy Raitt for the end-of-the-month Johnnie Walker

Championship. But Euan is only first reserve; he needs someone to withdraw at the last minute.

Euan waits for some news on the driving range each day where coach Bob Torrance casts an eye over his swing. It is quite common, even with a couple of days to go, for a pro to pull out of an event with an injury, so Euan is quite chipper as he chats to fellow players and caddies. He likes the Gleneagles course and is primed for a good event. He just needs for someone else's misfortune to give him a chance.

During the pre-tournament days, there is talk on the range of niggling injuries among some of the star players and even the impending birth of fellow pro Sam Little's baby that might cause the Englishman to drive to the hospital at any minute. However, the wait proves fruitless – all the players on the entry list above Euan make it to the 1st tee and he returns to his home in Glasgow.

Waiting for the next opportunity is something Euan understands. "I've spent over half my life waiting; I'm waiting right now for Q School and maybe a planned schedule and some stability that would come with a Card. It would be great, in an ideal world, to have a wife and kids and be financially sound and playing regularly on Tour, but that will have to wait too. Until then, it's work, work, work on the golf."

Strangely, Euan is calm about the lack of play. He has started only 15 tournaments in total this year, but made six out of eight cuts on his limited Main Tour opportunities. He has played only one really poor tournament – the 9 over for two rounds at the Open de Saint Omer in June – and then there has been the benefit of spending more time with Bob Torrance. His previous lack of a strong work ethic is well behind him.

"Bob shows great belief in me and I'm starting to believe a little more in myself each week. It's taken a lot longer than I thought it was going to. I was tipped to be quite successful by him and because of that I didn't work hard enough. Nowadays, he's never totally happy with my work rate, but he's definitely more pleased to see that it is increasing."

At the end of the day, Q School has been Euan's long-term goal this year, the only thing on his mind. "It's all about the mental side; it's just taken me a long time to see that. I'm not frightened of Q School because the Main Tour is where I think I should be and, if I don't get my Card, then I'll to find golf somewhere around the world. There's Canada or America, but the European Tour Card is the goal. Getting it is the hard part, but the ultimate dream is to keep it."

Someone with his mind a long way from the Tour right now is Martyn Thompson. He has spent the summer focusing almost totally on his job as club pro at Parkstone. As recently as six months ago, Martyn made a commitment to place Q School at the centre of his world, but that pledge is still shelved because he feeds his family with work as club pro not a tournament pro. Only occasionally has he found time to hone his game for the School.

Martyn spent £800 to see one of Europe's most renowned putting coaches, Paul Hurrion because lack of success with the flatstick has always plagued the club pro, even though most amateurs would grade him quite high as a putter. Martyn continually adjusts his grip, the ball position, the takeaway of the club and the follow through of his putts and hopes a few sessions with Paul will provide a breakthrough. But the coach's advice is a disappointment: his core muscles are not strong enough; there's not technical fix.

So Martyn continues to play fast and loose with his determination about Q School – he will insist one moment that he is desperate to make the most of his chance this year, but then his Q School application form has sat on his desk for months waiting for a signature. There is a disconnect going on and Martyn finally realises he needs the full backing of his whole family in order to go to First Stage with his mind and conscience clear. He has always been aware that success at Q School – however much it would be against the odds – would change his family life immeasurably and even risk their security. Yet Martyn is still to have this key conversation with Sally, his wife.

"At the start of August, the whole family was going to be in Majorca for two weeks and I got out the Q School forms and signed them before we went. I left them ready to go, but wanted to talk to Sally about it while we were on holiday. We were having dinner one night with a couple of friends and Sally was hearing all this talk about how good a player I am. My friends said I should go to Q School and Sally agreed, but she also said I had to think about all the other things going on in my life. We sat down afterwards and I said she couldn't stop me going, but I wanted to know that I had her support. Finally, she said 'yes'. So I called the pro shop and told them to send off the forms. At a pro-am after the holiday, I played really well and Sally joined me on the back nine; I made six birdies. She said that seeing me play good golf made her understand why I wanted to go. Sally sees the bigger picture. She knows that I don't really like being away from home these days, but here I am entering a tournament that could take me away from home a lot. She just asks why am I doing it because success would be a double-edged sword. I like playing competitive golf, but I would miss my family, for sure. It's always been my dream to be out on the European Tour and the dream's not out of me yet."

Martyn's journey to Q School is definitely going to be an unusual one. Compared with his rivals at Q School, he will probably have played less competitive golf than any of them. Not only that, he has spent all year being the best club pro he can be rather than the best practicing tournament player. If he succeeds, it will still almost be despite himself.

Luckily for Martyn, he still believes that golfing fairy tales do happen and now he has to hope they happen to him.

Chapter 10 – September 2007

First Stage

"(Q School) is a weird old week. You want to go there playing well, but the thought of playing bad kinda plays on your mind even more. You're under a lot of pressure"
– Kenneth Ferrie of England, a three-time winner on the Main Tour

The six tournaments that make up the First Stage of Q School are probably among the weirdest in any golfing year: they are spread over two separate weeks in early and mid-September, three at a time. On the face of it, they look like normal pro golf tournaments: fields of over 100 players; professional PGA tournament directors in charge; top quality courses; and a high level of intensity among the players. But compared with tournaments on the Main Tour, the differences are stark. Q School First Stage events attract almost no crowds instead of thousands of fans who watch Monty and friends every week; the Q School prize funds are a few thousand pounds compared to the millions fought for by Padraig *et al*; and there is an air of near-desperation among many Q Schoolers whereas Sergio and his colleagues ooze confidence. But perhaps the biggest difference is the cast of golfing characters that turn up at First Stage – some would shock even the most experienced tournament watcher.

First Stage of Q School is where seasoned pros line up alongside the aspiring teenage amateurs; where the fortysomething, long-time underachievers take on the slim-hipped, hair-gelled next generation. This is not the Main Tour's weekly circus with hospitality tents, courtesy cars and thousands of adoring fans. This is Q School where the tiny tournament office can be stuck in the old trolley shed; where the players search for their own stray shots in the deep rough; and where golfers of different colours, creeds, hopes and fears meet at the annual crossroads in their careers.

In 2007, the cast list at First Stage included Europe's latest potential superstar golfer who might one day be a genuine threat to Tiger Woods; over half the recently defeated GB and Ireland Walker Cup team; and national and regional champion golfers from more than 40 different countries as exotic and distant as Paraguay, Algeria, New Zealand, Canada, Kenya and the Bahamas. These golfers might not hold the greatest titles in the world, but they have all been winners at some level of the game and this is their best shot at the big time.

Dig a little deeper and the back stories are more worthy of fiction than fact – a Romany gypsy who was also a former London champion boxer and bare knuckle fighter and the English teaching pro based in Spain who uses the tournament as an excuse to visit his ageing mother in Lancashire. First Stage of Q School is definitely not your conventional golf event.

Then there is the entry fee of £1,200 (a huge chunk of money for many fringe players) that offers only long odds of success. Only about 200 of the near-700 entrants at First Stage will even progress to Second Stage let alone play the full 14 rounds to get a Tour Card. And, to make the story even gloomier, of the near 500 who fail at First Stage, around half will leave the tournament after the three-round cut. This is truly the nightmare scenario – you will shell out £1,200 for 54 holes (that's £20.22 per hole) and simply waste a lot of money on playing a lot of bad golf.

No one enters Q School to make a profit; it is about the dream. A First Stage winner receives £1,500, second gets £1,000 and third £700. Seventh place wins a player £100, not even enough for a round of celebratory drinks. Q School is about jam tomorrow, not today.

Mix all the players together in the six tournaments in four different European countries and there are countless stories of derring-do, triumph over adversity, abject failure, car-crash-type collapses and sheer bad luck. And, make no mistake, there will also be golf of an incredibly high quality as well because these men are all good players on their day. Plus, a very small handful of First Stage players will eventually win themselves a Tour Card in November. But at this moment it is impossible to pick them out of the crowd.

The Oxfordshire

The one totally outstanding player at the 2007 European Tour Q School is playing at The Oxfordshire less than a week after starring in the Walker Cup. Described as the best player to turn pro in Europe in the last 10 years, Rory McIlroy is the Northern Irish teenage amateur who won the Silver Medal at the 136th Open in July at Carnoustie. The fact that his first round score was better than Tiger Woods' pleased both the headline writers and the public. American Ryder Cup player Scott Verplank's comment was perhaps the most apt: "He's a fine player. He's 18, looks 14 and plays like a 28-year-old."

Rory's talent has been obvious for many years to those following European amateur golf and he is one of several dozen from the unpaid ranks testing themselves at Q School. It is rare but not impossible for an amateur to sail through the three stages and win a Tour Card – Rory's Walker Cup predecessor Oliver Fisher achieved the feat last year and immediately turned professional so he could join the Tour. The difference between the very best amateurs at this year's Q School and the returning professionals is mostly experience. Amateurs feast on lots of matchplay, fourball and foursome events rather than just a steady diet of strokeplay, the week-by-week tournament format of the professional game. Amateurs also rarely play four consecutive strokeplay rounds and so Q School is often a test of technique and concentration. Whereas both amateur and pro can go low with a burst of great shot-making or a white-hot putter, the professional will most likely manage his game better and for longer, limiting risk and often using a superior short game. Over a four round strokeplay tournament, the amateur's occasional inspiration is rarely going to defeat the pro's rock-solid consistency. The difference may be only one or two shots per round, but that is often what separates a champion from an also-ran.

Rory is expected to make the amateur-to-pro transition with ease. His swing is silky smooth and his confidence sky high; top pros like fellow Northern Irishman Darren Clarke have long predicted the brightest of futures for him. Still technically an amateur at this event, Rory's pro career is mapped out because he has agreed to join the likes of Clarke and Lee Westwood at International Sports Management (ISM) agency and will turn professional next week at the British Masters at The Belfry, a tournament promoted by ISM which wants to manage the anticipated media hullabaloo for the benefit of the Tour event and its sponsors. In fact, ISM is already lining up Main Tour invitations for Rory over the next few weeks while, at the same time, guiding him through Q School.

Rory attracts the eyes of many of his rivals at First Stage because they know he is a superstar in waiting and is a hot favourite to glide through to a Tour Card. There is another advantage for Rory at this event: he has a Tour-hardened caddie on his bag in Gordon Faulkner, another friend to ISM, whose thoughtful experience balances the 18-year-old's youthful impetuosity.

Rory's idiosyncratic "bouncy" gait as he approaches the first tee seems to be modeled on Padraig Harrington's. A dozen players leave the practice putting green to watch his opening drive of the tournament, an honour not bestowed on any other player here. Rory is that good and also very calm about what lies ahead in Q School "I didn't feel any nerves really," he says after his first round. "I just kind of cruised. I want to get through, move on and concentrate on my European Tour invite events. I'm not trying to put too much pressure on myself, but it's definitely different than the Walker Cup. It's like playing in a library here."

The library-type atmosphere might not be to Rory's liking, but the weather is. It is roasting hot and The Oxfordshire is also unseasonably calm without the usual high winds. This is the strongest and largest (108 players) of the three fields in the first week, the young Irishman realises that par golf will not be good enough here. His opening round of 2 under par 70 is perfunctory.

After a 67 in round two, Rory is coasting towards Second Stage along with fellow Walker Cup star Lloyd Saltman, a tall, chatterbox Scot. But being a top amateur is no guarantee in the pro ranks, as Llewellyn Matthews, another Walker Cupper of a week ago, finds out. In his opening round, the notorious par 3 5th – a 202yd tee shot almost entirely over water – suckers the young Welshman who takes a horrible 9. Amazingly, he plays the other 17 holes in one under par, but a 77 is virtually the end of his hopes. He improves to a 73 the next day when really a 63 was required. After 36 holes, Llewellyn finds himself, ironically, nine shots off a passport to Second Stage.

By contrast, James Conteh has had nothing like a Walker Cup to hone his game. He travels to The Oxfordshire from his parents' home each morning rather than his own because mum Veronica is again chauffeur and caddie. Ideally, James would stay in a local hotel and hire a professional caddie, but there are financial considerations; his golf earnings this year consist of a few thousand pounds from EuroPro or Jamega Tour events plus as much again in sponsorship. James is one of many pros at First Stage who have to watch the pennies.

There has been no indication that 2007 will be James's breakthrough year, but he hopes the intensity of Q School will unlock his best form. A few mini tour players always burst through unexpectedly, and so his first few holes will be crucial.

James made it through from First Stage at The Oxfordshire last year and hopes those good memories will calm his nerves and help him settle into a rhythm. On the opening hole, he has a birdie chance, but misses it and then hits a reasonable tee shot on the par 3 second to within 30ft. This should be another regulation par, but James's major worry prior to this week has been his putting; he fails to lag the first putt close enough and the second slides past. A three-putt bogey is careless and, immediately, James's mind is jolted by thoughts of how a potential 1 under score has already somehow turned into 1 over after just two holes. He is clearly not tournament-hardened, forced to practice too much rather than compete because of his struggle for cash. He needs to eliminate the negative thinking quickly.

Two pars and then he faces the next par 3 – the 5th, the same hole that fooled Llewellyn Matthews. The Englishman avoids the water, but his ball gets stuck in webbing covering some rocks in front of the green; a double bogey 5 is the result. He is 3 over already and desperately searches for good memories of 2006.

James takes a few deep breaths to settle himself. For the next few holes, he manages some much-needed par golf; he is hitting fairways, but the one thing that distinguishes the best pros from the rest – the ability on and around the greens – has totally deserted him. Then at the 10th he loses a ball after his drive and takes another double.

His mother watches silently. There is little that Veronica can say to help and little that her son wants to say in explanation. James plays the final eight holes in level par; a finish that is almost a relief, but 5 over leaves him tied 85th and seven shots off the cut mark. He is massively disappointed; he has been waiting all year for his Q School moment and now this. He is already facing his worst-case scenario – First Stage elimination. To grind out pars is one thing, but the leaders are enjoying a birdie-fest and that is much tougher for the out-of-touch golfer who has managed limited amounts of competition during the season.

James spends a little time on the putting green before a quiet drive home where he talks to his father. However, although John Conteh was a long-time professional sportsman and has his own experiences of overcoming hardship and adversity in his boxing career, he cannot provide any real comfort for his son. "I try to put myself in his shoes," says John, "but I can't really. Golf is a whole different kind of pressure than what I had with boxing." Being the father of a sportsman is never more difficult than this. "You want your kids to be successful, you want the best for them, but I suppose it boils down to how I probably always see him as a kid when he's really a man with his own life. He has to make his own decisions."

In fact, James *is* a man who can solve his own problems, but he does tend to internalise his emotions and so spends the evening working out his strategy for the next morning on his own. He made two very bad mistakes and not a single birdie; improvement needs to come on the greens.

On day two, James arrives two hours before his round for putting practice. Another two-tee start means that he begins at the 10th hole and his birdie plans focus on is the 11th (his opening par five) and the short par 4 14th.

The day is again hot with very little wind – perfect golfing weather – but James's luck has not changed. After six holes, he is still dropping shots and not making those birdies; his frustration is growing, especially as his two playing partners seem to be holing putts at will.

James tends to stride ahead of Veronica down the fairways as he continues to search for inspiration. It fails to arrive. His second round score is exactly the same as his first, a 5 over 77. He is tied 95th and, with uncommon swiftness, his Q School is just about over before it really starts. Afterwards, he verbalises his pain: "This is a huge kick in the teeth. I got through last year, but this year I just can't get the ball in the hole. It feels like a real step backwards. I might not even bother to come back tomorrow."

James is profoundly tired, he has none of the adrenaline he needs; talking about his disappointment does not help, so he says no more. He feels bad for his parents who want him to succeed so much; his father can understand why James may miss the third round. "If it was me, I'd probably throw in the towel," says John. "Golf can drive you mad." But to return to The Oxfordshire is the professional thing to do. James will be on the first tee in the morning.

Martyn Thompson rolled up to the tournament with his usual mixture of renewed determination and self-defeating casualness. His decision to play at Q School may have been a last-minute one, but once he is here (with son Josh as his caddie) then his competitive instinct kicks in and his determination and ambition soar. He even arrives at The Oxfordshire a day earlier than normal and spends three hours of his first evening putting.

Parkstone's club pro is perfectly relaxed, although far from over-golfed; his competitive preparation has been limited to a pro-am or two and the pattern of his round shows a lack of sharpness. Martyn hopes for a par 72 on the opening day of his first four-round tournament of the year, that would be acceptable, but it proves too optimistic and he finishes day one with a 77.

Strangely, Martyn is calmness personified after the round. In 2006, he opened with a poor round and then improved each day. He believes that he plays his best golf under pressure and is confident that his recovery of last year can be repeated. He decides to spend three hours in the evening on the range ironing out any swing problems – the kind of practice that is usually anathema to Martyn, but tonight it is a mark of how seriously he is taking the challenge.

And, indeed, on day two, he returns to some form; his driving is top class and he picks up two early birdies; he is back to just three over. Martyn's plan seems to be working. However, he trips himself up on two par 3s on the back 9 and eventually just holds on to level par which means only limited progress up the field – from tied 85th to tied 74th. He is now 5 over, eight shots away from the anticipated score needed to qualify for Second Stage. Martyn is back in the hunt, but only just.

After two rounds, the leaders are on 11 under par while the score to qualify for Second Stage (that is, 29th place and ties) is currently 3 under. By the end of round three the first batch of Q School hopefuls will be checking out of their Travelodges; anyone not within seven shots of 29th place after 54 holes will not play the fourth round. To avoid that fate, James Conteh needs a miracle of biblical proportions – something maybe in the low 60s; he is currently 10 over par and the anticipated three round cut is probably 3 or 4 under. James's demeanour is dark; he has travelled up from Hertfordshire without his mum today, his chances are so slim that her caddying duties are no longer required. James is truly alone as he tees off; no one else can save his golfing year from being another disappointment.

Despite his best intentions, the inevitable happens quickly: another early double bogey takes away even his slimmest of hopes. He trudges through the rest of the round with his mind racing; he wants this to be over and, not surprisingly, his feeling of distress is reflected in his final score, a 4 over par 76. James ends the tournament 14 over par and tied 95th.

Pro golfers can usually find something positive even from the worst rounds, but James is finding this is a difficult tale to spin. He is shocked and empty; this is his most disappointing Q School ever. "It is heartbreaking. Q School is the focus of my whole year and I didn't even get out of the blocks. I didn't ever get the pace of the greens, it just didn't happen from the very first day. But if I'm to carry on playing professional golf, then I have to sort out what is wrong." James turns on his heels and leaves The Oxfordshire as quickly as possible. Another 42 of the original 108 starters depart with him after round three, but to be one of so many is no consolation for him.

James's latest attempt to move up the golfing ladder has ended in a whimper. There was no drama, no chance almost from the opening few holes; it is the most unsatisfactory moment of his sporting life. Back home, his mother and father hear the news with sadness. John, in particular, feels powerless and wishes there was more he could do to help his son. "James has to learn through defeat. It's painful to talk about his golf and, yes, thoughts about him giving up [being a tournament pro] come into my head. I think about the fact that if he hasn't made it by now [to the European Tour], will he ever? But I also think 'Why talk about his future? Why go so deep?' I'm not sure if I should even say those things, if it would de-motivate him, but at the same time, you have to see the reality of the situation. It gives me headaches. James is still fighting, he's still on his battleground. I just hope he makes it."

Up to now, the Conteh family still only has one member who has reached the top of the sporting world; John is the father with a world title and James is the son with just a dream. Yes, there is still time for James to rise to the European Tour, no one wants to deny him the chance to keep improving and hoping. But this latest Q School failure leaves him asking himself how many more times he can suffer the same torture. No one's father can make that decision; it is one for the son alone.

For Martyn Thompson, his third round mission is simple: make it to day four. But on the 1st tee, Martyn experiences the ultimate scare – he feels like he has lost his golf swing. Out of nowhere, he has no clue if the ball is going left or right; the gentle right-to-left draw – his stock shot – has deserted him. For any golf pro, this kind of lack of control is both bemusing and frightening. Martyn is facing the most important round of his year with no feel for his swing at all.

This has happened to Martyn just three or four times in his golfing life, the last time in 2006 at Q School Second Stage. He wonders whether it is linked to pressure, but more likely, it is the change of routine; perhaps his time on the driving range at The Oxfordshire has hindered him more than helped.

This experienced campaigner has made a rookie mistake. Martyn decided after day two that, against all his normal regimes, he would spend some hours on the range ironing out the wrinkles in his game. Usually, his solution to problems is the exact opposite: less time practicing to allow his natural game to emerge. But Martyn is suffering from Q School craziness and hours of hitting ball after ball (something he had not done in years) has put more questions into his head than answers.

He starts his third round tentatively, trying to grind out a score. Somehow it works. And he ekes out a 2 under par 70 for his best round of the week. It leaves him on 3 over for the tournament, but as an early finisher, he has an anxious wait for a few hours to see if that score is good enough. While he and his son stage their own family putting contest, Martyn's fate is announced – he has sneaked into day four. He stays with his son on the putting green until dusk in a satisfied state of mind. After 54 holes he is tied 64th with 29th place as his target tomorrow.

The fourth round will be death or glory for many of the golfers at The Oxfordshire. The Q School field is full of super players, but you would hardly know it given the tension here. Some players carry a worn-down look; their faces capture some of the sadness that the event causes when careers are stalled – or even ended – by failure on an annual basis. It hurts if you are a player who is better than 99% of all the golfers in the rest of the whole world, yet still not good enough at this one particular place.

Such a player is Warren Bladon, a good friend of Guy Woodman's and a former British amateur champion. Bladon has a reputation for a *laissez faire* demeanour, but is actually still mightily determined to live up to the promise of his early career. On the course, Warren maintains the appearance of someone out for a casual stroll in the sunshine; stories about him are legend. A favourite describes how he walked in after nine holes of a practice round at the 1997 Masters with Jack Nicklaus. This round was a courtesy given to the British amateur champion by the greatest pro player of the era, but at the halfway point, Warren turned to his distinguished partner and told him he was returning to the clubhouse; he was too tired to play any more. "Nobody can believe I had the best player in the history of the game as my playing partner and I gave up after nine holes. He was gracious, and it's no wonder he had a confused look on his face. But I was tired,"says Warren.

Those that know Warren tell the story with amazement; it sounds like an urban myth, but it is absolutely true. He had just turned 30 at the time and his best years of golf should have been just ahead of him. However, that trip to the Masters would actually be the best experience of his golfing life. Now at the age of 40 and a pro for almost a decade, Warren has never got within touching distance of his Tour Card at Q School nor ever seen Mr Nicklaus again. He has enjoyed an occasional invitation to the Main Tour, qualified for the Open in 2006 and even appeared with Guy on TV's *The Big Break*, but none of these achievements are the same as being a regular European Tour player.

At The Oxfordshire, Warren is playing the course with a mate as his caddie and a couple of additional friends following him for support. He chats to everyone as he walks the fairways seemingly without a care in the world. However, Warren does care; his desire is so strong that he will renounce a normal life in order to try to make it happen. He is working part-time as a picture framer in his hometown of Coventry to make ends meet. However, this is not how champion golfers are made in the new millennium and he is doubtful about his chances this week.

"It's difficult working and playing golf. I've only played seven EuroPro events this season because I have to fund it myself and it's expensive. Sometimes I hate the game and sometimes I don't mind playing. I've been hating it a lot recently. But I never give up when I'm out on the course, not unless it's mathematically impossible. It might look like it, but I don't. Picture framing doesn't earn me great money, but if I don't work then I don't earn anything. If I play golf and play badly then I don't earn anything there either. It's tough."

Warren begins with a ring rusty 74, but a second round 66 is one of the best of the day and lifts him to 24th. His third round starts well, but any loose shots lead to double or triple bogeys rather than single ones and he falls to another 74. "The thing that upsets me is hitting shots without thinking enough; I've done that a few times. That's my weakness, it's what winds me up, it's why I walked off some EuroPro events this year. There are a lot of good players here who play all the time and I don't. That's why it's hard."

Warren is back in the chasing pack after day three at 38th, but still in sight of the magical top 29. He will need to shoot well under par for his last 18 holes to succeed because of the inevitable cavalry charge of dozens of players in a similar position.

Martyn Thompson is further behind. His day four starts with a smile after he re-discovers his swing. He believes it has something to do with his father-and-son putting session. To spend so much time practicing is not in Martyn's nature, but to simply enjoy golf with Josh in the beautiful surroundings of a top class golf course is the kind of relaxation that every father understands. Whatever the outcome of today, Martyn has enjoyed a memorable trip with his son and the world does not seem such a bad place.

What Martyn wants on the final day is bad weather so that those already within the top 29 will not birdie themselves out of his reach. Instead, it is the hottest and the calmest day of all; nerves might raise the scoring, but these conditions will actually be perfect for going low and that will lengthen Martyn's chances. Still, he is calm and chooses not to pound balls on the driving range. Instead he does his normal, short warm-up and this return to normal practice regime is immediate – two birdies in the first three holes. The words 'Hello, I could do something here' go through his mind and he knows it is within his ability to go on a birdie blitz, so why not now? Martyn has an opportunity to shoot the round of his life.

He registers a few pars and then misses a real chance on the 9th but recovers by birdieing the 10th. At three under with eight holes to play, he needs another three birdies at least; there are no scoreboards to tell him what everyone else is shooting, so he must trust his instincts and simply score as low as possible.

On his 12th, Martyn misses a straight 10-footer for another birdie. However, he picks up a shot on the next hole and a fourth birdie on the 16th keeps his unlikely hopes alive. Two final holes and one birdie needed, if not two. He must now risk everything.

After a solid drive on the tricky par 4 8th (Martyn's 17th), he requires a finessed 9-iron to the green. It is not a difficult shot, but Martyn has to put the ball close to a pin that is tight against the edge of the green; he catches the ball thin and finds water. A double bogey and his week and his Tour Card dream are suddenly and definitely over. One shot with the pressure full on and it proves too much. His 18th hole passes without incident and Martyn walks off the course with a rueful smile.

The reaction of one of the handful of club pros at The Oxfordshire is stoical; Martyn had made it through to Second Stage the previous year and that had really been his minimum goal for 2007. But a poor start, the uncertainty of his swing and the acknowledged lack of preparation came back to haunt him this time. Although tired and deflated immediately afterwards, Martyn is still proud of his achievements.

"I don't feel like a second class citizen or out of place or that I don't belong here. Having said that, after today I am thinking 'Is it too late, am I kidding myself? At 37, am I good enough, young enough or fit enough?' I had good expectations going into this week and I haven't achieved those. The way I feel right now, there's part of me thinking that this is the last go I'll have. I'm not thinking 'Great, I can come back next year'. After all, how many club pros are here? I'm sure my attitude is different because on Saturday morning I can go back to my job and my family."

Right after the tournament is a difficult time for Martyn to properly gather his thoughts. "I still have ambition, but the more time I've spent here this week, it's put my life in perspective. I don't feel a real hunger and desire this year. It doesn't feel like it really matters. I'm pissed off the way I played and I'm disappointed that I haven't done what I set out to do, make Second Stage. But already a big part of me is looking forward to going home and that's not a Tour pro mentality. I've enjoyed being at the tournament, I love the banter and being out there and having Josh on the bag. But at the end of the day, getting through Q School just doesn't matter enough to me. I'd love to do it and if somebody said you could have 20 tournaments, I'd go like a shot. But I played badly, my swing let me down under pressure. Maybe the game's trying to tell me something."

The drive back to Dorset with Josh is pleasant in the autumn sunshine and family life plus his daily work for the members at Parkstone will go on. Q School is over for Martyn this year and only he can decide if it is over for good.

At the other end of the scoreboard, an unknown 25-year-old Zimbabwean Tongo Charamba wins the £1,500 first prize by a shot from Welshman Alex Smith and two Englishmen Matthew Morris and Paul Waring. Saltman finishes tied 7th and McIlroy eases into tied 13th. Lewis Atkinson from the Wentworth Club is the only man to make Second Stage after an opening round above par; his 78 start was worse than both Martyn Thompson's or James Conteh's opening 18 holes, yet he finishes with two 67s to progress exactly on the cut mark of 4 under.

There are more disappointing stories than victorious ones. Warren Bladon was five shots better off than Martyn Thompson heading into the final round and needed about a 3 under score to sneak into the top 29. However, the pressure of Q School causes mistakes and two crippling triple bogeys relatively early on in the round – both on par 3s – means it is not Warren's day. His 79 is the second worst score of the day. Failure sticks in his craw and he walks away from Q School with little to look forward to. His situation is not uncommon among his fellow pros who ply their trade on the mini tours and his self-esteem as a golfer is damaged.

"I'm not really a pro; I play golf when I'm not working as a framer. Between now and next April, I probably won't play unless there's a EuroPro Tour Championship."

Warren has had a series of jobs to keep the wolf from the door including being a pub manager; he earns enough money to keep his pro golf dream alive and is one of the players who suffers because the game he loves – and at which he has an outstanding talent – does not provide him with a living. He plays his golf in a kind of twilight zone where his hopes of a full-time pro career fade with each passing year. He might attempt to show indifference at failure but hidden behind each off-the-cuff remark is someone who still believes it is his destiny to be on Tour. It's why he returns to Q School each autumn.

"I played well early in the year, but hit it bad over the last four weeks," he said before leaving The Oxfordshire. "Q School is a big tournament for me and it's a long old haul to get through but I'd rather play and miss out than not play in it at all. It's better than sitting at home wondering if I could've got through. But every day here I've had at least one triple bogey and you can't do that; just stupid shots. Mentally, I wasn't fully focused on the job in hand."

Warren is one of the mini tour pros who keeps returning to Q School in the hope of catching a wave of good form. He knows such a thing could happen. "I'll never give up, much as I feel like it, even when I'm 50, I'll want to be on a Tour. I'll be back next year."

Warren has a resigned, doleful look about him as he prepares to load up his car; he will attend a wedding later the same day even in his melancholic state. At 40, he represents so many fellow pros who adopt the never-give-up-type attitude, continually trying to succeed against the odds. But also like those counterparts, Warren has not succeeded at Q School. Not yet, anyway.

Others among the frustrated failures are Llewellyn Matthews (his opening round punctured his chances) and, more surprisingly, the 2006 US Amateur champion Richie Ramsey of Scotland. Twelve months ago, Richie was almost the Scottish version of Rory McIlroy, a young man carrying some of the future hopes of a nation on his shoulders. He was the first Brit in more than 100 years to win the US Amateur title, an event open to the best players in the world outside the pro game. The title earned Richie invitations to test himself at this year's Masters, US Open and Open Championship. Straight after Carnoustie, he turned pro, cut his teeth on a couple of Challenge Tour events and should have been a shoo-in for a Tour Card via Q School, just like McIlroy. But it is a shell-shocked Richie that stands in the scorer's office after a final round 71 left him three shots short at First Stage Q School.

"I had four similar days. I took 32 putts in an early round and you can't do that. (On the last day) I double bogeyed the fifth and came back with some birdies, but only holed putts that were inside six feet. I actually three-putted from five feet once. When you get down to it, putting is half of the game and it doesn't matter about tee to green if you don't have a short game. Of course I'm disappointed, but you've got to take it on the chin."

Chart Hills

The other UK-based tournament in the first week of First Stage is an hour's drive from London in the Kent countryside at Chart Hills where Guy Woodman knows the competition will be fierce. Winning his first pro event four months ago may have put victory here in his mind, but just to progress to Second Stage is more in keeping with his early Q School ambitions.

Guy is a player who can suffer from brittle self-confidence even though he looks the part of the tournament pro: he is one of the best turned-out players on any Tour, he talks with expertise and knowledge about his own game and he knows both his strengths and weaknesses. But there is a fragility that exists quite near the surface. His EuroPro title at Collingtree Park should have allowed him to aim for a top five of that Tour, thereby gaining him a Challenge Tour card for 2008. Instead, he only added just over £1,000 in prize money for the rest of the season, missing four cuts out of 10 events. Q School is a daunting place for anyone with little or no form and an opening round 76 – 4 over and tied 70th – is a severe knock to Guy's brittle confidence. Plus, spending time earning a living wage in the pro shop at Stoke Park GC all summer instead of practicing was not ideal preparation. "I've played most EuroPro events this year, but I'm either in the shop when I'm not playing or I'm at a tournament, so I'm actually not getting time to work on my swing."

After round one, Guy spends almost six hours either on the practice range or the putting green. It is dark when he retires for supper. "The pattern for me this year has been a bad first round, but backing it up with a good second. I need to just keep it in play and make a few putts. I had a good chat with my coach last night because I was pretty down. I'm quite tough on myself because I thought I'd pretty much blown it, but then I looked at the scores and realised level par was still in the cut range." So that is his plan on day two – shoot four under to counter four over on day one.

Next day, however, there is nothing but panic on the driving range. Thirty minutes before his tee time and Guy is unhappy, he isn't feeling any power at the top of his backswing. He tries all his normal solutions, but nothing works. Finally, he throws down a few last-minute practice balls away from the other players and comes up with an answer. "It's not too technical. It's just a case of getting more onto my right side going back and then feeling like I'm hitting to a firm left side on the follow through." Finally, he is ready.

The opening par 5 at Chart Hills is the perfect chance for a fast start and Guy takes it: a booming drive, 3-wood to 25 yards short of the green, a pitch to a foot and a tap in birdie. This is classic Guy – and also true of so many young pros – that he has progressed from disaster on the driving range to fantasy golf on the first hole in the space of 20 minutes. With his new assurance coming to the fore, he makes the turn at two under and his target of par after 36 holes is in sight.

It is a birdie, bogey, birdie start to the back 9, but it is wrong club choices rather than any swing issues that cause his dropped shots. Three more pars and onto the last three holes.

Now at 3 under for the round, Guy's best chance of his desired fourth birdie is the par 5 16th and completes the hole in the required four strokes. Onto the near-island green 17th which is found with a 9-iron right over the flag; two simple putts from 25ft delivers a par and so to the last, a 449yd par 4 with the pin sadistically placed near the front and on a devilish slope.

As Guy walks to the 18th tee, he knows his strategy should be one of safety first on a tricky hole: he has fought all the way back to level par and that needs to be protected rather than risked. Any mistake now and there will be no chance of redress until tomorrow. Yet a tiny part of Guy cannot resist the thought of another magical birdie.

His drive is straight and true and his approach stops just 10ft behind the hole. Then the greedy little imp in his mind gains control and the 18th hole becomes a birdie opportunity. Guy's first putt is bold, however, the viciously-breaking downhiller slides just over 2ft past and the slippery return putt – a left-to-righter – lips out. Bogey. Instead of walking off the final green in triumph, Guy looks like he has been whacked across the head with a 4-iron. He is not that far from tears. All that work undone by a little hubris.

"I didn't trust the par putt and closed the blade on it. I normally miss putts like that on the left side and it's sod's law that I missed this one on the other side." That single shot leaves him in the chasing pack tied 35th rather than inside the Tour Card mark, but to his credit this is the turning point for a positive week.

Guy scores solidly in round three for another 69 to put him on 2 under for the tournament, tied 20th. He then manages a solid 2 under par 70 on the last day to finish 14th and ease into Second Stage with a veteran's calm. To put his performance into perspective, only one other player comes back to qualify after a first round worse than Guy's opening four over par. Among those who miss out is Wentworth pro Ross Fisher and fellow Surrey pro, Sam Osborne, a player of some promise who even had one of the world's most experienced caddies Pete Coleman (former clients including Bernhard Langer and Seve Ballesteros) on his bag.

Sam was the epitome of steadiness for much of the week and sat at 2 under for the tournament with one hole to play, just inside the cut mark. Then, Q School craziness struck – despite a perfect drive on the 18th Sam duck-hooked a 5-iron approach out of bounds. It was his worst shot of the event at the most important moment and a triple bogey 7 meant he missed the cut by two shots.

There are plenty of players at Chart Hills who sympathise – including Guy Woodman – because they know that 'a Sam Osborne moment' at Q School can be just around the next corner for them and, by the grace of God, this time it happened to someone else.

St Annes Old Links, Fleesensee, Bogogno & Moliets

At the other four First Stage venues, the usual triumphs and tragedies occur in equal measure. At Fleesensee Golf & Country Club in Germany, the Scandinavian contingent makes its mark: two Danes, Kasper Linnet Jorgensen and Knud Storgaard, share the first prize, but the cruelty of Q School is again illustrated by near neighbour Kalle Edberg of Sweden who led after round one only to shoot 75, 77 and 70 and miss the cut for Second Stage.

At Bogogno in Italy, local boy Michele Reale is in control early on, but is eventually beaten to the winner's cheque by 21-year-old Austrian Bernd Wiesberger who shoots the best round of the day, a 65, over the final 18 holes.

At Moliets in France, the assembled field is more than a half filled with either French or Spanish players, yet one of the joint winners is an English pro, James Morrison, who takes top spot along with Spaniard Carlos de Corral. They both finish on 16 under par and head a total of 34 qualifiers.

Moliets is noticeable for the best last round performance of the First Stage. Thirty-two-year-old Frenchman Sarel Son-Houi, who had failed to make a cut in any of his Challenge Tour starts this season, shoots a remarkable last round 64 to sneak into the final qualifying position. This kind of last-minute low score was what Martyn Thompson and so many other First Stagers were hoping for on day four of Q School. Not surprisingly, such performances are incredibly rare.

The most dramatic of the other four tournaments is St Annes Old Links, not least because of the heavy rain and high winds, weather that missed all five of the other venues. In the first three days, the rain on the Lancashire coast is so fierce (on day two alone, 2mm of rain falls in just five minutes) that Blackpool Tower, only a couple of miles away, is lost from the horizon. St Annes is a place for hand warmers, thermal underwear and double-thickness wind jackets as some of the scoring goes skywards. Tees are moved forward because of gusting 30mph winds.

This all takes place on one of Britain's classic links courses. St Annes Old Links is a fabulous example of an English seaside course with a classic clubhouse, a façade that mixes red brick with pebble-dash. The building boasts high-ceiling rooms, oak-paneling, a snooker room and enormous honours boards with ornate wooden sculpturing all set off by a large colour photograph of the Queen at her most regal.

The players are disinclined to be outside practicing in the awful conditions preferring to sit in the dining room with its all-day breakfast menu and Sky Sports on the television showing live coverage of the British Masters at The Belfry. Of course, the Q Schoolers are all dreaming of being at that TV tournament next autumn, so watching the action from The Belfry provides a painful paradox to their own current situation.

By the final day, everyone is exhausted with the weather and the long delays as the grounds staff tries to prepare the waterlogged course. On day four, the rain is so heavy that there is talk of the event drifting into a fifth day and Q School nerves are now at breaking point.

Tournament Director Kevin Feeney watches helplessly as another downpour begins. Although 95% of the course is fine, a few key areas are unplayable. Small amateur events can easily be abandoned for the day in such conditions, but not the pro events, not the Q School. Eventually, the weather relents and the first groups eventually peg it up at 12.45pm – more than five hours after their original start times. Hanging around drinking coffee with nothing to do but wait and worry is not ideal preparation, but it is part of the life of a pro. The last groups – including the leaders – may struggle to finish before sunset. Thoughts of possible missed planes or an extra night in the hotel are put aside; it is game on.

The players at St Annes include the usual mix of Q School hopefuls, but also some much more experienced candidates. These are players of substance, men who understand how much strain this tournament can cause to the psyche. Scotland's Murray Urquhart knows his way around European Tour events; Q School has played a full part in the story of his career.

In 2002, Murray made it to Final Stage and a par on the last hole gave him the 32nd out of 36 Tour Cards handed out that year. The extreme nervousness of the occasion is burned into his memory. "I was right on the bubble and the whole of the last round; you're pushing and trying to be cagey at the same time. It's a horrible feeling. Going down the stretch you're numb, especially the last three holes, I had a double bogey on my 16th from nothing and I had to finish at least par, par. But coming up the last, you really don't know what I needed for sure. It's a unique experience. I've never had that feeling since. My knees were shaking. It's different from winning a tournament, a totally different kettle of fish. That last putt for par was from two feet and it felt like twelve."

That story is from five years ago and Murray's following season on the Main Tour was poor. He has returned to Q School every year since then. This is his 10th visit. "I won myself a Card in 2003 but got only 14 starts and none at the bigger events, so I was always chasing my tail. Now Q School's getting harder every year, less spots available realistically. There are almost 1,000 entries, guys trying to do what they dream of doing. Actually, the Challenge Tour is the better way in nowadays for me because you get a better category and more starts."

Murray is among the older group of players who admits that attending Q School is now a strain on his family life. "I think I'll stop coming eventually; the cut-off is about domestic changes. It's harder being away from home. It's a young man's game and it's getting younger, more guys in their mid-20s, with 10% body fat and hitting it miles. Nowadays you have got to be fearless."

Murray's 2007 Q School adventure is not his best; he is tied 55th after day three. "It's the old story that you should just go out and enjoy it, but I've still to discover how to do that. For something as important as this for a pro, you are ultimately trying to relax and, if you're holing putts and playing well, then you do enjoy it. But I've struggled on the greens all week, so enjoyment doesn't come into it; it's more of a grind."

Murray eventually cards a disappointing 75 on day four and, not surprisingly, flees St Annes as fast as he can. "The big cash has gone for a year. From my perspective, I have an exemption to the Scottish region events and there are lots of pro-ams, but it's not my dream, not where I want to be."

Among the more exotic and fascinating stories from First Stage are those with the smallest chances of a Tour Card. One such player is Samuel Kemp, a former police constable from the Bahamas and self-taught pro golfer, who is making his second attempt at the European Tour Q School. He misses the round three cut, finishing at 10 over after 54 holes. He has spent $5,000 (including travel expenses) for the privilege of failing at the School and admits to never having played in winds as strong as those at St Annes. Plus the cold means he is forced to wear so many clothes that his golf game is hard to find. Somehow Samuel manages a giant smile before making a long trip home.

Another big-time dreamer is Lee Nuttall, an unpretentious 48-year-old ex-pat Brit who has been working as a teaching pro in Spain for the last five years. Lee's friends talked him into entering Q School, even though he had only ever played once on a links course. His opening 87 is the worst round by any player all week and he finishes 30 over par, in 116th and last place. Lee's only compensation is that he has fitted in a rare visit to his parents in nearby Bolton, something he had planned from the start. "I perhaps should've gone to France where the conditions are similar to Spain, but I wanted to see my parents because I don't have much contact with them any more."

But the most remarkable First Stage Q School tale is that of Joe Smith, a Romany gypsy and former bare-knuckle fighter. Joe's big smile never disappears at St Annes even though his chances of a Tour Card are astronomical. His quest is one of romance over common sense. At Q School, he is like a child in a sweet shop; his every action, every conversation, every shot is filled with a joy of life. Joe has none of the airs and graces of so many pro sportsman of the modern era who live in a gilded cage of privilege. From him, there are no complaints about the bad weather; he doesn't moan about receiving no freebies from the equipment companies or lacking a sponsor. The speed of the greens doesn't phase him, neither the state of the bunkers. Joe Smith is just happy to be alive and to be playing a game he adores.

Refreshingly, Joe's ethnic background – unusual within topline professional sports – is not something he hides from; his golf balls are logo'd with the words 'Gypsy Joe', but almost inevitably, his journey as a golfer has been bumpy. He felt victimised for being a gypsy while playing junior golf at Home Park (nowadays known as Hampton Court Palace GC). Nowadays, the incident that happened in the mid-1980s, seems horribly trivial after he had won several tournaments including a London junior title. Joe was playing in a club tournament and was given a plate of sandwiches to eat for free; he did not feel hungry so gave them to his father. Inexplicably, a club official challenged Joe's father about the sandwiches with an inference that he had taken them without paying for them, otherwise known as stealing. This accusation was untrue, but the seemingly innocuous incident which could easily have been dismissed as a simple misunderstanding sparked a major row.

"My father didn't feel he should pay for something that his son had given him, but he was reported to the club committee and asked for his resignation. We both left the club. I then had to go to a public course where the practice facilities were not very good and it had a bad affect on me." It was extremely difficult for Joe to devote himself to golf to the same degree after the incident. His game suffered, although he did turn pro at 20 and tried to make his way in low-level mini tour events. "It was racism (at Home Park) and it is still a bad memory. They thought they could stamp me out of golf and my way of life, but that's not happened."

However, over the years, Joe fell in and out of love with golf and even returned to boxing, the sport that he took up at age seven. "I got to the stage with golf where I needed to let some steam off, I was becoming frustrated. Also, I thought that I'd never know how good a boxer I was unless I tried, so I joined the IBA ranks and had 12 fights. And 12 wins." Joe won the London heavyweight title in 2003 and with it came his self-respect and a feeling that it was time again for golf. That's when his Q School dream really began.

Joe has come to Q School for the last four years but has yet to make it past First Stage. Aged 36, he is at St Annes to test himself (his regular tournament golf these days is over two rounds on the Jamega Tour) and even making the third round cut would be a major result for him. He opens with a 1 under par 71, but crashes to a 78 on day two, leaving him tied 67th.

He has made friends with lots of his rivals at St Annes and all of them truly wish him well for day three, but he shoots a disappointing 75 which leaves him at 8 over and on the bubble. He is one of the earlier finishers so has to wait for several hours to see how the rest of the field performs. He nervously practices putting below the tournament office, regularly sending his children – one his caddie, the other a ball spotter – up the metal staircase to check the scores. As it turns out, his score is right on the mark and he makes the final day. The joy on his cherubic face is priceless.

The next day Joe will need to shoot a 63 to reach Second Stage and, in such unhelpful, cold conditions that would be a world class round by anyone's standards. His chances may be remote, but his enthusiasm is undimmed. "Fairy tales do happen and I'm in there with a shout. If I can get the flatstick working then who knows. Somebody shot a 64 on day three, so you don't know when 63 is your day. It just happens."

For his final 18 holes, Joe sets off in hope, but reality bites early: he just cannot hole a putt and the weather is too tough for the required number of birdies. He keeps his poise and tries his hardest, but it is not to be. He walks off the 18th green with another 3 over par 75 and the same smile he has offered everyone all week.

"It's frustrating, very frustrating. I hit 17 greens in regulation and the one I missed I had a bad bounce into a bunker, splashed out to 5ft and only just missed the putt. But I'm happy because I played good. I was a bit off the pace, I suppose, and even the best round of the day wouldn't have got me in. But I could've shot 65 the way I played tee to green. This is the second time running that I made the fourth day. I was a bit closer last year, but all in all it's not been too bad. The Q School is like the FA Cup: we can all play, we hit it similar, some longer than others and we're all trying to find that magic button to press to turn the scores around. It's not a waste of a week; it was a great week."

By the time Joe finishes, sunset is less than 20 minutes away. On the other side of the course, the leaders are being urged on in near-darkness by worried tournament officials; no one wants to come back tomorrow to finish a couple of holes.

Finally, at dusk under purple-pink clouds, Walker Cup star David Horsey completes a round of 68 to win the event with ten minutes to spare before the conditions became impossible. While David checks his card in the scorer's office, Joe Smith is already on his way to Blackpool Pleasure Beach with his two sons. He has played his heart out over the whole four days, finished tied 81st out of 121 golfers and earned himself a good time among the autumn holidaymakers. Even at the First Stage of Q School, some losers are also winners.

Chapter 11 – October 2007

Last Man In, First Man Out

"When I got my Card back in 2002, I shot 67 and 66 on the weekend and that 66 is one of the best rounds I've ever had, probably not the best, but under the circumstances it's right up there" – Paul Broadhurst, Tour winner, Ryder Cup player and three-time Q School attendee.

The month of October is when Q School takes a break – Second Stage and Final Stage will both take place in November, so this is a time when other stories from within the world of professional golf are written. However, the School is never far away because this is a month for the last couple of European Tour events to take place and their results will decide who joins the First Stage qualifiers in a few weeks time and who will earn their 2008 Tour Card by their Order of Merit position.

However, the average golf fan is largely unaware of these dramas. The millions of armchair golf fans around the world are fed a constant diet of live coverage of the top European and American events these days thanks to the growth of cable and satellite television channels over the past couple of decades. The focus is on the superstars and the leaderboards, yet there are a myriad of sub-texts developing at each tournament further down the field. In fact, almost every player in every event is a story. Certainly by October each year as the season comes to an end, the chase for a first prize cheque is not the only tournament drama.

Right now, every euro earned by every player can have a profound effect on his season. First place at the European Tour event will win mean a huge cheque – usually around 16% of the total prize money – and the money gradually reduces until those finishing around 70th receive little more than loose change, a few thousand euro. But every euro won or lost affects someone's position on the Order of Merit (previously known as, more aptly, the money list) and the higher you finish, the better the tournaments you can enter next season.

The trick to staying on the European Tour is to finish the season in the top 115 of the Order of Merit; such a position means a Category 7 playing status next year, guaranteeing entry to most of the big money tournaments. Finish 116th or worse and you face lower level tournaments, less prize money and perhaps the start of the slippery slope to golfing oblivion.

In any one season, over 350 players actually play in one or more European Tour tournaments during a season, but there are hundreds more waiting for their turn and, as standards continue to rise, a place at the top table becomes increasingly hard to both win and to maintain. It is the after effects of Tiger Woods' emergence as a professional more than a decade earlier – he both inspired a generation of young players and also helped grow prize money in golf to previously unimaginable levels.

So if golf isn't frustrating enough, imagine how a tournament professional feels at the end of a season when he has sweated through as many as 30 events, scores of competitive rounds, thousands of drives, irons, chips and putts only to be told at the end of it that he's not good enough to come back next year. And the margin of failure might be just a handful of euros. Each season, there is always at least one player who drops out of the top 115 at the year's final tournament, overtaken by a rival or two charging through the field at the last minute. That 116th Order of Merit spot is a deadly place to be and means a trip to Q School, while the 'last man in' at 115th spends the winter planning a new assault on some of the world's richest tournaments.

In 2007, things are slightly complicated because the official Order of Merit – as often happens – includes some players who are affiliate members of the Tour not full members and therefore not eligible for a Tour Card. When this happens, the affiliate members are ignored when the 115 Cards are handed out; this year there were two affiliate Tour members well inside the 115 places, so 'last man in' is actually the 117th finisher. Even though the rules seem convoluted for many fans, the players know exactly what's going on, particularly Lee Slattery from Lancashire who sits in the 'last man in' position as the final tournament begins.

The last two tournaments of the European Tour season are staged in the Mediterranean, both in Spain – the penultimate on the mainland in Madrid and the final one of all on the island of Mallorca.

Madrid's most fascinating Tour Card story is Emanuele Canonica of Italy, one of the longest hitters in Europe. His 6th place finish in Spain's capital is his best showing of the year and takes him from the 120s in the Order of Merit to 110th – he avoids Q School with one week to spare.

Hoping to join Canonica is England's Sam Little, a player well used to end-of-season battles for a Tour Card. In 2005, Sam made an up-and-down from a greenside bunker on the final hole of the final tournament to get his Card. He hoped he would never be in that position ever again.

However, it has been a miserable season for Sam only made memorable because his wife gave birth to twins in August. As the season draws to a close, Sam has had one top 10 finish all year, so tied 7th in Madrid earning almost €20,000 is most welcome. He moves up to 153rd in the Order of Merit and now needs a top 8 finish in Mallorca to save his Tour Card once again.

In the season's finale, Sam forces himself into a position of reckoning and potential glory. He is 4 under after 16 holes of his opening round before hitting a driver out of bounds to drop a shot. A magical 4-iron to one foot on the par 3 18th gets the shot back and he is just one behind the leaders. Astonishingly for a man under such pressure, Sam's post-round interview shows a golfer enjoying a rare spiritual calm. "You've got to enjoy it because if you don't enjoy it, you're going to play badly. The last two months have been difficult for me, but the last three weeks I've played great. I'm trying to enjoy my golf and I'm getting the rewards."

Days two and three pass without more weather delays. As for the 'last man in' story, Lee Slattery is in trouble; he misses the cut. Still in with a chance, however, are Ian Garbutt (117th), Alessandro Tadini (118th), Jarmo Sandelin (119th), Steven O'Hara (123rd) and Robert Rock (130th) who all make the cut along with Germany's Marcel Siem (139th). Just 11 months ago Marcel celebrated winning the WGC World Cup with partner Bernhard Langer; such are the vagaries of golf.

When the third rounds are completed (actually on the morning of day four because of earlier delays) Sam sits 5th, but the next 18 holes will be among the most stressful of his career. The problem is, does he attack for birdies or just avoid bogeys? Does he risk the brave shot or play for the centre of each green? At least those further back like Garbutt and company know that there is no alternative but to play aggressively.

However, early birdies take the pressure off Sam who is lying 2nd with eight holes to play. The final holes at Mallorca are known to be tough and birdies are not littering anyone's scorecard, but Sam's form is majestic and there are no last-minute hiccups in a 3 under round of 67. Three weeks ago, Sam was 164th in the money list, but with €222,220 for this 2nd place he is catapulted to a staggering 76th place on the Order of Merit.

Watching the players close-up in these situations you cannot help but empathise with the pressure and read it on every expression on their face. After Sam's round, he is interviewed live on *Sky Sports* and is choking back tears. The enormity of what he has achieved – one of the most gutsy rounds of the year – is beginning to dawn on him. "Take a minute," says Sky's Tim Barter who had followed Sam's progress and can sense the player's bottled-up nervous energy that makes it so difficult for him to speak at all.

Eventually, Sam talks from the heart: "When I holed my putt for birdie on the 16th I actually thought I might have a chance of winning the tournament, but this (Tour Card) is a wonderful consolation. I can't control what other people do, I can only control myself and because of that, I am really proud of myself for coming through this week. This was my great escape."

To perform so well when there is no other alternative is remarkable. It is one of the ultimate tests of guts and heart. What Sam – and others who have done the same thing in the past – will always wonder is this: how does a player find such form under the most intense pressure but not in other tournaments earlier in the year? If any golfer ever finds the answer, then they will bottle it and make billions. Most pros will tell you that winning a golf event comes when your game is in good shape, so for Sam to perform under this kind of end-of-season stress after months in the doldrums is all the more remarkable. In a way, the accomplishments in Mallorca by Sam are straight out of the Q School handbook.

However, not everyone can be a hero this week. The list of "fallen" is long. Robert Rock, Steven O'Hara and Marcel Siem all fall well short of their targets for the final day and never look like moving into the top 117. Meanwhile, Ian Garbutt drops three shots in his final two holes, shoots a last round 74 and ends up one shot (or €188 short) of a Tour Card, while Alessandro Tadini is left haunted by a bogey on his very final hole; the dropped shot costs him his Card as well. The luckiest man in Mallorca is fun-loving giant Jarmo Sandelin: he finishes the tournament a lowly tied 50th to win just €8,600, yet it is enough to take his winnings total for the season above that of poor Lee Slattery. While Jarmo now sits in 117th place in the Order of Merit, Lee is left just €77 short of that 'last man in' position. Now that is heartbreaking.

The only tiny consolation for those who fall just short of retaining their Tour Cards (Slattery, Garbutt and *et al*) is that they avoid Second Stage of Q School and go straight to Final School. That applies to anyone between 115 and 145 in the money list.

This same scenario of final-tournament-histrionics and near-misses is played out almost every year because the difference between 'last man in' (Sandelin) and 'first man out' (Slattery) can be agonisingly small over the course of an entire season; in playing terms, it can be a single bad swing or one lucky/unlucky bounce. Either way, the smallest incidents translate into prize money which is the only true measuring criteria.

In the most pitiful cases, the monetary difference between death or glory has been less than a tenner, in fact £9.39 (€14 in Tour currency) to be precise. The man whose career was thrown into chaos for an amount equivalent to a couple of drinks was Australian Jarrod Moseley in 2004.

One of many Aussies on the European Tour, Moseley had enjoyed a decent amount of success after bursting onto the scene in 1999 with a stunning win in at the Heineken Classic in his native Australia only 18 months after turning pro. A rising star, he then settled into life on the Tour earning money and plaudits.

But 2004 was a bad year; he played 25 events, but made only 10 cuts. He had started the season brightly, yet through the summer slipped inexorably down the Order of Merit. By the final tournament – in 2004 it was the Madrid Open – Jarrod was in desperate straights at 114th on the Order of Merit; he first had to make the cut in Spain and then hope that a handful of rivals would not outscore him. This season, 'last man in' would be in 116th place, so a dramatic finish to the season for Jarrod was guaranteed. Of course, when form is lost it will not magically reappear on demand and Jarrod missed another cut in Madrid so had to spend the next two days watching three fellow pros try to pass him in the rankings, their own careers on the line.

It was like death by a thousand cuts for Jarrod as his rivals fought their own intense battles: South African Richard Sterne, Wade Ormsby (another Australian) and Sweden's Robert Karlsson all made the cut and were all trying to edge past Jarrod. Sterne, in fact, was in the best form of his pro life and went on to take the title by two shots with final rounds of 66 and 65. The €166,660 that he won didn't so much as edge Sterne past Moseley as rocket him from a place in the mid-130s to 70th in the Order of Merit.

Ormsby, meanwhile, who was in his rookie year on the European Tour, did his fellow countryman no favours. He shot a remarkable 66 on the last day for tied 6th place to earn his second biggest pay cheque of the year – €30,000 – and also surge past his helpless Aussie pal. But it was Karlsson's performance that really hurt.

The tall Swede, who had five Tour titles to his name, had been out of touch for several seasons; at one time he contacted a life coach to help him relax both on and off the course, but any changes had yet to bear fruit and tied 16th was his best finish of 2004 before Madrid.

In this final tournament, Robert sneaked into the weekend right on the cut mark of 1 under par and then shot two very ordinary rounds to finish tied 77th, joint last but one. Yet, to the horror of poor Jarrod Moseley, that seemingly awful finish took Robert's season-long income up to €145,868 compared to Jarrod's €145,854 – the difference was the aforementioned €14. Celebration for the Swede, devastation for the Aussie.

To make the whole episode even more excruciating for Jarrod, the player who finished dead last in Madrid – Spaniard José Rivero – earned precisely €14.50 less than Karlsson. Therefore, if Rivero and Karlsson had swapped places then Jarrod would have been the one to keep his Card, but only by the even more agonising amount of less than a single Euro. There is no finer example of how a pro golfer's life can turn on one good or bad shot.

However, this whole affair had a happy ending – the Australian turned up at Q School a few days later and, to his eternal credit, shot a 70 in the final round to earn the 25th Tour Card. It obviously pays to keep a level head in professional golf.

But these machinations at the lower end of the Order of Merit are just one indication of how each tournament – in fact, each Euro won by each player – can turn out to be vital. There might only be one champion at each event, yet every pro golfer is battling for something. Maybe it's the Vardon Trophy – that is, No 1 on the Order of Merit; a top 15 place on the money list that means automatic entry into all four Major championships; the top 60 to be invited to the money-fest that is the Volvo Masters at Valderrama at the season's end (€4 million in total prize money and €15,000 even for finishing last).

Where is there the most pressure in professional golf - at the top end or the journeyman end? The question has many shades of answer, but the Q School experience always gets a special mention when hardened pros talk about the subject.

Many current Tour high-flyers know how difficult it is to struggle for their livelihoods at a golf tournament. For Nick Dougherty, for example, the most stress he has felt on Tour did not come when he was fighting for a title. "The most important shot I've had was in the German Masters when I was struggling to keep my Card, not when I've had chances to win. It's about when you play for your career. Q School is a huge amount of pressure; the enormity of what it means is actually what holds people back."

Nick knows how lucky he was to pass through Q School so young and on the back of a Walker Cup winning effort as well. "I finished third in Final Stage in 2001 and it felt almost straightforward, but knowing a bit more now and seeing guys who've gone back and forth there, it's not that easy. I was fortunate. I can see that the more you go there the harder it is. And for guys who need to make a living and have a family to feed, you have to go back; I hope I never have to because it's not something I'd cherish."

Tour elder statesman Barry Lane was forced back to Q School seven times, but still went on to win a veritable fortune in prize money – including $1 million in the 1995 Accenture World Championship of Golf. "Q School's an absolute nightmare. I got my Card four out of my seven visits, but it is so nerve-wracking. You have to be fit and playing well for the whole of the tournament. It's even tougher now because you may have to play through two qualifying rounds, but in my days you pretty much only had to enter and you were through to the final and that was only four rounds not six like it is today. I remember missing by a shot and waiting for another year to have another go. Horrible."

And for the 47-year-old Lane and many fellow pros, that is the overriding problem with the School – lose a little form on Tour and there's always next week, but if your game crashes and burns at the School then there is nowhere to go but downwards.

"It's a daunting prospect because it is your whole livelihood," says Barry, now happily able to play on Tour because of his position in the top 40 Career Earnings List. "That one week means everything. The pressure is unbelievable and so the golf that is played is fantastic. It's so easy to miss your Card. I have admiration for all the guys who do it because you look around the Tour and almost everyone has been through it. More than 75% of the Tour has had to go through Q School and I think it's a fantastic idea."

Paul Broadhurst is an inspiration to Q Schoolers because the Englishman is one of the few to win before *and* after a visit to Q School. The first time at the School seemed like a breeze to the then 23-year-old West Midlander in September 1988 and the next few years were a dream as he won three times and played in the 1991 Ryder Cup. But 9th place on the Order of Merit in 1996 proved to be a summit that he would fall from quite dramatically. His end-of-season finishes in the next three years were 25th, 35th and 47th before, in 2001, he slipped to 157th mostly because of a hand injury.

By now the previously free-wheeling bachelor Broadhurst had been replaced by the family man with three young children who was also closer to 40 than 30. Forced back to 2001 Q School, he failed to gain a Tour Card and his career was in jeopardy, his pride badly bruised.

"I went back to the School with no confidence whatsoever, didn't expect anything, completely different circumstances than the first time. I was 15 years older with a family to provide for and the pressure was really on. Going there not playing well is really difficult. I made the four-round cut, but finished nowhere."

Paul felt an understandable numbness, but his standing within the Tour was not forgotten. "Afterwards, I didn't know what to expect. I was hoping I'd get a few invites on the basis of playing Ryder Cup and winning a few times. I had a few days at home of not knowing what was going to happen, then I had a call from Ken Schofield (Executive Director of the PGA European Tour at that time) who said not to worry. I played about 20 events the next year on invites and was grateful for that."

His 2002 season was not auspicious, but he did find a little confidence to take to his second consecutive Q School where the 37-year-old finished 17th. "Touch wood, I haven't been back since and my career has moved on a bit since then."

In fact, Paul is living proof that a comeback via Q School – even in your late 30s – is possible. His return to the big time was confirmed in 2005 when he won the Portuguese Open, a title he went on to defend in 2006. Therefore, Paul is the perfect person to answer the age old question: is attempting to win a European Tour title more pressure than trying to gain a Q School Tour Card? "Not even close. When I got my Card back in 2002, I'd been out on

Tour for nearly 15 years and I had nothing to fall back on. I shot 67 and 66 on the weekend and that 66 is one of the best rounds I've ever had, probably not the best, but under the circumstances it's right up there. To play six under when you know your livelihood is on the line, I took a lot from that. Maybe Q School is not as much pressure for someone who's just starting out because they have plenty of other chances, but for someone like me it is."

Meanwhile, the final tournaments of the 2007 European Tour season are unkind to both Andy Raitt and Sion Bebb; they both play just one event (the Open de Madrid) and fail to make the cut. They will now play Second Stage along with Euan Little (who dabbled in the Challenge Tour over the autumn, but found no real form) and Guy Woodman whose First Stage performance was outstanding but whose chances for further competitive golf after that never materialised.

Phil Golding – as a recent Tour champion – is slightly luckier. He will vault past Second Stage straight to Final Stage but lacks tournament sharpness. He faces the prospect of trying to overturn the effects of two torrid seasons and the threat to his whole career in six rounds of in the Q School cauldron. Almost any scenario would be better than this, but Phil – like all his counterparts – is heading off to San Roque next month for the European Tour's version of the last chance saloon. He has no choice.

Chapter 12 - November 2007

Second Stage

"There are certain people who won't get through [Q School], they are just not good enough or they have a full-time club pro's job or other aspirations. But if you dedicate your life to it then it can happen. The people who are passionate about golf and who give it the time, they are the ones who should keep trying at Q School"– *Nick Dougherty, multiple Tour winner and Q School graduate 2001.*

Second Stage of Q School is a strange affair. It's like the mid-point in a trilogy or being the middle child of three – it's neither the start nor the finish, there's an awkwardness about it, it's a twilight zone of tournaments. It is also distinctive within the Q School format for a particular reason: playoffs. First and Final Stage tournaments operate a system whereby players can be tied for the final spot and still progress or even win their Card. However, the four Second Stage events need to send through exactly the right number of players to fill the 156 places available at Final Stage, so there have to be playoffs to sort out who moves on and who goes home. Second Stage playoffs are necessary, but still perhaps the cruelest of all ideas invented by golf administrators.

For this reason, fear of failure at Second Stage tournaments is different from other parts of the Q School journey; it's like losing in a semi-final, a match that is only truly memorable if you win. You can wear a Final Stage appearance as a badge of achievement, but no one wants to know you fell just short.

There is one significant absentee from Second Stage. Rory McIlroy turned pro the week after he got through First Stage at The Oxfordshire in September and then proceeded to play on the European Tour via invitations. In just his second pro start, the remarkable Rory finished second at the Alfred Dunhill Links Championship, pocketed €211,000 and promptly won his Tour Card for 2008 without further recourse to Q School. Golfers in the four Second Stage tournaments hear McIlroy's news with a mixture of admiration and jealousy; if only they had such invites maybe they would also be avoiding this month's trip to Spain.

The four 72-hole Second Stage tournaments take place similtaneously this month on courses in southern Spain to provide the best possible European conditions at this time of year: plenty of light along with some sunshine and warmth.

Three of the four venues – Costa Ballena, PGA de Catalunya and Sherry Golf in Jerez – are familiar to regular Q School attendees; only the fourth, Arcos Gardens (also near Jerez) is new. It is impossible to choose four courses which are precisely the same, but the Tour acts fairly and allocates players to each venue not by preference but in an effort to balance each event. So the 198 First Stage qualifiers are spread evenly across all four courses while the same happens to the 109 new players joining straight from the Main Tour (players who finish outside the top 145 in the money list) and Challenge Tour (players between 45th and 90th in the end-of-season ranking). That makes 307 players fighting for 64 spots, approximately a 1 in 5 chance of qualifying for Final Stage. Just 10 rounds to go – for many players, that is an exhausting thought.

Arcos Gardens

For Guy Woodman, Second Stage is not foreign territory, but he has yet to progress beyond it. Being drawn at the new venue, Arcos Gardens could be of benefit because, like most of his rivals, he is playing the course for the first time.

Since First Stage, Guy has continued searching for his mid-summer form. He has been forced to spend up to 50 hours a week working in the pro shop at Stoke Park to make up for all the hours he missed at early season EuroPro Tour events, so he is now short of practice and confidence. A trip to the EuroPro Tour Championship at St Andrews Bay in Scotland was disappointing; he finished tied 46th finish and very heavy winds blew away chances of positive practice.

Perhaps determination and belief will be enough, yet those qualities look inadequate when Guy sees the near-7,500yd-long course and the wind that accompanies it. This track is for the big hitters and Guy is not among them; in practice rounds, he is 50 yards behind some players. "On one uphill par 5 into the wind, I'm hitting driver and my best 3-wood and don't get there in two; the young German guy I played with hit 5-iron for his second shot onto the middle of the green. I'm hitting driver then 3-iron or rescue club into lots of par 4s; there aren't many par 4s like that on the EuroPro. I'm not as used to it as some of the other guys. I am surprised about how far some of these kids hit it. It's out of my comfort zone." Despite a lack of distance off the tee, Guy's opening round begins brightly and he is 2 under after nine holes. Then the first disaster strikes – a four-putt at his 10th hole (the 1st on the actual course) for double bogey. As the pressure ramps up, Guy's fails to respond and his round ends unimpressively when he finds water with his second shot on a par 5 that is even reachable for him in two hits. He had hoped to pick up a shot, but instead drops another; a possible 73 turns into a 3 over par 75 to leave him tied 53rd. Only 19 spots are available for Final Stage here and Guy is four shots off the pace already.

Day two is the same tale of woe – very windy and too many multiple putts. A 74 is a slight improvement, but Guy is going backwards against the field, he is tied 61st. The young Englishman is still in with a chance and he is hitting the ball better, but he has to tighten up every aspect of his game, particularly his putting. He grits his teeth for one last effort; unless he can shoot well under par in round three, his trip to Spain will be in vain.

Guy tries to stay calm and searches for inspiration, but all his problems remain, especially the three-putts and he finishes his third round tied 53rd, eight shots off the cut mark. Guy phones his parents and, while they don't say it openly, they all know Q School is all but over once again.

Desperately wanting your dream is one thing; playing well enough to achieve it during one specific week of the year is another. With only pride to play for, Guy's body-constricting nervousness is diminished and he shoots his best round on the last day, a 2 under par 70 including five birdies in the last 14 holes. It is still nowhere near enough.

"I had it going at times, but nine three-putts and one four-putt throughout the week was what killed me. I'm standing over a 6ft putt with a foot of break on a really quick green and I'm not as used to that as the others playing on better tours. It's a huge disappointment, but it's another experience where I came away thinking I could have done it. My comfort zones need to change and I need to compete at that level more often. I would make faster progress playing this kind of difficult course more often; it would either bring the best out of me or I'd fail miserably."

Guy actually enjoyed his fourth round. "That's how I needed to be from the first hole of the tournament, I struggled to get into that state. You so desperately want to do well, you're over-trying, you get tired and over-analyse instead of just getting on with it. I had one of the better scores on the day. It's ironic; you come away thinking 'What if'. I've got to learn from it, but you think how many more learning lessons have I got to have? I've improved this year, got the win and achieved some of my goals. The frustrating thing is that now I've got to wait another year. Maybe a shot better every round is what it comes down to."

While Israel's Birgir Hafthorsson wins, among those out of Q School at Arcos Gardens are Michele Reale, David Horsey and Lloyd Saltman who all had high hopes, but the Q School does not lie; this year, they were not good enough.

Guy hides behind a veneer of hope himself, but this kick in the guts is hard to take. His is a classic case of the young player whose desires are continually a finger-tip out of reach. Yet he will not be deterred. "I'm still desperate to play on the European Tour, I think I can compete there. I'm going to continue pursuing the dream. I'm not going to give up."

Costa Ballena

Over in Costa Ballena, there are no obvious favourites in what looks like one of the more open fields. An opening 7 under par from Northern Ireland's Damien Mooney gets everyone's attention and shows that this course can be tamed. By day two, 10 under is leading after two 67s from Australian Adam Bland. After round three, Bland is joined by French amateur Adrien Bernadet at the head of the field on 13 under. With 20 places for the 81 players, there is the usual cavalry charge over the last 18 holes before Bland wins on 17 under and Bernadet takes second. Mooney only gets through by a shot despite leading on day one and 46-year-old Welshman Mark Mouland (a former World Cup winner with Ian Woosnam) snaps up a place with four solid rounds. Elsewhere, Lee S James (202nd on the 2006 European Tour Order of Merit) never looks in danger and finishes fifth; while Scot Craig Lee shoots the best round of the final day – a 65 – to burst into the top 20.

Those missing the mark include: Adam Frayne (the man who lost out to Guy Woodman for the EuroPro title at Collingtree earlier this season) who manages one of the alternate spots after a six-man playoff; the older Saltman brother, Elliot; Walker Cupper Rhys Davies; and veterans Darren Prosser and likeable Aussie Terry Price.

Catalunya

At Catalunya, Andy Raitt is in the smallest field (just 72 players) which means less places available, just 17 (compared to 18, 19 and 20 elsewhere). Although this slightest of differences seems inconsequential at first sight, it will be significant to someone at the end of four rounds. That someone will be Andy himself.

The London-born golfer enters Second Stage after a season of wild inconsistency. To start Q School in poor form is a common problem for many players; if they had enjoyed a good season then they probably would not be here at all. Andy hopes that his experience of eight previous Schools will count in his favour. However, he suffers the mother of all poor starts.

"I hit 3-wood off the 1st tee fairly far right; it's quite thin rough over there. I was a bit edgy. I hit a provisional ball, just in case, and then couldn't find the first one. I couldn't believe it. I made triple bogey; I mean, the first hole of the tournament; it's very stereotypical of the way I've been playing." Somehow, his experience and patience prompts some birdies and he reaches 1 under after 13 holes before eventually finishing level.

During the second day after starting at the 10th, Andy has a horrific Groundhog Day moment when he reaches the 1st tee again. Although now at a remarkable 4 under, he cannot put yesterday's troubles out of his mind.

"I hit a 2-iron off the tee this time. It went right again, but it looked like it was just off the fairway in light rough. I got down there and couldn't find it again. I thought I was going crazy. I had to walk back up the hill to the tee and hit another. I took double bogey." Five shots dropped on the same hole over two days and yet Andy proves his skill by fighting back to 1 under for the day and the tournament. While the leaders have reached 11 under, Andy is in a group of no less than 11 players in joint 13th place. With 17 spots to play for, the Catalunya tournament is going to be a tight affair.

Day three and another 1 under score means Andy holds his position and lies tied 14th with four other players. Now he hopes for better luck. Life and golf have treated him badly recently, so surely it is his time for some good fortune.

On the last day, the previous horrors on the opening hole evaporate as he holes a birdie putt on the 1st green. However, Andy's loose shots are never far away because of his tendency to 'lose' the club on his down swing and he makes four bogeys on the front 9, slipping to 1 over for the tournament, a long way from the cut. He knows a birdie blitz is the only answer and he gets them on 10, 11 and 12. But one more is required and misses from 4ft on the 15th and then from 15ft on the next. On the final two greens, further birdie putts lip out; that little bit of extra luck has eluded him again. Andy's fate now rests in the hands of others. "When I putted out on the last I thought I was on the mark. Then I looked closer at the scores and thought it was 50-50. There were five groups behind and, basically, I needed a couple of those to mess up." Unfortunately, no one did. Andy's 1 under finish is one shot too many. If just one of those first-hole horrors had not happened, then he would have been inside the mark with a shot to spare.

Immediately after his final round, Andy is in a state of shock; so much has happened to him and so much of it has been bad that another slap in the face seems almost normal. He is emotionally empty. "Ten years ago I missed at Q School a couple of times by a shot or two and, in those days, I really wanted to play in those big tournaments. I was more disappointed then, it really hurt. But this year I don't feel so bad. Maybe compared to the other issues I've had in my life recently, it's no big deal really. I'm surprised I don't feel so upset. It isn't as painful as I thought it might be."

The next day, Andy becomes more reflective and starts to feel the hurt. "Competing is probably over for me now. I don't have a stock shot or a stock swing or a stock grip. When I play social golf I might finish a couple under par because I'm relaxed. But on Tour, every day has been a struggle. In my heart of hearts I know next year I would struggle even if I had got my Card; I'm not suddenly going to grip a club and feel it is secure. I do play better than I used to on occasions, but I won't ever be able to play at my best. Everyone else is getting better and I'm struggling day-to-day."

Talking to Andy is not like talking to any other professional on Tour. His story is unique and you cannot help but feel sympathy for him and admire his bravery. But Q School 2007 may be a landmark. Andy could be one of the many golfers whose pro tournament career ends after crashing into the Q School buffers just one time too many.

"Every shot's a struggle. There's no natural element in my game any more. It felt like hard work all season and yet I thought it was going to be easier and easier this year with all the surgery I've had. I've had significant improvement with my arm and shoulder and I do have good days, but as far as building my game again? Well, I don't have the same strength through my wrist to know where the club face is and I'm using the index finger to grip too hard and that relates to my shoulder."

Andy can explain all the technicalities that only fellow pros might truly understand, but essentially a player of his ability knows the direction of the ball immediately on impact; his feel for the club is so finely tuned that a blocked shot or a duck hook is instantly apparent. But with Andy, this is what is missing.

"Everyone has tendencies and fears a particular shot, but no other pro would hit a shot and not know where it's gone; they could tell you if they've hit it left or right. But because of my wrist, I don't know where the ball is at impact. I've been working on the premise that if my shoulder is neutral then I can swing neutral and allow my body to control the ball without using the strength in my hand. But at the end of the day, it's such a disadvantage. Now I tee up waiting for a mistake. Maybe it's rose-tinted glasses, but I never used to feel that way; I'd look at the fairway and try to hit it instead of just trying to avoid the big error."

There is a sadness in Andy's voice and he sighs when he recounts the details of his troubles, but he never asks for sympathy or that anyone make allowances for his injury even though his money troubles have returned; he earned just €50,000 in prize money this year, not even enough to cover his expenses. There is a little consolation in being 5th alternate for Final Stage after a one-hole playoff. This means he will need five players to drop out of Final Stage in the next week for him to take up an unlikely place at San

Roque. One or two dropouts perhaps, but not five. For Andy, it could be the end of his Tour career.

"It'll be a nightmare if I have to bring it to an end like this. If I'd given up a few years ago, I'd be in a different frame of mind. But I'll have a chat with Lindsay, my girlfriend, about what I'm going to do, but maybe it's time. Maybe I should do something else." The decision will be the most difficult one of his life.

Meanwhile, among those celebrating at Catalunya are Spain's Gabriel Canizares who shoots a best-round-of-the-week 65 on the last day to take first place and two regular Q Schools from the UK, Scotland's David Drysdale and England's Andrew Marshall.

Sherry

The construction of Sherry Golf Club was completed only three years ago and still has the feel and smell of newness. The course is very open and relatively flat (just the 1st and 10th provide a few meaningful slopes) with manageable Bermuda rough and sparse trees close to the fairways. There is, however, plenty of water on the back 9 and a tad of wind could cause havoc. For three days, however, there is hardly a breath of a breeze and it all suits one man – Sion Bebb.

With newly-acquired bagman Gary Marshall at his side, Sion's passage to Final Stage is virtually secured by round two. His opening 65 is paired with a 68 and he is already six ahead of second place. The Welshman has gained huge amounts of confidence from his top 10 finish in Switzerland in September and walks around Sherry like a winner. So it proves as a 70–73 finish takes him to an easy victory at 12 under. None of the other four Q School Second Stage events are so dominated by one player.

But at the other end of qualifying, there is gut-wrenching drama involving Euan Little. Euan has put in plenty of hours of practice, but is not 'match fit', so it is masterstroke to employ experienced Tour caddie Martin Rowley. This veteran carrier is one of the masters of his trade; Martin was with Ian Woosnam for eight years and has even been head of the caddies association for almost 20 years. He gained fame with his candour in Lawrence Donegan's seminal book on the caddie's job, *Four Iron In The Soul*. If Q School progress comes down to one correct club choice or lining up a particularly tricky putt, then Martin is as good as anyone. Plus, the Euran and Martin are friends and the caddie wants one of the nice guys on Tour to succeed

However, "Rowls" will put friendship aside when some necessary harsh words need to be spoken. "There's no point in not speaking the truth and that's my way of motivating the player; if they want someone just to save them carrying their own bag, then they should employ someone else. Euan's problem is that he needs a frontal lobotomy. He thinks too much sometimes. He's got the talent and he just has to be patient. Players at this level aren't always good enough to force it, but they can all get birdies. It's what they give back to the course that counts."

Despite Martin's attentions, Euan suffers a shaky opening 75 which is not surprising for someone with so few competitive rounds under his belt; it leaves the Scot tied 53rd. The player then leans on the caddie heavily as he recovers during a second round 68 and third round 70 which move him up the field; at 3 under par, he is tied 14th and one shot inside the score he needs to make Final Stage. However, holding onto that position will take all his skills because there are 29 players at 1 under or better fighting for 18 slots and, to make matters worse before the final round gets underway, Euan is still trying to diagnose problems with his swing. There is a lack of completion to his turn that means his hands are working too hard and the ball is shooting left. It is mostly tension that is causing him to question himself – is it ever thus at Q School?

On the range before the start of day four, the talk is of 3 under being the required score to make progress if the conditions are calm and 2 under if the wind blows (although it has not done so all week). Martin thinks par will be enough for Euan, but the bagman is cautious and highlights holes like the par 5s – the 5th and 11th as well as the driveable par 4 16th – as the potentially "smelly ones" for his player. He also thinks all the back 9 pins – especially the last hole – are in totally brutal spots, either very near water hazards or the back fringes where overshooting would mean killer downhill chips from nasty lies. Patience and calmness will be the watchwords.

Euan starts confidently with two pars; he is playing with experienced Frenchman Olivier David (who starts on 4 under) and a young Italian pro Lorenzo Gagli (3 under) who both start well. On the par 5 3rd, the Scot comes alive himself. His drive unluckily finds the rough and an uphill lie means no chance of going for the green, so he clips a 9-iron to around the 115-yard mark and then flicks a gap wedge to 10ft. "Keep you head still," says Martin before the putt gently drops for a neat, early birdie. But the first of the "smelly" holes, the 5th, unfortunately fulfills Martin's prediction – Euan finds water with his second shot. He recovers and has a 6ft putt for par, but it lips out. He is back to level par for the round.

As is so often the case at all levels of golf, it is putting that will bring success or failure. For the first four holes, Euan hit very cautious putts, all dead-drop speed, but on this crucial 5th hole, he changed his tactics trying to hammer the ball through the break. Martin's response is caddie-style black humour at its best: "If you play like a c***, then expect to get f****d". Harsh, but fair.

Euan starts to feel the pressure; he begins to pull away from shots, unable to settle; the enormity of the day is weighing on his shoulders. Meanwhile, the pace of play is already at a crawl, exactly what he hates and to make matters worse, the dreaded wind is blowing stronger than at any time during the week. However, pars on 7, 8 and 9 are the perfect answer to Euan's growing list of worries. He is still on 3 under and that should be good enough.

As Euan heads for the 10th tee, the players are met by a scorer who asks their current number for the tournament so it can be entered on a makeshift paper scoreboard. Over par scores are in black, level par in green and under par is signified by red on the large sheet. Not surprisingly, black is the most popular colour of the day.

This scoreboard is primitive stuff and an indication that Second Stage of Q School is a long way from the Main Tour, but it is helpful to the players who can see that the early starters are falling back – a sign that conditions and nerves are taking their toll.

Euan strikes a fabulous drive on the 10th and then a towering 8-iron level with the pin only three feet away; this is his moment to push for home and leave the dramas behind. However, the putt that Euan eventually nudges towards the hole is hit with no confidence and falls away to the left. His par feels like a dropped shot; Euan may not get an easier birdie chance on the tough back 9.

Setting aside such disappointments is never easy at Q School and it is doubly difficult when Smelly Hole No 2 follows immediately. Euan hits his tee shot at the 11th right into a sand trap on the corner of the dogleg. When he arrives at the scene of his crime, he finds the ball plugged near the face and he can only hack it out some 30 yards. This leaves an extremely difficult, long third shot into a narrow green with water all down the right and a sucker pin near the wet stuff.

Euan takes plenty of time and stays well left, but is short, just off the green. The noose is tightening as Euan's fourth shot – a short chip – comes up about 12ft shy. There now follows a long debate as both Martin and Euan read the crucial par putt differently. The player eventually bows to his caddie and Euan strikes the ball firmly into the hole. This is a huge let-off. Two pars in the last two holes, but totally different feelings for Euan. Not surprisingly, he is now playing very cautiously. Had Euan known what was happening around him, his guts would have been even more in turmoil.

By now, the early finishers are coming into the scorer's office. England's John E Morgan is in the first group home and scores a remarkable 67 leaving him 4 under for the tournament. That's one of the 18 spots at Final Stage filled, so it's bad news for Euan although he has no knowledge of it and just continues to maintain his position in ignorance of unfolding events elsewhere. Then at the 15th his drive finds another bunker, his second is

40 yards short and he has to summon all his courage to hole a 4-footer for another par. He knows that too many knee-knockers like this will eventually catch up with him; he wants tap-in pars not scrambles. Of course, it does not help when those around you have all the luck. Also at the 15th, his playing partner Olivier David hits an even worse drive than Euan, then almost goes out of bounds with his second before playing a poor lob wedge onto the green. But the vagaries of golf are apparent when he holes a 45ft putt for par. Oliver comes off that green looking like a man whose death sentence has just been reversed, while Euan has not holed a long putt all day and, somewhere in the back of his mind, he feels like he deserves one. He remains 3 under.

Another rudimentary scoreboard near the 15th green shows that Euan's chances are narrowing. With 20 players at 3 under or better, the message is simple – Euan's current score will only be enough for a playoff for a Final Stage spot; a birdie will be a triumph and a bogey disaster.

At the driveable 16th, Euan elects for a 5-iron, but immediately cries "big bounce left" after hitting it. To his relief, the ball misses the worst of the trouble and lands in the rough. However, the Scot will have little control of his second shot to a pin cut so close to the water at the back of the green that it looks almost in the lake. It will be a brave man or a complete idiot to mess with this pin. As it turns out, Euan slightly duffs his approach, leaves his lag putt 4ft short and then holes for his regulation four. Another tiny scare, but also another par.

By now Martin is trying everything to keep Euan calm, while at the same time ready to cheerlead him through the par 5 17th and a par 4 18th. "Eight more shots," is how Martin outlines their plan for the next two holes; that will mean a birdie-par finish and definite progress on 4 under.

It looks good when Euan hits a long, bold drive down the right on 17. The green is certainly reachable from 260 yards with his 3-wood, but he fats it horribly and the ball comes up short, 40 yards from the hole on an awkward hanging lie. Euan's third shot is just as nervy (a 24-handicapper shot, murmurs Martin) and he finally holes another knee-knocker from 6ft for a par. This means a 4 under final score is almost out of the question because the 18th is not a place for birdies, it is more like an accident waiting to happen.

Euan's drive misses not only the water all down the right, but also the fairway on the left; he now has a second shot from a slightly hanging lie to a pin on the top half of a two-tier green with heavy rough and more water ready to catch anything a little over ambitious. The approach shot causes another debate between Euan and Martin, both expect the ball to fly out of the rough, so an 8-iron rather than a 7 (which would bring the water into play at the back of the green) is the club of choice.

The club swings, but it is not Euan's best effort; he catches the ball slightly fat and sends it straight into the bunker just short of the green. The last thing Euan needs is a 30yd bunker shot to a back pin with water (aka disaster) awaiting beyond, but he makes a good fist of it and flies the ball to the top level. He is still 20ft short and the putt will be a double-breaker. "Do you think I need this?" asks Euan plaintively. "I know you do," is the best that Martin can say. There is much studying, but although the putt just reaches the hole, it breaks 2 inches to the right and leaves Euan with a bogey.

You can almost see the air being sucked out of Euan's body. A 2 under finish looked like one too many at the start of the day, so Euan strides to the scorer's office to discover the worst. There are no cameras here, no computerised scoreboards, so any news – good or bad – is slow to reach Euan who can only think the worst. He cannot talk, he cannot think, he wanders to the car to find some quiet. His mobile phone is already screaming with voice messages and texts from friends and family who are checking the European Tour website for scores. Euan is too brain-dead to call anyone; he sends one text to his mother saying that nothing is finalised yet and he will phone later. "I can't speak to my parents. I know the disappointment for them will be terrible." As Euan waits, there are exactly 18 players on 3 under which means all spots for Final Stage are taken, but 12 players are yet to finish, all of whom had started the day on better scores than Euan. If one of those players slips up, then there may be a lifeline.

The next group to finish is probably Euan's only chance and the player under the most pressure is South Africa-born Justin Walters who lives in England and is a friend of the Scot's. He began the day on 4 under but is currently 3 under with one hole to play. Justin is an emotional player on the course – on the 11th tee he hurled his driver away in frustration after blocking the ball into water – but on 18, he tries to remain calm. In the end, he has a 5ft downhill putt for par, but it slides past the hole. Justin slams the putter head into the palm of his hand and curses. He has slipped to 2 under, the same score as Euan, so there will be a playoff for the 18th and last place at Final Stage.

Euan hears the news in the bar where the players have been gathering after their rounds. The playoff will actually feature three players: Euan, Justin and a young Austrian Florian Praegant, who had shot a creditable 1 under final round score. Euan immediately goes to the driving range with Martin and fellow Scot and long-time friend, Scott Henderson. Team Euan has little to say except that their man is the most experienced of the three and that should be to his advantage. The playoff is sudden death with one player going straight to Final Stage, one to be handed the 2nd alternate spot and the third to receive the 6th alternate position that is, realistically, a ticket home.

Martin tries to bring some levity to the proceedings as all three players arrive on the 10th tee; he takes a driver from his player's bag and pretends to hit the first shot. "I'll pay the green fee," he jokes. Half smiles only. Euan is trying to tune out of everyone else's emotions.

After drawing lots, Euan will drive second. He is the shortest off the tee, but strikes a solid approach to the back right hand corner of the green and gets his par. His opponents both show nerves, but also scramble fours.

They move to the 18th. Euan's two rivals both hit irons off the tee, but the Scot hits driver again almost to the exact same shot as in regulation. He is in the best shape of the three, but he fails to take advantage with a poor approach that he tugs left. The tension is too much for all of them; Euan misses from 8ft for par and three bogey fives are all the group can manage. Back to the 10th.

Euan has wasted one golden opportunity while his two rivals are feeling relieved; adrenaline is now in short supply with all three looking sunken-eyed and exhausted. There is little joy in a Second Stage playoff even for the winner; the key feelings will be either relief or despair.

At the third playoff hole, Florian hits a short hook left and Justin a massive block to the right. Euan hits his best drive of the playoff down the middle and is again looking the man-most-likely; he even manages a smile after his second shot finds the heart of the green. Yet, somehow Florian and Justin continue to scramble successfully; both eventually hole par putts leaving Euan with his third chance to wrap up his place at San Roque. It is a 25ft putt and he has already seen Justin's effort that is on a similar line. Rather than risk going a few feet past, however, Euan tries to drop the ball in with dead weight and it shaves the hole through lack of pace. The excruciating playoff goes on.

At playoff hole No 4 (again the 18th), Euan's driver once more overpowers the irons of Florian and Justin who then both hit poor approaches: Justin puts his second 50 yards short of the green while Florian blocks a shocking 5-iron into the lake. Surely, Euan can grab this chance now. But the tension has become unbearable and he misses the 18th green for the third time today; this attempt flies left leaving him a difficult chip out of a scrubby lie.

Florian's mistake is fatal and he is heading for a six; the Final Stage spot is now between Euan and Justin. The Scot plays first and chips to within 6ft, looking good for a par. The man feeling the tension now is Justin who needs a miracle chip-in for par or a rudimentary chip-and-a-putt from the back of the green for a five to at least exert some pressure on Euan.

But Justin's chip is poor and he then misses a short, downhill putt to score a six (the same as Florian). This allows Euan the luxury of two putts to secure his place at Final Stage. He uses them both. This is easily the latest finish of all four Second Stage tournaments, so Euan has gained last place in the field at San Roque next week. Yet his face looks empty; the well of emotion is completely dry. There are a few perfunctory handshakes before the other two players move on to settle the alternate spots.

Euan finds it difficult to make sense of a crazy day and the wild playoff. "I've had it all, I've really been through the ringer. I felt I had an edge with

Florian, but I know Justin well and know he can play. Those two guys were playing the wrong tactics; they should have gone for it (on 18) because there was only one spot. You can't play irons off the tee there, it gives you too much to do. It's driver, 7-iron. In a way, they gift-wrapped it for me."

But honesty about his own struggles is not far away. "I've played poorly myself, though, and still got through. That's golf. After all that, you're not tired, it's like a great empty feeling when you think you nearly missed it and then someone gives you half a carrot; it's not even a full carrot. I was so convinced I could do it and I really wanted it; I thought somewhere down deep inside 2 under had a chance. Everybody said last year 'you only missed by one shot', but you miss by one shot because of yourself and what you do. I got sucked to the cut line today and maybe that's something I've got to rectify in the future. I definitely let my mind get carried away out there because it's tough not to; I'm thinking of my coach, my family, my best friend. I probably don't look happy, but it's incredible the feeling I've got inside, I could run a marathon. I'm elated. I'm not ready for next week, but I soon will be."

Euan's 2006 experience when his final putt lipped out at Final Stage to deny him a Tour Card was agonising and today almost ended with the same emotion. The fine line between triumph and disaster is as thin as ever. The Scot is relieved, euphoric, tired, energised and shell-shocked all at the same time. As a professional, he is already thinking ahead to San Roque, but the scars of days like today sometimes heal slowly.

Meanwhile, Justin Walters misses another short putt at the next playoff hole and allows the young Austrian to take the 2nd alternate spot. As he packs up his clubs and leaves the clubhouse with his wife close by, Justin's face is deathly white and his brave words (he will be 6th alternate for next week) are not enough to hide momentous disappointment. "I played good all week, but I've pretty much come up with nothing for the year. It's tough. You kind of beat yourself up (after dropping into the playoff) and then have to pick yourself up again. I wasn't really nervous. I've been a pro for five years and you get used to it. The hardest part about it is knowing the consequences."

The 18th at Sherry GC will never be on Justin's top 10 list of favourite holes. "Me and 18 are like oil and water. I haven't figured out how to play that hole yet. My biggest mistake was my fourth shot (on the fourth playoff hole), the chip. It came out soft; it was probably the nerves. If I put down a bag of balls there, I'd probably get it up and down 90% of the time."

Not surprisingly, tears are starting to form in his eyes. "I don't really know what I want to do now. The hardest thing to ask yourself is 'Where do I go from here?'. I missed Q School First Stage in the US by one shot and now this. I've got my wife here, so it's not the end of the world, I guess." His remark is slightly unconvincing; this job of tournament professional that he has chosen has just stuck a knife in his belly. His dream of playing on the best golf tours in the world has taken him across continents and is the most important thing in his life. Will there be tears, he is asked. "There probably will," he says and walks quickly away.

To prevail at a Second Stage playoff takes immense strength of character; it is a level of intensity far in excess of what a normal club golfer might experience. This is golf at its most brutal. The rewards loom large and the consequences of missing would cause most players to curl up and hide. Yet there are always teasing examples of what Q School success may one day lead to.

Twelve hours after Second Stage finishes, there is another tournament coming to an exciting climax on another continent: Phil Mickelson, Lee Westwood and Ross Fisher are involved in a playoff of their own, this one, for the prestigious HSBC Champions title in China on the European Tour. The differences between this three-man, sudden death challenge and the one at Jerez are vast. The winner in Shanghai (Mickelson) takes home a trophy, a massive cheque and lots of World Ranking points, while even the losers (Westwood and Fisher) have the compensation of walking away with €300,000 in prize money. In Spain, however, the playoff victor (Euan) wins only the chance to battle through another six tortuous rounds on his journey to a possible Tour Card, while the Q School playoff losers (Florian and Justin) walk away with absolutely nothing. No wonder there will be tears in Jerez.

Chapter 13 - November 2007

Final Stage

Day One

"The Tour School is the ultimate reflection of you as a golfer. When you don't match your expectations then you have to realise your game wasn't good enough and you go back to the drawing board" – Murray Urquhart, 12-time Q School attendee.

Southern Spain in the second full week of November 2007 is dazzlingly sunny and warm, just as the Q School Final Stage golfers ordered. The two San Roque courses are in excellent order and 156 Tour-Card-hungry players are ready to start the six-round tournament to decide which 30 will receive full exemption to the 2008 European Tour season.

A total of 876 will have taken this journey by the end of this week and exactly 720 have already fallen by the wayside. For Final Stage rookies, this week will be unlike anything they have experienced before, while for the veterans of this six-round torture, there are different feelings: a reluctance to be at golf's last chance saloon missed with a quiet confidence that their experience is now a valuable commodity. Q School often feels like a meeting of those on the way and those on the way down, both sets of players will only endure Q School rather than enjoy it and, by the end of it, everyone will have suffered both agonies and ecstasies, the kind that sport so uniquely delivers.

The field is a strong one, certainly on a par with anything in recent years. The highest ranked player is Alan McLean of Scotland who sat in his home in Ontario at the end of the 2006 season as his place in the top 115 of the Order of Merit disappeared in the last three tournaments, none of which he was able or invited to play in. Alan's Sony World Ranking is 251 while Sion Bebb is 426th and Euan Little 485th. In all there are 22 players here inside the top 500 in the world

This illustrates the level of the Q School contestants – these are players of high quality operators who, for some of us, already are among the very best.

But, of course, top 500 is not top 115. Nor is it top 50. There is always another rung on golf's ladder of meritocracy to climb.

The 156 hopefuls arrived in many different ways: 75 won through from Second Stage; 15 qualified directly from the Main Tour by finishing between 117 and 145 in the Order of Merit; 26 are from the end-of-season Challenge Tour rankings between places 16 and 45; three places each are allocated to leading players from the Asian, Sunshine and Australasian Tour money lists; two are either a previous Q School winner or a Challenge Tour winner from 2006; and one is on a medical exemption (Raymond Russell of Scotland). But the most interesting category of player is the winners on Tour from the last 10 years.

This year there is a total of 21 former champions, the most high profile being ex-Ryder Cup players Andrew Coltart of Scotland and Joakim Haeggman of Sweden. Others include Scots Dean Robertson and Andrew Oldcorn, England's David Carter and Gary Emerson, David Park of Wales and Jarrod Moseley of Australia. Phil Golding also qualifies in this group as the winner of the 2003 French Open, but Coltart is their main spokesman. "I am here to win and I am strangely looking forward to it because I am hoping this can kick-start the career again," he says during practice. "I still haven't achieved all that I want to achieve; I have lots of unfinished business."

The former winner of the Qatar Masters and Great North Open has over €5 million in career earnings, but at 37 he returns to the School for the first time since 1993 after finishing 168th on the money list with just €127,000. Coltart knows how to create a confident mental attitude, but he is currently struggling with his game and will need a steady start.

"Mentally, I'm fine being here. What's frustrating has been wanting to improve and get better, still having goals, dreams and ambitions, but seeing them getting further and further away. You hear about how hard the guys are practicing, whose doing well, but you can also practice hard and not do well. Practice makes perfect? That's not necessarily true. Perfect practise makes perfect."

Another interesting sub-group is the 13 Tour Card winners from last year's Q School (including Sion Bebb) who have had to return to San Roque. The other nine of the successful class from 2006 – such as Andy Raitt and the joint winner from last year Alexandre Rocha of Brazil – have already been knocked out this year.

Meanwhile, three Q School reserves are hearing good news. England's Ben Evans is 1st alternate and replaces Alvaro Velasco who flies home to Argentina four days before the contest begins because of the death of his brother. Austria's Florian Praegant – who lost so dramatically to Euan Little in the Second Stage playoff at Sherry – gets a starting spot when England's Ian Garbutt drops out with an eye infection. Then on the morning of the first round, Sweden's Oscar Floren finds himself in the tournament because of a wrist injury to Italy's Massimo Scarpa.

Praegant is particularly grateful to be at Final Stage for the first time, especially after his dramatic playoff. The 25-year-old with a fine amateur record broke his neck in 2006 in a swimming accident placing his career in doubt. But he recovered and has been learning his trade on the ALPs Tour. "I am obviously a little bit surprised to be playing here, but I am not nervous. It would be amazing if I got my Card because my year was not really that good. My best finish on the ALPs Tour was only 5th place," he says.

However, although three men had their wishes granted, the next man on the list, 4th alternate Adam Frayne who had hung around during the practice days, quietly hoping he might be lucky, makes the depressing journey back to England without hitting a ball outside of practice. Fifth alternate Andy Raitt never actually left home; he always knew his chances of playing were somewhere between slim and none – and so it proved.

On the morning of day one, the conditions are benign – temperatures in the mid-to-high 60s – although the forecast is for the weather to deteriorate towards the end of the tournament. The experienced players have brought along winter clothing and wet weather gear because they remember 2006 when the event suffered two days of postponements due to torrential rain plus a last round storm delay of almost two hours. So the opening day tactic for most players is to make hay while the sun shines, get some early birdies. If the weather forecast for days five and six is true, then today is a perfect time to get below par.

One question on everyone's mind is what score will ultimately be needed to earn a Tour Card? The statistics from previous Q Schools indicates that, even if the weather stays benign, level par over six rounds will not be far away, while anyone shooting consistently one under each day will walk it. The players often discuss 'the mark' as they sit relaxing in the clubhouse bar, but a second key question is slightly more controversial: who is *good enough* to succeed here?

It is accepted wisdom that one fifth of the 156 players have no chance; these are players with a weak mental attitude, those who are surprised just to be here and are already half-expecting to fail. Another 30 or so are in poor form including many who finished low in the Tour money list or who are returning former Tour winners lacking in vital competition fitness. Any Q School veteran will then dismiss another fifth who will fail gloriously, losing out because of either fatigue or nerves or both. That leaves the number of potential Tour Card winners at 60. So the final question for all the players is: are you one of this "chosen" 60?

The more astute players will therefore lift their spirits today with the thought that they have a one in two chance of grabbing one of the 30 Cards available – you have to admire anyone whose mental fortitude can deliver this message on day one of such a pressure-cooker tournament. It's a marvelous example of positive thinking although, of course, Q School is never quite that simple. That's because many Tour Cards are won by golfers committing the fewest, grievous errors rather than by shooting the most birdies. San Roque will be a place where steady golf is the order of the day because there is no safety net to capture a big fall from grace, no next week to make amends. The term 'grinding' could have been invented for Q School and, if there is ever a time to find your 'A' game, then this is it. After all, Final Stage is one of the toughest tests in golf.

Unlike First and Second Stages, this week at San Roque feels like a real European Tour event. The field is bigger, the course set-up is more challenging, there are more officials, referees, caddies and even a smattering of spectators, plus there is a huge scoreboard in sight of the clubhouse bar. The format is simple: each day, the field is split in half as all the players will play four rounds – two each on the New Course and the Old Course, both par 72s – over the next four days. To mitigate against possible weather interruptions, there are two tee-off starts every morning.

The players are placed in the same threeballs for the first two days after a random draw and then there is a re-draw for days three and four based on scoring. After four rounds, the top 70 and ties will go through to the fifth and sixth rounds; tee times will again be decided on scoring so that the leaders start off in the last group of the day. After the final round, the top 30 and ties receive Tour Cards that provide full exemption for European Tour events throughout 2008.

Of the two courses, the Old is considered slightly more difficult, perhaps by one or two shots, but both are set up in similar fashion each day to avoid benefiting one group of players over another. The greens will be cut to run between 10 and 11.5 on the stimp metre depending on the wind; if the worst blustery conditions prevail then the speeds will be towards the slower end of the scale.

Every player is now desperate to just get started. Q School director Mike Stewart knows that this is a crucial day and, along with day four and day six, the most nerve-wracking. This morning, everyone from the golfers to his own team of officials and the dozens of local volunteers are feeling a little twitchy. Mike took on this job in 2001, so he recognizes the tense atmosphere; he knows that appropriate levels of encouragement or sympathy for the players will be needed depending on their daily results and there will be plenty of both from him and his team throughout the six days.

Sion Bebb is off in the very first threeball on the 1st tee of the Old Course at 9.00am, while Phil Golding is also an early starter but on the New Course at 9.10am with Euan Little 20 minutes behind him.

From the very first hole, Sion carries on where he left off at Sherry less than a week ago. He is bursting with confidence and begins with two birdies. This kind of start allows him to play the game he prefers: steady golf to reduce the chance of a major error. Gary Marshall is on his bag again and they are making quite a formidable team; in just a few tournaments together they have had a fourth and a win.

The Welshman's drives are long and straight, his iron play more than adequate and he is holing his share of putts, especially the sneaky short ones. It is these kinds of putts that require so much attention and Sion gets quite animated over them. He has a habit of moving a little quicker than normal when lining up his key putts and is apt to lie flat on the ground in an effort to read the breaks on the subtle San Roque greens. Putts like the three and a half footer for par on the 17th are classics; both Sion and Gary get low to the green before deciding on line and pace. Sion holes this one and goes on to record a 71. He is angry that the four par 5s did not give up a single birdie, but 1 under par is bang on his target.

Phil Golding is playing his first competitive round since the Kazahkstan Open in September on the Challenge Tour when he finished tied 51st. He has been working particularly hard with his coach Jason Banting – who will also caddy for him this week – on his short game and suspects that he might feel a little off the pace to start with. His prediction proves to be the case.

Phil is level par at the turn, but then suffers a horrible four-hole stretch; bogeys on 12, 13 and 14 are followed by a double bogey on 15 – he is only partly through his first round and is already 5 over. This puts unwanted pressure on a player who is already a little tournament rusty. The 16th, however, on the New Course is an inviting par 5, especially with a quiet wind and Phil takes his opportunity with a damage-reducing birdie. Then a par on the short 17th leaves him at 4 over standing on the tee of the famous final hole, the 453-yard par 4 18th that is a disaster zone for so many Q Schoolers. Phil knows that this is the most nerve-inducing hole on the course, so a birdie here would really lighten his mood at dinner tonight. He hits driver, 8-iron to a relatively comfortable flag; he is 8ft from a birdie and his putting stroke has looked smooth all day, so he sees the line clearly before easing the ball straight into the hole for a 3 over par 75.

The veteran's mind focuses on the high-pressure birdies at 16 and 18 that have shaken the cobwebs from his game; he thinks less about his unwanted spate of bogeys. Five over would have seemed like Everest; 3 over reduces Phil's task for the rest of the week to something more like Kilimanjaro. His self-penned report card reads: must do better.

Euan Little's joy after his Second Stage playoff drama last week is already a thing of the past. He hardly had the energy to celebrate on the night of his triumph and, instead, collapsed into a 12-hour sleep once the adrenaline had subsided. Next day, he drove down to Cadiz and met up with is sponsor, Willie Crowe from the Tipperary Golf Club in Ireland. Euan's pre-tournament routine at San Roque then amounted to just one practice round because these are courses that he already knows well. There is no need to pound the driving range in search of his swing; all that work is done. There is no Martin Rowley on his bag this time – instead, another experienced Tour caddie, Brian McFeat, a fellow Scot is his caddie – but Euan feels ready. He is staying in a beautiful apartment a few miles away overlooking the ocean and Willie is providing both moral support and his cooking talents, he was a head chef long before becoming course director at Tipperary.

However, despite the assured build-up, Euan suffers a little wobble on opening day. The par 3s on the New Course are causing him problems: he drops three shots on them. Luckily, though, there are also plenty of birdies out there to balance the books and Euan grabs four of them to finish at 1 under par.

As day one unfolds among the rest of the field, there is plenty of drama. The round of the day is on the New Course where England's Robert Coles cards a six under par 66, two better than the next best. Robert says either a new putter or becoming a father for the first time just six weeks earlier are reasons for his good form. Meanwhile, the Old Course is proving tougher and 68 is the best score by four players. Andrew Coltart manages a level par 72 and says a 69 was possible, but is happy with his opening 18 holes.

There are plenty of steady rounds of golf – 29 players hit the most popular score of the day, one under par 71 – while a couple of Frenchmen (Jean Pierre Cixous and Raphael Eyraud) both shoot 80 for the title of worst-rounds-of-the-day. They are among about two dozen players who are already almost too far behind.

As dusk approaches, the driving range and the putting greens finally empty. No one rests easy tonight: those with solid scores hope for good form, while the players at the back of the field crave a change of fortune. They all know that golf is the most mystifying of sports and everything could change tomorrow.

Day Two

"This is probably one of the worst tournaments you can play, it is hard to be focused over six rounds" – Sven Struver of Germany, three-time Tour winner and seven-time Q School attendee.

Day two is all-change day at Q School because the players who teed it up on the Old Course yesterday move to the New and vice versa. It is also an all-change day in terms of the weather. There is a definite increase in the wind strength, a brisk easterly blows for the first time this week and both courses are suddenly considerably more tricky. It's a distinct disadvantage to those here for the first time, they only practiced in calm conditions.

The two courses are set to bare their teeth and the contrast between them is now more apparent. Whereas the Old requires greater driving precision, the New is a place to open your shoulders a little more. The horror holes on both courses will take some victims: the Old is dominated by the tough stretch from the 5th to 8th while the New is memorable for the 16th to 18th that are mostly into the teeth of the prevailing wind.

Today Phil Golding is under pressure. Yes, he knows that Q School is a long week and, yes, an opening 75 is retrievable, but the time to play well is now. He cannot contemplate another 'sabbatical' year, especially in his mid-forties. He is one of many players whose entire career is on the line this week; no Tour Card and there will be nothing but corporate days, pro-ams and a bit of coaching for years to come.

Phil begins on the Old Course at the 10th with two experienced pros, David Drysdale and Robert Rock and looks the part of a European Tour regular, his demeanour is that of the accomplished professional. He knows both David and Robert and chats easily with them during the round. Phil's momentum from yesterday's final holes holds good and at the turn, he is 3 under for the day and back to level par for the tournament. He is hitting the ball with precision, notching up easy pars and giving himself plenty of birdie opportunities. This is perfect Q School golf. His 20-yard chip to the hole-side on his 8th hole (the 17th on the course) is proof that his short game in particular is sharpening up. His back 9 is less spectacular – only one birdie – and his only bogey of the day arrives after he finds a bunker at the par 3 7th (his 16th). A 69 on the more difficult course on a windy day sends Phil's confidence soaring; it is one of his best rounds of the year. He is now level par, tied 51st.

Afterwards, he is cautious about too many celebrations and sticks to the routine that he and Jason have set up: he practices elsewhere rather than at San Roque so as not to remain immersed in the tournament tension and only hits balls for a short time after his round. After that, he reflects quietly on his day, has a bite to eat and gets an early night.

In addition, Phil is studying old journals that he has kept from previous tournaments in which he makes notes of feelings or physical aspects of his game. He reads about slight changes that he has made to his game in the past, perhaps a different posture or his position to the ball at address. He then incorporates the feedback from tournaments past into his present day feelings about his swing. It is an unusual thing to do, but shows his dedication to finding a solution to his poor showing at Q School last year. It all puts Phil in a comfortable mood.

Also on the Old Course, but starting at the 1st is Euan Little. He tees off at 9.20 while the wind is at its calmest, but fails to cash in on this good fortune. He is hitting strong drives and flushing his approach shots, but no early putts drop. Instead, bad luck is following him and any poor shot or swing is being punished. He finds bunkers on the par 3 3rd and the par 4 6th and suffers a bogey each time.

His back 9 provides a birdie on the 10th and he finishes on a 73, level after two days. Only one birdie in 18 holes is frustrating, but Euan is alongside Phil tied 51st and safely in the pack.

Sion Bebb, however, is enjoying the extra space available on the New Course. Just as yesterday, he starts fast: three birdies in his first seven holes. But, as the wind blows stronger, Sion's golf becomes slightly ragged and two three-putts on his back 9 from just 15ft and 20ft leave a sour taste in his mouth when he signs for another 1 under par 71. Still, he is 2 under for the tournament and in tied 18th place.

Compared to Sion's start at Q School last year (he was 6 over par after two rounds and in tied 110th position), he is in great shape. His routine is like Phil's, that of a veteran of Q School: very little practice, a quiet evening with some supper and, by a little after 9.00pm, he takes to his bed almost unable to keep his eyes open. The mental demands and levels of concentration for five-hour-plus rounds are as tiring as the physical demands. Sion knows surviving the fatigue is one of the keys to a successful week.

By the end of today, every player has sampled both courses and the leaderboard is starting to take shape. Spain's Pablo Larrazabal is on top after shooting a best-of-the-day 66 on the New Course for a 7 under total. There are already 50 players at 1 under or better and some surprising names are making a move including first alternate Ben Evans, aged just 20 and a two-time winner in the Faldo Series who only turned pro on the opening day of the tournament.

Ben actually says he felt more pressure at First Stage than he does this week, but the thought of a Tour Card adds a serious tone to his voice. "It would mean everything if I got through," he says without hesitation. Ben looks even younger than his 20 years; his body is still filling out and his face is that of an adolescent. But he talks with authority for one so young and his talent is obvious.

Of the other Final Stage rookies, Austrians Florian Praegant (69 today) and Roland Steiner (71) are well inside the top 20; Craig Lee of Scotland, a survivor of the horrid First Stage weather at St Annes Old Links, cards a 68 to lie tied 5th; and England's Gary Boyd (one of only two amateurs still in the field) manages consecutive 71s for a 2 under total and tied 18th.

But not everyone is settling into the six-round marathon. Andrew Coltart shoots a torrid 77 on the Old Course and is now tied 120th on 5 over; unsurprisingly, his mood of optimism is no longer apparent. Other past Tour champions like David Park (5 over), Malcolm MacKenzie (7 over) and David Carter and Raymond Russell (both 9 over) are already staring into the void.

However, Australia's Peter Senior is showing that there is life in the oldies; his 67 moves him to 4 under for the tournament in his first ever visit to the European Tour Q School. The event's oldest player at 48, Peter is warming up for the Seniors Tour more than he is in desperate need of retaining his Card, but it would be a considerable blow to his pride if he failed here and he intends to fight hard.

Some players feel the full force of the difference between days one and two. Robert Coles's opening 66 was a great start, but Q School is like a man-trap waiting to snare unsuspecting victims and the Englishman slumps to a catastrophic 79 on the Old Course today. "My 66 was a surprise, but not as much of a surprise as this. It was a bad day. I've had a massive high and a massive low now. I had a four-putt and a three-putt early on and was giving away shots too easily. It's difficult to get those shots back at Q School," he says. Coles was leading by two shots yesterday; today he is tied 66th with 16 others. At least Robert is not alone in his agony; Sweden's Frederik Orest followed a 68 with a second round 80 and fell from joint second to tied 109th.

Golf is no different for these experienced tournament pros than it is for millions of amateurs – just when you think your game is sorted, it turns around and bites back. The few spectators and the players' families and friends at San Roque can hardly believe the drama – and this is only day two.

Day Three

"If you don't get your Card one year, then you don't know if you'll ever make it back on Tour again" – Alastair Forsyth, Tour winner and four-time Q School attendee.

Sometimes the pain that golf imparts is just too much. Euan Little is one of the best-humoured and chattiest players on Tour. He is a hail-fellow-well-met guy who has a word for everyone and knows how to enjoy life. But day three of the Final Stage of Q School must feel like one golfing disappointment too far.

For much of Euan's third day, he is in control of his game despite more blustery conditions. He is playing well within himself on the New Course again and is steadily pushing into the very heart of the event. He comes off the 9th green 2 under for the tournament and is starting to play to his potential. Then, from nowhere, his touch deserts him: a needless three-putt bogey on the par 5 11th and two double bogeys on 14 and 17 mean five unforeseen dropped shots. Euan's problem is a slight swing fault: he is getting stuck underneath the ball at impact and relying on his hands to get him out of trouble. To make matters worse, he is over-analysing his situation and it is sapping his confidence. As he picks the ball out of one hole late in the day, he suddenly feels slightly light-headed; it is the tension, the intense concentration, his overwhelming desire for a Tour Card. Q School is taking its toll and proving it really is no ordinary tournament. Euan had put himself into the top 20 after 9 holes today only to stumble through 41 shots (5 over) on the back 9. Just one player on either course (young Englishman Seve Benson who was on his way to a 14 over par three day total and second-to-last place) played a worse 9 holes.

This is precisely the wrong score at the wrong time and Euan's 75 means he has gone tumbling backwards; even a par score today would have moved him up the field. When golf is your life, you learn to take the blows. There is only ever one champion in a tournament of 150 or so players. The perfect round or simply the perfect shot, is sometimes unobtainable and, most of the time, players understand that golf is a game of imperfections. Not every iron is crisply hit or putt sent directly on line and, with the courses set up to provide the toughest of tests, the players learn to roll with the inevitable punches.

But for the first time in over a year of talking about Q School and his dreams of returning to the Tour, Euan is almost speechless. He is angry with himself, numb in his body and sick to his stomach. He says only a few words outside the scorer's tent before leaving. "That's as mad as I've ever seen him," says one of the Scottish golf writers Jock MacVicar who has known Euan for many years.

Euan has plenty of support – Willie Crowe, his sponsor, is by his side here; his coach Bob Torrance is ready to take a phone call; and friends from the Tour like ex-Ryder Cup player Philip Walton are constantly texting best wishes. Yet no one can console him today. Euan is now tied 77th on 3 over with the predicted four round cut mark most likely two over. Missing the cut tomorrow would leave Euan in pro golf's limbo land next season; it is an outcome he cannot contemplate. His mood had been sunny before today, but Q School just got deadly serious. The Scot is caught up in the chasing pack instead of hunting with the leaders. A handful of these players on the fringe of the cut will come through tomorrow, but will Euan be one of them?

Others also fall foul of the last few holes on the notorious New Course at San Roque.

At the other end of the scoreboard, Sion Bebb is moving relentlessly upwards during his first nine holes (the New Course back 9) and is again one under par for the day. But on the back 9 the Welshman has a crisis. A sudden gust of wind and a bad kick sends his 6-iron tee shot on the par 3 4th (his 13th) into a hazard and, after a penalty drop, Sion writes up his first double bogey of the week. All the good work of the first part of the round is now cancelled out. He gathers himself and drains a good 4-footer for par on the 5th, but then misses a 6ft birdie on the next. Sion is grinding and almost ready to settle for level par when the unexpected happens: he hits a sand wedge to 5ft on the 7th and a 4-iron tee shot to 1ft on the 8th for two easy birdies.

On his final hole, Sion's drive ends up behind a tree to the left of the fairway and he decides to gamble with a 7-iron from 186 yards and over water. It is a calculated risk, but the strike is perfect and the ball lands 15ft from the pin. A third birdie on the bounce gives Sion a 69; out of almost nowhere he has one of the best scores on a very difficult day. He is tied 9th halfway through the tournament, but absolutely refuses to show complacency. A couple of friends congratulate him, yet he chooses to deflect the praise and talk about how hard he needs to concentrate tomorrow. A few practice putts as the afternoon ends and Sion is off to watch some football on the TV. Another day over, another good job done.

However, one of Sion's playing partners did an even better job today. Florian Praegent is having a fine time thanks to his caddie, a local retired English stockbroker named Barry who is a long-time friend of the Austrian golf team coach Anders Forsbrand. "Putting is the weakest part of Florian's game," says Barry as he shoulders the bag for another stroll along a fairway. "I'm reading every one of his putts for him because I know the greens better, I've played here a few times." The father-and-son-style partnership is working as Florian holes some unlikely putts – even one from the fringe of the 16th for birdie – and finishes with a 67 to climb up the field into a tie for 3rd on 7 under.

Phil Golding's day three was always going to be a profound test of his character. On day one, he showed inevitable rough edges while on day two he was assured and silky-smooth – so which side of his game would show up today? A bogey-birdie start on the New Course has Phil still wondering himself, then he three-putts the par 3 4th for a second bogey and his prospects look grim. However, two birdies and an eagle on the back 9 reverse his fortunes. Outstanding iron play starts to set up birdies and he almost pitches in for an eagle on the par 4 14th; he finishes with his second consecutive 69, a score beaten by only three other players all day.

Phil is particularly pleased with his putting, especially because he gambled with a change of flatstick before the tournament began. He rarely changes his putter, but explored his garage five weeks ago and re-discovered an old White Hot Odyssey he had never used before in any tournament. According to Jason his coach, the Odyssey sets his hands slightly forward and in a better position for a more consistent stroke. In golf, the smallest adjustments can mean the biggest improvements. Phil lies joint 13th on 3 under for the tournament, five behind joint leaders, the two Spaniards Pablo Larrazabal and Luis Claverie on 8 under. Considering Phil was 5 *over* after just 15 holes, it's no wonder he can afford a smile before leaving the course.

This has been a sombre day weatherwise, the first with thick, low clouds to match a gusting wind. Many players were dressed in black or other dark colours as if the more mournful weather reflects their more serious mood. The scoring also reflects the growing anxiety. On day one, 58 players broke par, today just 33 players managed the same feat. There is always a cavalry charge on day four by all those just outside the predicted cut mark, all desperate to make the last two days. A round under par tomorrow might eventually be worth a great deal of money and even save a career.

And there are plenty of careers on that tipping point here. Former PGA Championship winner Andrew Oldcorn, ends with a 76, leaving him at 4 over; Robert Coles does not match his day one 66 on the New and limps to a 73 for 2 over total; and Oscar Floren's good luck at being the last alternate to get a place at San Roque runs out with a 75 to take him to 5 over.

On the Old Course, Andrew Coltart's struggles begin to overwhelm him as a 75 has him at 8 over and with one foot on the plane home; David Carter is even worse off on 12 over after the same third round score. David Park keeps himself in the hunt with a 71 for 4 over and now, like Dean Robertson (also 4 over) and Andrew Marshall (5 over), needs to find a round in the 60s just to play the last two days.

Even for hardened pros, poor rounds of golf at crucial times like these are tough to accept. For the ordinary amateurs, missing out on the monthly medal with a three-putt might mean an extra pint in the bar afterwards to drown their sorrows, but the pro has to immediately eliminate negative memories and move on to the next round otherwise he would be paralysed with fear of making another mistake. There will be dozens of golfers fighting for their livelihoods and careers tomorrow and tonight they are all looking for inspiration. There are no free spaces on driving range this evening.

Day Four

"Not making the cut at Q School was the worst feeling ever because you basically get no playing rights and it meant I had to go back to playing EuroPro events" – *Graeme Storm, Tour winner and four-time Q School attendee.*

Q School is a compulsively fascinating event because there is tension in every single shot and every single player will have a significant story to tell by the end of it. Day four of Final Stage is probably the second most awful day for the players; if they fail to make this cut then, not only do they miss the final two rounds – the contest for the top 30 spots and a Tour Card – but they are also denied any worthwhile playing category for next season's Main Tour.

The cruelest drama of day four of Q School is the interminable end-of-the-day wait to see who leaves and who stays. The main scoreboard, referred to by everyone as the wailing wall, near the outdoor restaurant and bar area of the San Roque Golf Club will be the focus for the hundreds of players, caddies, friends and family. The cut mark will move up and down during the day in keeping with the fluctuating fortunes of the players.

As dawn breaks with bright sunshine and no wind, the cut mark is 2 over par and the chatter in the locker-room is speculation about whether that score will still be the mark at the end of the day. The general consensus is that 1 over will certainly make it; 2 over might be cause for anxiety; and anyone on 3 over will almost definitely need to settle their hotel bill. So, the strategies are clear: those players inside the cut need par at least; those around 2 over will want to shoot under par just to make sure; and anyone further back will need to go low.

Euan Little begins the day on 3 over and tees off on the Old Course in the first group on the 10th tee. He knows what is required. His mood is one of concentrated calm; he now needs a convincing start.

However, his nerves are tweaked after playing partner Gary Lockerbie's opening drive; somehow, on one of the easier driving holes, the Englishman hooks his opening drive out of bounds. The knot in Euan's stomach might have tightened, but he plays the hole without drama and logs a par on his scorecard. Lockerbie – playfully nicknamed 'Disaster' by his friends – eventually takes a double bogey 7.

Then, on Euan's third hole, he picks up his first shot against the course and is now 2 over for the tournament. Four more pars follow and the Scot is looking composed and confident.

There is, however, an emerging distraction. The third player in the group is the young German Benjamin Miarka who is living up to his reputation as one of the slowest players on any tour.

Inexperienced tour pros are not always in tune with speed of play at top-level tournaments. They often still use elaborate pre-shot routines that should be left on the practice range or they want to spend extra time visualising their shots or they slow to a crawl when weather conditions are poor. A few decades ago, a threeball would race around 18 holes in three and a half hours; nowadays, rounds of professional golf too often last for over five hours and the younger players know no better. Slow play is seen as a cancer within the sport and many senior pros are irritated – even angered – by it. For some, the slow play is tantamount to cheating.

The rules state that players are allowed one minute to complete a putt and 40 seconds for all other shots once it is their turn to play, but Miarka is taking almost twice his allotted time on some shots. The threeball is 'on the clock' after only a couple of holes (that is, followed by an eagle-eyed official and in danger of penalty strokes); they manage just seven holes in two hours. Miarka is eventually personally warned about slow play, but this is the kind of disturbance no Q Schooler needs and is especially frustrating for the two players innocent of any infraction. Euan stands well away from Miarka at every opportunity; he tries to relax into his own space to guard against letting the situation get the better of him, but it is a tough situation in such a vital round.

By the par 5 17th (the group's 8th hole) Euan hits what caddie Brian calls a 'Bing Crosby' (a drive that flies straight down the middle). The Scot then lays up with his second and hits a 129yd wedge for his third to give himself a 12ft birdie chance. He holes it and is back to 1 over, a position definitely good enough for a Card. After another solid drive on 18 (his 9th), he has almost the same wedge shot as the previous hole and, although the ball lands 20ft from the pin this time, Euan grabs another birdie. That's level par and he is thankful for a putting tip he received last night after complaining of feeling a little trapped in his posture on the green. A fellow pro suggested he move a couple of inches backwards, away from the ball and the suggestion seems to be working: he is now at level par for the tournament and last night's dark mood is far from his mind.

Euan is inside the projected cut mark, but the more difficult 9 holes await him. The spring in his step as he makes the long walk from the 18th green to the 1st tee is a little premature. "Beautiful day," he says to no one in particular as the group walks behind the scoreboard outside the clubhouse restaurant. He does not give in to the temptation to check any scores; he is thinking only of holding his position.

The most difficult holes on this section of the Old Course are the 6th, 7th and 8th, none of which seem to fit the eye of the majority of the players including Euan. The strategy is to build up a head of steam in the first five holes, hang on through this three-hole stretch before a final birdie chance on the par 5 9th.

However, trouble can emerge from anywhere at Q School. The 1st is an ordinary par 4: the fairway slants wickedly to the right away from a massive bunker all along the left hand side. The required tee shot for the right-handed Euan is to aim at the right edge of the big bunker with a slight fade. Anything that ends up far right will be awkward at worst, while no one really worries about being too far left (that is, over that bunker) even though that area is out of bounds.

Euan takes driver and is first of the group to hit. As soon as he strikes the ball, he knows something is wrong. Instead of fading off the right hand edge of the bunker, the ball is hooking to the left, heading towards a cart path. The ball hits the concrete and then veers sharply even further to the left. No one on the tee is actually sure where the ball lands, but for sure, something freakish has happened. Euan hits a provisional tee shot just in case and his second tee ball lands in the fairway bunker. The long walk to find the first ball is excruciating. Euan hopes for the best, but expects the worst. He repaired so much of yesterday's damage in his first nine holes today, yet now he might have undone everything with one errant shot.

As they approach the bunker, every player, caddie and spectator in Euan's entourage scans the sand and the rough around it for his Titleist ProV. After a couple of minutes, the Scot spots his ball on the nearby practice range, definitely out of bounds. By striking the edge of the cart path, Euan's ball dived 40 yards offline. Despite a second ball par, Euan has dropped two shots and returns to 2 over for the tournament.

With the toughest section of the course still to come, Euan's back is firmly against the wall, so the words of his coach Bob Torrance now come to his mind. Bob is his mentor and the older man knows how successful golfers overcome adversity. Euan can hear Bob's voice: "Head down, bum up, plough on." It is now or never; the Scot must get himself out of the mess he has got himself into.

A birdie chance on the 2nd from 8ft misses just to the right, yet he unexpectedly holes a birdie from 20ft on the par 3 3rd, the ball falling into the cup with its very final ounce of energy. Back to 1 over. The 4th (a short par 4) and 5th (a reachable par 5) both provide more birdie chances, but Euan misses the crucial putts by a fraction each time. On the 5th his putt actually sits on the very edge of the hole and refuses to drop.

Now his margin of error is small with the tough holes 6, 7 and 8 coming up. Euan needs pars on each of these as well as his final hole to finish on 1 over and make the cut, but if he drops just one more shot then 2 over is likely to mean the end of his tournament, while falling to 3 over is unthinkably bad. Euan has to dig deep because three of the last four holes have been absolute bitches all week.

The 6th hole on the Old Course is a relatively short par 4, but both the drive and second shot require total precision. The tee shot is a long iron or rescue club because the landing area for driver would be in the middle of the fairway lake. A bunker on the right of the fairway catches plenty of tee shots and there is a drop- away bank to the left, so the fairway is quite tight, no more than 20 paces wide at best. Euan aims right and his ball bounces through the fairway bunker and onto a grassy downslope; actually being in the bunker would make for an easier second shot.

The green is elevated with a deep bunker cutting into the front left edge, plus it is two-tiered with the pin on the top level. Euan has a tall cork oak

50yds away slightly blocking his shot so he tries to hit a 6-iron with some fade to the back of the green. He decides to grip slightly down the shaft because of the downslope, but that takes a crucial few yards off the distance and the ball finds the deep front bunker. It is not an easy sand shot and Euan's ball gets no backspin and runs 15ft past the pin. The par putt then slips beyond the hole on the right. Bogey. Two over.

Slow play in front then causes a delay on the 7th tee, unfortunately allowing Euan to stew about his latest bogey at exactly the wrong time. In fact, the pace of play may be partially to blame for Euan's dropped shot; he much prefers a faster pace. He knows a birdie in the next three holes is a must, but this par 3 has surrendered few of those today. The pin is back left and Euan tries to draw a tee shot off the right hand side. The ball does not obey his command and holds its line, landing on the fringe of the green. He has an improbable 40ft chip for a two and the ball comes up 4ft short. With no hint of nerves, Euan makes the short putt for another par and remains 2 over with just two holes to play.

This Scotsman has been in plenty of tight situations over his 11-year pro career, not the least of them last week at Second Stage, but these closing holes are testing even his nerve.

The 8th hole is another beast. Again the tee shot has been causing problems all week. There is another right hand side fairway bunker which is attracting plenty of drives and, further to the right, light rough drops into a small swale with a couple of olive trees; anywhere here is bogey country, while on the left is out of bounds.

Luckily for Euan, the obvious shot here is a draw, his stock shot. He aims over the right hand bunker expecting to bring the ball back onto the fairway, however, the tension of Q School is removing the authority from his swing and the ball stays blocked to the right. His body was moving a little too quickly through the swing and he got slightly ahead of the ball that negated any draw spin. He has not hit a drive like that all day and this shot takes him by surprise. He has no certainty where the ball has landed; all he knows is that he is the swale beyond the right side of the fairway. Things are not looking good.

As he walks towards the swale, Euan ponders that with even half-decent luck he could escape with just a mid-iron to the green; after all, there is only light rough even a dozen yards from the fairway. But when he gets closer and sees the damage, he shakes his head in disbelief. The ball has landed right under a small olive tree; Euan can maybe get a wedge on the ball and punch it back onto the fairway, but not much more. Again, he is staring at a bogey. He needs to get as much distance as he can with his second shot and studies his chances, thinking he can play a clever chip shot past one of the other trees nearby to get close to the green. It is a risk worth taking.

Euan strikes the shot firmly, but the ball hits an olive tree branch and ends up back in the rough only about 60 yards away. His third shot is a gap wedge that flies over the flag and lands in the first cut of rough at the back of the green. He is then faced with a chip onto a green sloping away from him and with the pin tight at the back; it is one of the hardest shots on the course and, although Euan makes a good fist of it for his par, the ball stays above ground. Another bogey. Three over.

This is now a dire situation. The scoreboards are indicating that even 2 over might be too many, so Euan has no option but to at least birdie his final hole. It is a par 5, so there is even an outside chance of an eagle.

Euan's final hole drive is long and straight but a couple of yards too far to the right; a fairway tree will partially block his second shot which needs to be a fade, not the shape that comes easily to the Scot. After plenty of thought and extra consultation with Brian his caddie, Euan tries for the fade, but instead he gets a "double cross" and the ball turns over to the left rather than swings to the right. There is another disconsolate walk before Euan finds his ball yet again in an unappealing spot: partly buried on a grassy slope to the far side of a greenside bunker.

A normal person would shake a fist at the golfing gods, but Euan keeps his poise and prepares for an all-or-nothing 50ft chip shot over the bunker from an uncomfortable lie as the ball is slightly below his feet. Hole it and he's pulled off one of the shots of the day to allow him two more rounds of Q School; miss it and there is no Tour Card and certainly no consolation prize.

Bob Torrance told Euan last evening that all he could do was give his best on every shot. Euan, for a change, takes extra time studying the contours of the green; he will land the ball about half way and let it roll to the hole. To give himself a chance of the eagle, he needs to be a little more aggressive than usual. After several practice strokes, he settles over the shot; one last look at the pin and he makes his swing.

The ball comes off the clubface a tad thin; it has a low trajectory and is a little more speedy than Euan wants. He stands up off the shot quickly and watches the ball approach the cup; he waits for his miracle. For a slow second or two, he is transfixed by the result of the most important shot of his golfing year. Just 12 months ago, Euan's Q School ended with an 18th green miss and here he is again. Will the outcome be different?

The ball misses the cup by a couple of inches and runs off the other side of the green onto the fringe. It was a shot of immense difficulty, a high tariff for sure; he may have been able to hole it one time in 20 or 30 attempts. Euan's face and body twitch almost imperceptibly as he walks to his ball. No chance of a 1 over finish, but he has a 10ft putt to get to 2 over and a sliver of hope.

It is a relatively easy putt, but the ball will travel over at least 3ft of fringe; that means a slightly less than perfect surface for another enormously important shot. Euan gives the shot the full treatment – he is low on his haunches studying it from all sides; he looks carefully at the edge of the hole; he has not given so much attention to a putt all day. Finally, he strikes the ball firmly, but it bobbles on the fringe and misses by an inch to the left; there is no birdie. Euan taps in for par to record a 72 and 3 over for the tournament. Again, his Q School is over.

As his playing partners putt out, Euan leans on his club and stares into the middle distance. He looks tired and empty as he completes the formalities of handshakes and walks to the scorer's tent 20 yards away. His experience of 12 months ago is not far from his mind.

In 2006, Euan left San Roque desperately upset; he had actually made the four-round cut only to suffer a crushing, last-round failure: a missed 8ft putt on the very final green denied him his Tour Card by a single shot. Back then his dream was almost in his grasp; this time he has fallen well short. His desolation is real, almost physically painful. Euan sits on a bench in the shade and tries to make sense of the last five hours.

At level par for the tournament with nine holes to play, he looked a shoo-in to progress to days five and six. But then a cocktail of bad luck and bad shots ended his hopes. For the second time in 24 hours, words are hard to come by. Any tears can come later; for now, he tries to understand what happened intellectually rather than emotionally.

"I am totally deflated. I really tried to overpower my negative thoughts in the last few holes to come up with what I needed, but I was just misfiring and I don't really know why. I would love to play without nerves and today I think I coped with them and I felt very comfortable after nine holes. But the result is the same as last year. I'm gutted."

Euan thinks that last year's experience was more agonising than today. "2006 was the worst I've ever felt on a golf course. To get so close and not get a Card, that was bad. I let myself down and my family down. Right now, I guess the feeling isn't quite so awful. I'm not as suicidal as I thought I might be. I think last year taught me something. I'm actually still furious about yesterday because I let it get away from me in the last few holes. At one stage I got really light-headed and I thought my head was going to explode. There were doubts in my mind. I was hitting bad shots that I hadn't seen for months."

It is less than half an hour after he signed his scorecard and time to meet up with

Willie, his sponsor, and drown a few sorrows. Euan will be one of over 70 players trying to comprehend what happened over the last four days before heading home. He struggles to find his normal sanguine self; this man, who is normally so loquacious, is drained by another tortuous Q School. In the end, he concludes sadly: "I suppose there's more to life than getting yourself wound up about this. Things just didn't work out."

By contrast later in the day, Sion Bebb and Phil Golding are both smiling broadly, especially the Englishman. Phil shoots his third successive 69 including a hole-in-one at the 7th hole on the Old Course. He moves to 6 under par for the tournament.

It would be the only ace of the week and Phil is slicing through the field at a rate of knots. From 5 over par after 15 holes on day one, his streak of good form is remarkable because no player has scored better over the last 54 holes. He is now tied 11th.

"I got a bit edgy on the back 9, so I've still got something to work on," he says afterwards. "I'm going to keep the same routine: a bit of putting and then hit 30 balls or so and get some rest. I'm still reminding myself it's process, process, process; no punching the air. It sounds a bit boring, but even on the hole-in-one – it was a 4-iron, two bounces and in – I just shook hands with Jason, kissed the ball and moved on."

Sion – playing the New Course – matches Phil's score and is now in third place on his own at 8 under. But after each day he looks a little more fatigued. "Every shot is mentally draining out there," he says after his round. "Another 36 holes to go; I'm happy with my score, but I'm not smiling until the very end." He returns to his apartment for tea and pizza plus as much sleep as he can get.

Elsewhere, Lee Slattery hits the round of the day, a 64. He started day four at 1 over par, on the fringes of the cut and climbs to 7 under and tied 4th. In the lead is Spain's Pablo Larrazabal and Thomas Aiken of South Africa, both on 10 under.

But the story of the day is not about the leaders, it is of those around the cut mark. Back in the scorer's tents, Jenny Janes and Carmel Treacy of the Tour's Field Staff are not only acting as official recorders, but also official deliverers of sympathy and advice to players on or near the mark. As the afternoon progresses, those on 2 over are increasingly in danger of missing the cut; the calm conditions are allowing a few crucial extra birdies.

England's Andrew Marshall is one Tour veteran on the edge. He has just shot his best round so far – a 3 under 69 – and is one of those on 2 over. But he is already talking of other options if his Q School implodes. "Every day's been a few too many for me. I was 4 under with three to play and shot a 69; it should have been 6 or 7 under. I needed another birdie, I suppose. It's tougher here every year and not making the cut will be hard to take."

As the hours tick by, the cut moves back and forth between 1 over and 2 over. At 3pm, with plenty of groups still playing, 1 over looks favourite, then just an hour later, after a few nervous players drop shots towards the end of their rounds, 70th place moves to 2 over. Those at the wailing wall are close to pulling their hair out with worry.

The drama is not over until the final group reaches the scorer's tent. In the end, a late birdie by Robert Rock – one of the last players to finish – kills off the chances of no less than 16 players on 2 over. Seventy one hopefuls finish 1 over or better and will contest rounds five and six while 85 players like Andrew Marshall will be leaving San Roque earlier than planned.

There are plenty of dreadfully sad stories. Frenchman George Plumet and Björn Pettersson of Sweden both double bogey their last hole to miss by one; Van Phillips of England, a former Portuguese Open champion, slumps to a 78 and a 6 over total when even par would have been enough; the 2001 PGA Champion Andrew Oldcorn finishes 7 over, the same score as Brazil's Alexandre Rocha, who was joint winner of last year's Q School. The list of quality golfers falling at this hurdle is a long one and includes several former Tour champions: Darren Fichardt of South Africa, Steven O'Hara and Raymond Russell of Scotland, David Park, Mark Mouland and Mark Pilkington of Wales, ex-Ryder Cup star Joakim Haeggman of Sweden and Wade Ormsby of Australia.

The leader on day one, England's Robert Coles, and Sweden's Fredrik Orest, who was joint second after the opening round, are both going home as well, but perhaps the most heart-rending story is Andrew Coltart's.

The 37-year-old from Dumfries in Scotland should really be in his prime golfing years; he has two Tour titles and one Ryder Cup appearance to his credit. He is well-liked by his peers and by the media, but this season's form has been dreadful, no top 10s and 18 missed cuts in 29 starts. A fourth round score of 73 leaves him 9 over par and 138th in a 156-man field. The tough Scot with the Sean Connery accent is still in a state of shock straight afterwards. "I haven't played well for a while and it continued in that vain this week; it's not enjoyable. It's no one single area of my game, it's just pretty poor in general. I didn't play well in the 2nd round (a 5 over par 77) and that gave me a lot to do. I couldn't get anything going." His eyes are hidden behind reflective sunglasses, but it is clear that Andrew is angry to find himself in this situation after 15 consecutive seasons on Tour. "I never envisaged missing out on my Card at all and I thought that was a good tactic, but it backfired subsequently. What now? I have no idea, some invitations, I suppose," he says. "I'll have a wee think about it in a week or so when my head has cleared a bit."

This was Andrew's first visit to Q School since 1993, but with so much talent bursting through every year, it may not be his last.

Day Five

"Final Stage of Q School is one of the only weeks of the year when I wished I had an ordinary 9-to-5 job" – Simon Hurd, Q School graduate 2004.

Q School is noticeably quieter on its penultimate morning. There is a sombre mood in the practice areas. The odd player who missed the cut or a newly-unemployed caddie ambles around the tournament office looking for travel advice or information on other golf events. The players remaining in the hunt for Tour Cards acknowledge the fallen and offer good luck wishes and a handshake. But there is not really much anyone can say.

There is plenty of room on the driving range and practice putting greens for a change as the contestants get ready for Moving Day. In a regular golf tournament lasting only four rounds, Moving Day is day three – the halfway cut has fallen and, if a player is going to win, then now is the time to make a move. At Q School, Moving Day is day five because all 71 remaining players now have a chance of a Tour Card; even those who scraped through on 1 over are just three shots off the crucial 30th place. Moving forward not backwards is the key, so the same tactics as the first four days still apply: take those birdie opportunities, play steady golf and limit the mistakes.

Again, there is much debate about what score will be required by the end of tomorrow for a Card. Currently, 30th place stands at 2 under, but the early prediction is 3 under. If the weather deteriorates (which is what the forecasters predict) then 2 under or even 1 under might be enough. Basically, all the players know that pretty much anything can happen over the next 36 holes.

The Old Course will be the site for today's action with the New Course providing the ultimate test tomorrow, that is traditionally how Mike Stewart, the PGA tournament director, plans days five and six and the players are placed in new threeball groups in order of scoring, again starting from two tees. The leaders will play from the 1st and tee off later while those at the back of the field will play from the 10th and begin earlier. The opening drive will be struck at 9.00am and there will be 10-minute gaps between the groups so that there will be plenty of light left at the end of the day in case of unforeseen delays (dusk falls around six in the evening here).

The day dawns with zero wind and blue skies. Although this is mid-November, the sun will still be quite intense by mid-afternoon, with temperatures well into the late 60ºs and even low 70ºs. With the surprisingly pleasant weather making the golf a little easier – despite the large amounts of nervous tension in the air – there might be some low scoring.

Phil Golding tees off the 1st at 10.10am in the fifth group from last and gets off to a dream start; after three holes he already has two birdies under his belt. Right now, he can do no wrong. Pars at the 4th and 5th keep him on track and, at 8 under, his name appears on the leaderboard for the first time.

Sion Bebb tees off in the last threeball of the day on 8 under with two 24-years- olds, Pablo Larrazabal and Thomas Aiken, who are leading by two shots. Pablo and Sion are the only players to have scored under par on each day, while Thomas (a regular this year on the American PGA's Nationwide Tour) has the length to take either of the San Roque courses apart.

The styles of the two young men and the more experienced Welshman could not be more different. While the twentysomethings fire for the pins, aiming to win the School, Sion has a no-risk philosophy, reckoning par to be a good score on each hole long. It bemuses him to see how his playing partners are chasing birdies.

Having said that, Sion seems a little out of sorts; he is not hitting his irons close enough and his putter is luke warm. His conservative tactics have been working so far, but he feels in the shadow of the two younger men; he drifts backwards after a clumsy bogey on the par 5 5th where he bunkers his wedge third shot and then three-putts. He has lost his rhythm.

Up ahead, Phil negotiates the awkward par 4 6th in par, but at the short 7th he tugs a 4-iron tee shot into the left hand bunker and cannot get up and down in two. It is his first bogey of the day. Nevertheless, another par on 8 is followed by a fourth birdie on 9, so Phil is 8 under at the turn with only five players ahead of him. It has been a remarkable run.

While Phil remains calm, Jason his caddie cannot help his mind from racing ahead; surely they can push on from here, he says, the trickiest part of the course is behind them.

Over in the final group, Sion actually comes through the tricky 6th, 7th and 8th holes unscathed and is 1 over for the day. His frustrations are building however, because Larrazabal and Aiken are thrashing the ball all over the course and somehow finding birdies. Some of their recoveries are startling. At 7 under now, Sion has actually dropped below Phil and is off the leaderboard. Meanwhile, Austrian Martin Wiegele is showing what can be done – he has five birdies of his own in the opening nine holes and has burst into contention.

The back 9 on the Old Course seems to be at the mercy of the players, but just to keep the leaders honest, the wind starts to freshen as they reach the turn. Nevertheless, Phil Golding pars 10 and also 11, but the 12th is a different matter: he three putts for a bogey and then repeats the mistake on the 14th. Just as Phil was expecting to push on, the course takes back a couple of shots. Then on the par 4 15th, he gets greedy and tries to flush a drive across the right-to-left uphill dogleg. The changing wind fools him and he finds more trouble. Suddenly, Phil has wracked up three bogeys and he is only 1 over for the day (5 under for the tournament) in the middle of the same kind of poor run that he had on day one. At the same time, Sion is being caught and passed by his rivals. His day is summed up on the 10th where he plays for a conservative par whereas Aiken slams a 330yd drive (with a 3-wood) to the middle of the fairway and then a 4-iron to 12ft before holing the eagle putt while Larrazabal is almost as impressive; he snags a birdie despite a wayward second shot into some trees level with the green.

It is 2pm and the final threeball has played just 10 holes in three hours. As predicted, the wind is getting up and play slows even more. While Sion looks tired, his young rivals are feeding off pure adrenaline. The Welshman continues to grind out the pars while fireworks flash around him; both Larrazabal and Aiken are heading for excellent scores.

Meanwhile, Phil has three holes to complete and a constantly changing wind to deal with. The crucial score of the 30th placed player is moving inexorably towards 4 under and Phil – who was 8 under at the turn – is just one shot better than that at 5 under. Whereas two hours ago a Tour Card looked odds-on, now he is near the edge. He really needs another birdie, but manages only an easy par on the 16th before missing from 15ft for his 4 on the par 5 17th.

Phil's confidence on the greens is disappearing. On the 18th, he plays a little too conservatively and is 35ft away for his birdie. It's an unlikely putt to hole and, sure enough, it misses by less than an inch. Phil gasps and is unconcerned that the ball slips two and a half feet past the hole. He just needs to tap in for a disappointing but adequate 1 over par 5th round still leaving him in the top 20 and at least one shot inside the Tour Card mark. Then the unthinkable happens: Phil misses the tap-in. It was an absolute tiddler by a pro's standards, a gimme in matchplay. Phil has not flunked a putt this short in any of the previous 89 holes; he is in shock.

His broad smile of a few hours ago is replaced by a face full of anxiety. Q School is playing its usual tricks, creating drama where there should be none. Phil is suddenly back to 4 under and right on the mark at tied 24th along with eight other players; tomorrow he will have no room for manoeuvre, no margin for error.

About one hour later, Sion approaches the last hole. The Welshman's back 9 has been a par-fest, eight in a row and he is still 1 over for the round. Even Larrazabal and Aiken have dropped a few shots as their luck slightly runs out in the increasingly windy conditions. However, Sion wants a below par round even though in the last group, he has suffered the worst condition; that means a last hole birdie. He has been averaging at least 3 birdies per round, but has had none so far today. On 18 tee, Sion hits his driving iron, then his approach comes up 20 yards short of the green. It is a bad mistake, the wind has fooled him and his concentration is running low after almost five and a half hours on the course. Sion's chip shot up the green is workmanlike and rests 10ft below the hole; no birdie, but a likely par. After a delay while Aiken holes out for double bogey (he has found the lake with his approach), Sion and Gary his caddie prowl around what they hope will be their final shot.

The Welshman tries his trademark full-body, horizontal position in one last effort to see the line. Then he sends the putt forward at a good pace expecting it to break slightly from the right. It looks set to drop and then lips out on the right hand edge of the cup. Sion is bent double with disappointment as if someone has kicked him in the guts; a second bogey of the day when he really wanted a birdie. His 74 – the same score as Phil – is his worst of the week. While 41 of the 71 players break par today, Sion and Phil are among a handful of the leaders to falter and fall back into the pack.

Sion's 6 under total for five rounds still leaves him tied for 11th, but 30th place is only two shots worse off at 4 under. Another 74 and Sion could ruin his week and all the hard work that he has put in. He had started the day on 8 under and level par today would have left him tied 5th going into day six, not only 90% certain of a Card, but probably a very good Card. Now four days of hard work is forgotten and the 10ft missed par putt floods his mind.

"I'm goin' home," is the full extent of Sion's post-round press conference. He waves everyone away and instead talks things over with Gary near the putting green for a few minutes before heading for the car park. He is seething. His Tour Card seemed secure for so long, yet now he feels like he has to start again from scratch.

Phil does not leave the course quite as swiftly as Sion, but he is also pondering his week so far. Tomorrow will be one of the most challenging rounds of his life. Will the fact that he has played very little this year come back to haunt him or can he find the kind of form that made him French Open champion three years ago.

As predicted, it was someone's big day. That someone was Martin Wiegele whose 64 leaves him on 15 under, worth a four shot lead from Aiken (who reached 14 under himself at one stage) and Larrazabal both on 11 and Lee Slattery two shots further back on 9 under.

Moving day has left a chunk of the field pretty much out of contention for a Tour Card, while a select few at the very top of the leaderboard can all but guarantee their 2008 season on the Main Tour. But 18 holes on San Roque's New Course is no push over and there is plenty of time for more heroes and fools to emerge. Unfortunately for the players, no one knows who will fill which roles.

Day Six

"You can miss out at Q School and just get lost forever" – Tony Johnstone, multiple Tour winner and 20-year European Tour pro.

The final day of every professional golf tournament is payday, the time when the prize money is divided. However, although there are a few cheques to hand out here, Q School is different. Yes, the £15,000 for winning Final Stage is nice, but today's winner – or even the player finishing today tied 30th – is looking forward to the chance of banking 10 or even 100 times more than that over the next 12 months on the European Tour. It is the prospect of these riches next season via a Tour Card that is the real prize.

So, the last day of Final Stage is less about the man who finishes 1st than what it takes to come inside the top 30. Miss out on a Card and you will have to survive on smaller, much less lucrative Tours or maybe live for a whole year off a few pro-ams and last-minute invitations; you might even give up pro tours altogether.

Whole careers are at stake and, if that was not cause for enough tension, then a howling easterly wind and predictions of thunderstorms add an exclamation mark. The strong breezes earlier in the week will feel like gentle zephyrs by the end of the day if the forecasters are right, so tournament director Mike Stewart takes no chances. The worst of the weather is due after lunch, so start times are moved up by 30 minutes to 8.30am. Given that it is still dark at 8.00am, this is as early as day six can begin and means that the first couple of groups off the tee have less than half an hour of daylight in which to warm up. However, after five consecutive days of 5 hour 15 minute sweaty-palm rounds, there are few golfers in a fit state to pound endless balls on the range this morning anyway. Golf pros are used to rolling with the punches of weird weather conditions and, although they might not always agree with every decision tournament officials make, this one seems a sound idea – get the whole thing up and running early and take out the possibility of a day seven.

The New Course at San Roque, neatly designed by Pete Dye and Seve Ballesteros, seems specially built to showcase today's prevailing easterly wind and among the two holes most affected, are the two most crucial, the 9th and 18th.

Under ordinary circumstances, these golf holes are relatively ordinary: long-ish, straight par 4s, each needing a strong tee shot and a precise approach with water protecting the greens (to the right of the 18th green and to the left of the 9th). However, played into today's prevailing wind and being the holes where the two halves of the field will each finish their tournaments, they will be the scene of many heart-bursting triumphs and head-hanging tragedies at the end of the day.

The 453yd 18th hole will be particularly under the spotlight as all the leaders and most of those players around 30th place will finish there. It is an uphill, blind drive to a fairway that is reasonably generous with only a few scattered nearby trees and almost no rough. But when players reach the brow of the fairway hill and feel the fierce headwind blowing into their faces for the second shot then the knots will tighten in their stomachs. The approach shot to a small green with its slight back-to-front slope can be anything from a 2-iron to an 8-iron. There is the lake all along the right hand side and a small swale to the left and around the back; today it will be both uninviting and intimidating. Plus there is a cart path dangerously close to the green on the left, an area that often acts like a golf ball magnet. The 18th at San Roque might not compare in European golfing folklore with the 17th at St Andrews or the 18th at Carnoustie, but in Q School history, it sits at No 1 in the difficulty charts.

Today sees another two-tee start and as the 8.30 groups hit their opening shots, the general mood is subdued as everyone – from the volunteers around the course to all players and caddies – knows how much is at stake. The early start is particularly good news for those players around 30th place because they will begin early and most likely enjoy the best of the weather while the leaders teeing off later will suffer the worst. Thirtieth place is currently on 4 under and the predicted bad weather means the Tour Card mark may drift backwards to 3 or even 2 under, so those players at the very back of the field feel they still have a chance. Only a couple of players are really without hope today – Fredrik Widmark of Sweden and Jordi Del Moral of Spain who shot 78 and 77 yesterday and are 4 and 5 over respectively – but Tour stalwarts like Robert Rock, Gary Emerson and Patrik Sjoland along with Gary Boyd (the only amateur left in the field) all on 1 under could still push their way in with a 68 or better. Somebody always bursts through the field on the final day of Q School, the question is who will it be.

By contrast, Sion Bebb and Phil Golding are inside the top 30 and rounds of even par 72 will probably be good enough for them. Yesterday evening's highly annoying bogeys on their final holes soured their evenings – Sion says with great understatement this morning that he was "cheesed off". The Welshman reports a poor night's sleep as well. "I had butterflies in my stomach because you're thinking of the good things that happen and the bad things as well." Deep down he understands that today could go either way: another stepping stone towards a lucrative Tour career or a return to the nowhere-land of regional events in Wales. His nightmare is another frustrating 74 like yesterday's, but Sion believes everyone is allowed one bad day in six rounds. At 6 under, his mood is one of quiet confidence.

Phil is a little more difficult to read this morning when it comes to his emotions. He tends to stay neutral and his years on Tour make him guarded about showing anything put a positive outlook. However, his coach and caddie Jason knows the true suffering of Phil's final hole yesterday. "That 3-putt really hurt him on the last," Jason says. "We were 8 under after 12 and all I could see was us finishing another one better than that or at least the same." Four dropped shots in six holes has left Phil in the danger zone. Only eight players shot worse than 74 yesterday, so his career is once again teetering on the edge of collapse and a second so-called sabbatical year could be tantamount to early retirement for him. He cannot allow it to happen.

The Englishman is off in the third group of the day from the 1st tee at 8.50am with Terry Pilkadaris of Australia and fellow countryman Lee S James, all of them on 4 under. There are some forced smiles among the group, but this is a day destined for endurance not enjoyment. Phil needs a solid opening few holes, but when he hits his first drive of the day it is everything he does not want. He pushes his shot badly to the right into a copse of cork trees, the ball coming to rest behind one of them; there is no other option but a chip-out.

How often does this happen to even the best pros? All the experience, all the rehearsals, all the muscle memory and they start a crucial round with a horrid shot. It happens even to the very best (remember Tiger Woods' first shot in the 2006 Ryder Cup hooked directly into water with a 5-wood?). Phil walks extra-slowly down the fairway, deep in thought. If nerves were not already bothering him, then they are now.

After the chip-out, he hits a very brave third just over a bunker to within 10ft; he tugs the putt slightly and it misses left. A bogey start is just what he and every other Q Schooler does not need on day six.

However, the dropped shot seems to get Phil's attention and the par 5 2nd hole gives up an easy birdie to him, so the damage is immediately repaired. Solid pars on holes 3, 4 and 5 show that Phil's head is dealing with any demons. He is helped by his two playing partners making similar errors to his own – Lee is continually over-clubbing his irons and Terry is also making mental errors and dropping shots. Q School, true to form, is working its evil spells.

On the 6th, there is another birdie chance for Phil from 6ft, but it is missed. The player lets out a big sigh; Jason grimaces. One third of the round gone and no real sign of how his day will end; he is still on the mark at 4 under.

Meanwhile, Sion is in the 7th group off the 1st tee, playing 40 minutes behind Phil and, by contrast, his game is transformed from the day before. Instead of being unable to hit approach shots close enough or not holing mid-range putts, Sion has turned both parts of his game around. Despite predictions of nerves – he birdies the 2nd, 3rd and 4th to suddenly re-appear on the leader board at 9 under. His 25ft putt on the 4th for the third consecutive birdie is particularly welcome because it is just over an hour into his round and the first really heavy gust of wind blows in followed by a few spots of rain. Spectators start to unroll their umbrellas.

The weather forecasters have got it right. The leading group of Thomas Aiken, Pablo Larrazabal and Martin Wiegele are still on their first hole as the wind and rain starts. The more birdies you have in the bag by now, the better.

Sion is in control of his own destiny again; he is five shots clear of the Tour Card mark (4 under) and does not need to press from this position. He can return to his tactic of pushing gently forward, accepting any birdies, but avoiding the slightest chance of a round-busting mistake.

Meanwhile, Phil has no such safety net and a bogey 6 at the par 5 7th means he has slipped out of the top 30. Then, another mistake: Phil's tee shot comes up short left of the par 3 8th when anything right is safe. It is a second bogey on the bounce and Phil has fallen to 2 under, in danger of slipping into all-out reverse. Jason starts working overtime on re-focusing his friend's mind.

The 9th is into the headwind that is now gaining power and Phil's tee shot is another push, not dissimilar from his opening drive. Yet this time lady luck smiles and his ball hits a tree trunk before bouncing into the middle of the fairway. He then draws a 4-iron approach shot in to 30ft, leaving him with a relatively calm two-putt par.

Phil turns in 38, 2 over par for the day and 2 under for the tournament. At this point there are 30 players on the scoreboard at 4 under or better, so the cut is right where it began the day and Phil is outside it. There is no sign of a burst of birdies from players behind him, so Phil is by no means out of contention. It is too early to predict the final cut mark, but Jason is keeping his eyes and ears open. When it comes down to the last few holes, Phil will need to know exactly where he stands.

Sion's story could not be more different as he moves to 4 under for the day and 10 under for the tournament. He has made as much progress through the field as anyone and is feeling confident about a high finish. Around him, however, there are raw nerves; Aiken, the young South African, drops four shots in his first six holes.

Meanwhile, a three-hole downwind section begins the back 9 for Phil; it is a great chance to recover his position. The long walk from the 9th green up a sharp incline to the 10th tee gives him time to reflect. He is walking well behind his playing partners spending considerable amounts of time selecting clubs and studying his yardage book. This unhurried pace helps him concentrate; he knows his score can still be turned around particularly after Jason reminds him he is averaging four birdies per round and he has achieved only one so far.

The rain has now stopped and the sky is actually brightening, but the wind is freshening and gusting, so choosing the right club is a difficult job.

Phil gets everything right on the 10th with a steady par and follows that with a birdie on the 11th thanks to his new, trusty Odyssey White Hot # 7 putter.

On the 12th Phil has an outside birdie chance from 33ft. As he surveys the putt, he thinks of his six-year-old son Lucas and a conversation he had with the boy the previous night after his annoying fifth round. "Why are you grumpy, Daddy?" asked Lucas. "You've had a hole in one and some birdies. Don't be grumpy." Phil's mind is filled with the picture of his son's smiling face; Lucas loves his daddy whatever happens on the golf course. Freeing his mind from the strain of the game, Phil drains the birdie. He is two-thirds through his last 18 holes and back to 4 under for the tournament. He is fairly certain that with the wind increasing, he now has a score that will be good enough. But there are no easy holes on day six of Final Stage, so hanging on to his score will require top drawer golf from.

While Phil's 13th passes without incident – a tap-in par – Sion's bandwagon is wobbling again in the worsening conditions. The three holes after the turn are supposed to be birdie chances – being downwind – but Sion finds a bunker off the tee on No 10 and three putts for a bogey. Then on the 11th fairway, Gary his caddie suddenly falls to the ground with a cry of pain; bizarrely, he has stepped into a drainage pipe hole covered only by a piece of replaced fairway turf. It is like a booby trap and Gary's first thought is that he has broken his leg. The hole is several inches deep and he badly gashes his right shin; there is blood everywhere. The caddie wonders whether he can actually continue, but adrenaline soon kicks in and he gets back on his feet after a few minutes, albeit limping quite badly. His leg is very painful, but there is a job to finish. The scary thing is that the hole was very near Sion's ball and the player probably missed suffering the injury himself by only a few inches.

Despite his reassurances, Gary is a little rattled and so, naturally, is Sion. The two men have formed a close working relationship in the last few weeks and this is their first real crisis of any kind. A bogey 6 almost inevitably follows. Then on the 12th, Sion three putts for his third bogey in a row. He has fallen to 7 under and his slide has to stop. Sion is annoyed, so Gary reminds him that he is playing well; just go back to the old routine of fairways-and-greens.

By now, the wind is a factor on every single shot, even the putts. Gusts over 30mph are sweeping golf balls off course; even those on the greens are in danger of being blown off their spots. Of all the types of weather conditions, a strong, gusting wind is the most disliked by pros. PGA referees around the course are carefully monitoring conditions and three reports about balls oscillating on the green will cause a delay. This near-gale has already blown over the event scoreboard near the clubhouse and will later divert flights away from nearby Gibraltar Airport. A gripping climax is about to commence.

With five holes to play and at 4 under, Phil Golding would settle for a run of no- nonsense pars, but golf is rarely a game of serene, untroubled progress. The 14th is a par 4 that is almost a rehearsal for the horrid 18th – the distance is almost the same, the headwind is in the player's face and there is a lake to the right of the green. Phil hits another powerful drive that leaves him with a 4-iron second shot that he can draw in from the right to the pin positioned left. "We need one more birdie," says Jason, but when the approach shot is in the air, no one is thinking of a three.

Phil pushes his ball a little too far right and shouts "Get down" almost immediately. He and Jason are frozen as they watch the ball hang out over the lake for a second; Phil's Q School chances hang with it. Somehow, the draw spin on the ball and a little right-to-left wind work their magic and Phil's lucky Titleist #3 lands on the fringe of the green less than two yards from the water. With a true sense of drama, Phil's ball then rolls a little further forward before stopping about two feet from disaster. It could just as easily have taken a hop into the lake or carried on rolling, so the word 'relief' hardly describes his emotions at this point. Phil has not sent a shot into water so far this week and this is about as close as he wants to get; the strain is beginning to show and an eventual par feels like a reprieve. But still the rollercoaster will not stop.

Phil's drive on the 15th is too near to a tree and requires a sliding cut shot for his second to a pin on the front of the green. Phil comes up short with his approach and decides to putt over a very bumpy fairway area. It is the right shot and the pace is perfect, but the ball bobbles six feet to the right. He fails to hole the par putt and the luck he enjoyed on 14 deserts him. Back to 3 under.

There are now 35 players on the same score as Phil, so the next hole – the par 5 16th – is very welcome because it is his best birdie chance. He hits a super drive and then a solid 5-wood that comes up just short of the green. A chip on to the top tier settles within 5ft of the pin and the putt drops. Sensational – a birdie and 4 under again; surely his drama is over.

The crosswind on the par 3 17th is Phil's next problem and club selection is the key. What he does not want is to bring the huge bunker on the right into play. Phil and Jason spend an age before choosing a rescue club, yet the player then commits the cardinal sin as he blocks the drive to the right and his ball dribbles into the sand.

It would not normally be a difficult bunker shot, but the circumstances make it so. In addition, Phil and many of his fellow players dislike the tiny crushed marble in the San Roque bunkers; they would rather play from normal sand that delivers the same amount of spin they are used to. Nevertheless, his 25yd sand shot flops majestically out of the bunker and comes to rest three and a half feet from the pin. All seems well, but the slightly downhill par putt lips out. Phil has just blind-sided himself and created yet more needless anxiety. Back to 3 under and the treacherous 18th will play a full part in Phil's latest Q School journey. He must at least get a par; there is now absolutely no leeway. He has hit 425 golf shots over six days, some fabulous, some ugly, some that deserved better and some that seemed plain jinxed. He has to place every one of those shots to the back of his mind, focus on making two good swings, a couple of good putts and grabbing that Tour Card. "Trust it" are the words of advice from Jason's lips.

Phil's driver fires the ball long and straight off the 18th tee; first job done. He still seems outwardly relaxed and, as he reaches his ball in the middle of the fairway, he can see the small crowd gathering at the scorer's tent. He can also feel the monstrous wind blowing almost directly into his face.

Phil continues to take his time; he removes his visor for a moment and bends down to snag a few scraps of grass and throw them into the air to check the wind direction. Meanwhile, Jason pumps up the positives reminding Phil that this 4-iron shot will be just like the one he successfully hit onto the 9th green; he says this is what Phil has been training and practicing for; this is his time. Everything seems to be moving in super slo-mo; real-life action is happening at the speed of dripping treacle.

Phil studies the shot some more; there is no rush. This approach shot could define the next few years of his career: he yearns to return to his glory days of high Order of Merit finishes, even another Tour win; he wants his peers to recognise that he truly belongs among European golf's upper echelon and that this year was just a blip. Phil is a proud man; his status as a European Tour professional is what defines him as a person. Twelve months ago, his career stumbled when he failed at Q School; it left him in a kind of fog, unable to believe his fate. It even crossed his mind that his time on the Tour was over.

Despite all these thoughts and like so many pros in similar situations, Phil eventually zeroes in on the immediate job ahead. He eyes up the green for a final time and remembers Jason's words "Trust it". Too aggressive and the ball will find the lake on the right; too cautious and he will risk a tricky up-and-down from the unpleasant valleys of rough on the left; the pin is far to the back of the green and certainly not offering any easy option. The wind blasts one last strong breath. Phil grips slightly down the shaft of the 4-iron and tries for a low, penetrating ball flight. There is no fear in his swing, it is grooved and fluid.

When a pro hits a good golf shot, there is a soft thudding sound on contact and a "whush" just after the ball leaves the clubface and pierces the air. He knows within a millisecond of making the connection whether the ball is well struck. This shot has to be perfection or damned close to it.

Phil's Titleist is in the air for between three to four seconds. Often, if the ball is going right, the pro will lean left in an effort to pull on some invisible string to bring it back on line. If the ball is on its way to the left then the body will lean the other way. If the shot looks short, then the pro will to urge it on with words like "get up" or "big bounce"; a shot that seems too long would prompt a swift "get down". There are no tell-tale signs from the player about where his ball will land, but he knew what had happened the very moment it left his club: Phil's ball lands in the right half of the green and bounces forward a couple of times to come to rest 25ft below the pin.

There is applause from the growing crowd at the back of the 18th. None of those watching know what Phil's score actually is or the tension that pre-empted that shot, but they definitely recognise great golf under pressure when they see it. Phil's chest puffs out ever so slightly as he strides to the green and marks his ball. He knows that the approach was his best shot of the day, especially given the circumstances.

While his playing partners chip onto the green, Phil stands on the fringe by the lake calming himself for what should now be the final two shots of a successful 2007 Q School: a solid lag putt and a tap in. He has done this millions of times.

Phil gives the first putt due attention and strokes the ball confidently right on line before it pulls up a foot short. He nods to himself and taps in for that vital par. He has finished the tournament on 3 under. All the scoreboards indicate this is now exactly the Tour Card mark. With the wind still blowing strongly, there is no way the mark will move to 4 under – Phil has made it by the skin of his teeth. He has now hit 429 golf shots in six days and, if he had hit just one more, then his face would be full of anguish rather than joy. His beaming smile demonstrates a job well done; the weight of a whole year of expectation is lifted; the persistence of one of European golf's most regular visitors to Q School has won through.

Phil extends his arms into the air and shares the moment with Jason who walks forward to give his friend a huge hug. There would be no more honest or touching celebration on the 18th green today. The accomplishment is shared; everything that the two of them had done during the last six days – the last six months – has been justified: the routine they adopted, the continual words of encouragement from Jason; the goal-setting; and the focus on Phil's short game. This is only the seventh time in 18 attempts that Phil has won his Tour Card at Q School. To make a comeback at his age and with so little golf during the season is a tremendous achievement. Many others far younger and with far more tournaments under their belt this season have finished well behind him.

As he and Jason walk off the green with arms around each other's shoulders, tears of relief – as well as of happiness – flood into the coach-cum-caddie's eyes. This week, Jason has been Phil's entire support team and if he did not shed a tear after the unpredictable ride that the two of them had shared then he would not be human. It is a poignant moment and Jason will not be the only person to cry at Q School this afternoon because the emotional cost of either triumph or tragedy here is overwhelming.

Meanwhile, Phil retains a professional calm; pros are taught to control their feelings in the golf arena. He signs his scorecard, receives congratulations from some colleagues and is interviewed by a TV crew. He is still smiling. He is back on Tour and how he deserves it.

As Phil's celebrations are beginning, Sion is reaching his crucial last few holes; he is now battling both a viciously gusting wind and the inevitable nerves. The advantages of starting early are now apparent. Francois Delamontagne – first off the 10th tee in a two-ball group – sped through his last round, finishing over an hour before Phil and shot a 68 to easily gain his Card. His score would be the joint best of the day.

Elsewhere, most players are just hanging on. Marcel Siem of Germany (the player who won golf's World Cup 12 months ago with Bernhard Langer) signs for a 71 and the crucial 3 under score, exactly on the mark. He then weeps with joy on the final green. South African James Kamte manages a 72 to finish 3 under and beams an ecstatic smile.

But for every success, there are more tales of woe. Another South African, Doug McGuigan, bogeys his final two holes to drop to 2 under; Peter Senior fritters away three shots in the last three holes and ends at 1 under; Bristolian John E Morgan cannot complete a dream week for his soon-to-be-born child and leaks five shots in the last five holes to complete the tournament on level par. And still Sion is on the course.

The pace of play is slower than ever as the conditions worsen. Club choice is almost guess work and there is the first report of a ball oscillating on a green. A couple more and the tournament will be delayed.

At the turn, Sion was in the top five on 10 under, but those three bogeys in a row sent him even out of the top 10. On the 14th hole, he suffers another bogey and the advantage of his four early birdies has been completely cancelled out by four dropped shots. Now 6 under, Sion is not alone in dropping shots, so he is reassured by what the scoreboards tell him: 3 under gets a Tour Card.

The Welshman gathers himself and hits a superb wedge to the 15th green from behind a tree and holes an unlikely downhill putt for birdie. He can think positively again, more about achieving a high finish than just grinding. Back to 7 under, only the golfing equivalent of the world's worst car crash will wreck his dream now. But such things happen regularly at Q School.

In the group just ahead of Sion is Derby's Stuart Davis who began the day in confident mood at 5 under; he had just shot his best round of the week on day five – a bogey-less 67 – to make a strong move for his first ever Tour Card. A Challenge Tour regular, Stuart just needed to stay calm to complete his most successful year since turning professional in 2004.

But Q School always devours someone and, unfortunately for Stuart, it is his turn. He had battled bravely all day, but bogeys on 16 and 17 were perhaps understandable as the pressure mounted. With one hole remaining, he is on 3 under; a par for his Tour Card. What happens next would send a chill through every pro who has played Q School's last hole with a Card beckoning because they know it could so easily be them.

Stuart hits a reasonable tee shot on 18, but then viciously hooks his approach to the green; it bounces wildly on the nearby cart path and leaps 70 yards offline. His mind is now in turmoil. Less than half an hour ago he had a two shot cushion, yet suddenly he needs a miracle chip onto the 18th green and then a par putt for his Card.

Instead of a miracle chip, Stuart airmails the green and the ball plops into the lake. A penalty drop, three more shots and it is a triple bogey 7. Stuart had one hand on a Tour Card almost all day and now it has vanished after five dropped shots in three holes. There are no words that can console the Englishman as he walks away alone from the scorer's tent. He is known for his fiery temperament and all those gathered around the 18th green leave him to his thoughts. It is hurtful even to try to talk to him at this time. A wound like this will not heal overnight, but the chances are that Stuart will be back at Q School next year if that is what it takes. Being a golf pro is Stuart's life and he will not give up. He will hope that next time a Tour Card is in reach, he has built himself one extra layer of courage to allow him to grab it.

As Sion witnesses Stuart's devastation, the Welshman's day is coming to a happier end. He has birdied the par 5 16th and bogeyed the par 3 17th to remain on 7 under with one hole to play. There is no triple bogey disaster on the 18th; instead, he manages a drama-free, regulation par. It has been a fine afternoon and a splendid week for him – only one round over par (just Pedro Linhart of Spain matches that feat); only one double bogey in six rounds; and his 71 today is beaten by only one golfer finishing in a later group. Sion ends the day tied 6th for the tournament and receives the 9th Tour Card. He has succeeded at Q School for only the second time in 12 attempts.

Sion's consistency has shone through. The spectacular shots are all very well, but they are risky and most pros steer clear of risk; they usually play the high percentage shot, hitting very few drives or iron shots with maximum strength. The majority of long putts are lagged rather than raced at the flag; such tactics are why they score so well so often. It is a question of being in control, understanding the value of course management.

By adopting those tactics, Sion's performance has been a Q School masterclass. Immediately after finishing his round, he shows only a small smile of satisfaction. No fist-pumping, no high-fives. He is a quiet man on the course and a sincere, family man off it who cares for others. He knows that dancing with joy is inappropriate as the dreams of some of his friends are being crushed. His celebrations will be elsewhere, in a more private place. He knows how to let his hair down, but it will not be now.

He has just enough energy for some honest reflection. "It's a crazy game, golf; and those were horrendous conditions. Level par is a great score today and it helped me that no one was able to come up through the pack. I got to 4 under for today, but it was obvious that the conditions would mean a bogey run at some stage. The six-footer on the last makes me feel better. I'm absolutely delighted."

Achieving a top 10 Tour Card shows Sion's improvement from last year when he finished 14th. He has looked the part of a real European Tour player in San Roque this time and finishing four places higher could make all the difference when it comes to gaining entry into some of the early season tournaments. That's because successful Q Schoolers are ranked on their San Roque finish 1 to 30 in Category 11b of the European Tour exemption list. That means the winner gets first option of tournaments eligible to players in that category and then the others follow in sequence.

This is all in the future though and, for now, it's time for Sion to thank his lucky stars. "It could've gone either way today. You see friends missing Cards. It's not nice. I'm happy inside, but I don't jump up and down because I know how other people feel. I'm looking forward to a relaxing week at home. A couple of beers tonight; I think I deserve them." Only a couple? Probably not. Sion has reached an age where he has seen the best and the worst that golf can throw at someone. It is hard to put into words how much this Tour Card means to him. His is a grown-up response. To him, the Tour Card is potential financial security of his wife and young daughters, it is the deep respect of his fellow Welsh pros, it is the proof of his talent to his late father.

Perhaps the most telling part of Sion's last words is that "it could've gone either way". On some days you control your golf game and, on others, golf controls you. Sion's self belief has increased so much over the past couple of months that he overcame all the demons this week. As a complete professional, he is already thinking of his first Tour event of the 2008 season. This is a very different Sion than at Q School 12 months ago.

There were several players who began the day in better positions than Sion Bebb and did not convert their chances. Two new young pros, Tiago Cruz of Portugal and England youngster Ben Evans, had both started on 7 under; they each had a four-shot cushion, but it was not enough. Cruz stumbled to a 5 over 77 while Evans's few short months as a pro were not enough to prevent an 8 over par 80. Evans is not tearful, he prefers to think how he competed earlier in the week and, like any 20-year-old, is already excited about the future. He is heading for Challenge Tour and could be a star in the making.

Although plenty of players went backwards today (four shot 80 or worse), someone always charges through the pack and Patrik Sjoland of Sweden was this year's last-minute hero. Patrik – a former winner on Tour – was tied 60th before the final 18 holes began and was still one shot outside the cut mark as he stood on the 16th. But when a 137yd approach shot dived into the hole for an eagle, the Swede's luck turned around; he would eventually secure the 22nd Card. Thankfully for the sanity of pro golfers, stories of stunning triumph like Patrik's are a balance at Q School to those of pure tragedy.

This year's School almost claimed a much more unlikely victim. South African Thomas Aiken was 11 under on the 1st tee at the start of day six, in joint 2nd place, but the more holes he played, the more ragged his golf became. The wind, the nerves, his relative inexperience, it all combined to turn Aiken's day into a near-catastrophe. He dropped four shots in the front 9; managed a couple birdies on the 11th and 12th, but then went spiralling downwards. By the time he stood on the 18th, he was just 4 under for the tournament (a frightening 7 over for the day). He was suddenly in grave danger of an unimaginable plummet from being in contention to win Q School to missing his Card. A Stuart Davis-type disaster on 18 and his week would be wasted.

Thomas's final drive was adequate, his second just crept onto the green, his lag putt was over-hit and he took two more to complete his round – a bogey five and, although he finished safely on the mark at 3 under, he would be handed the 30th and very last Tour Card because of his horrid final round of 80. And golf fans wonder why players at Q School lie awake at night worrying.

But while Thomas Aiken's post-round smiles were of relief, those of England's Paul Waring and Craig Lee of Scotland were of unfettered elation. Both men had begun their Q School journeys at First Stage – Paul at The Oxfordshire and Craig at St Annes Old Links. Before this year, neither player had even reached Second Stage let alone Final Stage. Today their stories are among the most remarkable.

Paul's grandfather – the man who had introduced him to golf – died three weeks earlier while the young golfer was out in Spain practicing for Second Stage. Paul had to choose between continuing his dream or returning home for the funeral. His family was adamant: stay and play because that is what your grandfather would have wanted. He then qualified easily from Arcos Gardens.

Heading into the back 9 on the final day at San Roque, Paul was 7 under, but running out of steam. However, there was a guardian angel helping him hold on and finish on 3 under to achieve a most surprising Tour Card. "I know my granddad's looking down on me now. He was a sport maniac and looked after me a lot when I was younger. I was asking him to guide me through. I think about him a lot and he'll always be there. He taught me that there are worse things in life than missing a 4ft putt on the last hole. I've already had a few tears and I'm sure there will be a few more later."

Meanwhile, Craig was originally determined not to attend Q School this year. His future seemed to be more about increasing his golf teaching than playing on Tour, while he also opened a custom-fitting club centre. He was building a new life away from tournament golf and he celebrated his 30th birthday by enjoying a more settled existence.

But many pros whose lifelong desire is to compete with the best players in the world are fooling themselves if they think they can give it all up so easily. Craig kept Q School in the back of his mind even while his life was changing and he sent in the entry forms almost on automatic pilot. With £2,000 worth of sponsorship help from a retired local businessman, he turned up at First Stage without any serious hopes and promptly finished 3rd.

"The £2,000 sponsorship paid for my entry and I had nothing to lose, but before Q School, I didn't practice much or play well in local tournaments in Scotland. My form at St Annes was a real surprise." He then went to Costa Ballena at Second Stage and managed 4th place. There are only a few days between Second and Final Stages of Q School, so Craig had little time to worry about what might now happen to him.

"I didn't know what to expect (at San Roque), so I didn't really have a plan. I just tried to play the best I could and see what happened. I've been up and down all week, but adrenaline kept me going for the last round; it was definitely very tough. This is a completely new way of playing golf, being defensive rather than pushing for more birdies. Today I just held on."

Like any first time Q School qualifier, Lee can hardly fathom what he has just achieved. "High as a kite" is how he describes his feelings and the thought of being on the practice range at every tournament with the likes of Monty, Padraig, Sergio and others almost makes him swoon. "This is just the best feeling ever," says the man who picked up the 21st Tour Card. "It's so much better than winning a tournament."

The success stories of Paul and Craig are wonderfully romantic and Florian Praegant's is another. The fact that the Austrian managed a place in San Roque was a shock to him because he lost the Second Stage playoff to Euan Little just 10 days earlier. From abject despair, his life has turned 180 degrees.

Florian was originally a Final Stage alternate, but when he was handed a last-minute place in the tournament, he played with stunning confidence and looked stronger after each round. His last day 72 and 4th place finish are a testimony to his skill.

"I was a little bit nervous at first today, but I started with two birdies and made a lot of good up-and-downs. Mentally now I am done; I don't want to play here any more," he says. "I can't believe that I finished top 5 and I will only realise it when I play on Tour. After losing the playoff at Second Stage, I thought I would be on the ALPs Tour next year. I am so happy to play with the top players in the world from now on; my parents will have a big party for me when I get home."

Pablo Larrazabal of Spain actually hits the very last shot of the 2007 Q School
– a 2ft tap-in for 10th place – while Austrian Martin Wiegele wins the tournament on 11 under despite his last round 76, easily his worst of the week and some 12 shots more than his previous day's 64. Martin finishes two ahead of Pedro Linhart and Lee Slattery.

Exactly 30 players have won their Tour Cards after six long days, while 126 players are left disappointed, many with their careers in a state of flux. A crowd of about 100 spectators, volunteers, officials, players and caddies applauds as Wiegele receives a silver salver from tournament director Mike Stewart in a short ceremony behind the 18th green. Then it is time to head to the airports.

Next year, Final Stage moves PGA Golf de Catalunya near Barcelona, a facility operated by the PGA European Tour's courses division. For now, San Roque has provided its concluding and, perhaps most compelling, last-day Q School dramas. The reputation of the event as one of the most gripping – and often most grotesque – in professional golf has again been enhanced.

The 33rd annual European Tour Qualifying School in 2008 starts in 10 months time and, naturally, most of the 846 pros who failed to secure a Tour Card this year will again test themselves over one, two or all three stages even though every single one of the failed pros would love to discover another, less stressful way to win that Card. Hanging on to the dream of playing regularly on the European Tour is very seductive.

Only a relatively few players ever climb up to that high level, yet there are many, many tens of thousands who want it, wish for it, even pray for it. Q School is the quickest pathway, but it is a torture chamber of an event and it will get tougher as every year goes by. The faint-hearted or the obviously untalented should stay away because it can break their hearts. But, like mountaineers drawn to Everest, Q School attracts the hopeful as well as the skillful; the tournament exists as an enormous challenge and can be conquered only by a select band of brave individuals.

The final word goes to Phil Golding, the man with so many Q Schools behind him. "This is one of my proudest moments," says the former French Open champion. Like so many other long-time tournament professionals, Phil rates his Q School achievements very highly indeed. Every single golfer who has trodden this precipitous pathway to glory would whole-heartedly agree.

Q School 2007 Final Stage Results

The following 30 players gained their European Tour Cards for full playing privileges for the 2008 season.

		R1	R2	R3	R4	R5	R6	Agg
1	Martin WIEGELE (AUT)	71	69	69	72	64	76	421
2	Pedro LINHART (ESP)	71	72	71	69	70	70	423
3	Lee SLATTERY (ENG)	69	76	72	64	70	72	423
4	Florian PRAEGENT (AUT)	73	69	67	72	71	72	424
5	Luis CLAVERIE (ESP)	69	71	68	73	71	72	424
6	François DELAMONTAGNE (FRA)	73	74	72	69	69	68	425
7	Lee S JAMES (ENG)	72	69	74	73	68	69	425
8	Alan MCLEAN (SCO)	71	69	69	74	72	70	425
9	Sion BEBB (WAL)	71	71	69	69	74	71	425
10	Pablo LARRAZABAL (ESP)	71	66	71	70	71	76	425
11	Richard BLAND (ENG)	73	69	71	73	71	70	427
12	Birgir HAFTHORSSON (ISL)	71	70	73	70	71	72	427
13	Joakim BÄCKSTRÖM (SWE)	69	74	68	70	74	72	427
14	Sven STRÜVER (GER)	71	71	68	72	72	73	427
15	Paolo TERRENI (ITA)	72	71	71	67	71	75	427
16	Benoit TEILLERIA (FRA)	76	71	71	69	71	70	428
17	Juan ABBATE (ARG)	74	71	73	70	68	72	428
18	David DRYSDALE (SCO)	70	75	73	70	67	73	428
19	David DIXON (ENG)	70	72	74	68	71	73	428
20	Matthew MILLAR (AUS)	71	73	69	71	71	73	428
21	Craig LEE (SCO)	72	68	75	70	69	74	428
22	Patrik SJÖLAND (SWE)	75	72	73	69	72	68	429
23	Marcel SIEM (GER)	71	72	74	70	71	71	429
24	James KAMTE (RSA)	71	70	73	73	70	72	429
25	Gareth PADDISON (NZL)	74	72	70	73	67	73	429
26	Philip GOLDING (ENG)	75	69	69	69	74	73	429
27	Paul WARING (ENG)	74	70	72	70	68	75	429
28	Jan-Are LARSEN (NOR)	72	70	73	70	69	75	429
29	Ulrich VAN DEN BERG (RSA)	70	71	72	71	70	75	429
30	Thomas AIKEN (RSA)	70	68	72	68	71	80	429

Author's Postscript

To their eternal credit, all seven players from my self-appointed Q School Class of 2007 attended the launch event for the original book about their lives, *Golf On The Edge: Triumphs & Tragedies of Q School,* in May 2008 at Hampstead Golf Club in London. Since then, I have stayed in touch with all seven to varying degrees. The strange fact about them as a group is that while all of them returned to Q School at least once after the first book was published, none of them ever gained a Tour Card again, those days of living the European Tour dream were confined to the past. However, each of them moved on and found a new kind of success.

Sion Bebb – The balancing act of a father with a wife and young family who still wants to travel the world in search of golfing greatness was something Sion struggled with for a number of years. Eventually in 2011 after another season on the Challenge Tour, Sion walked away from the life as a tournament professional and in 2013 took a club pro job at Morlais Castle Golf Club in Merthyr Tydfil, South Wales. "It wasn't a difficult decision," he says. "It was getting to a stage when I was trying so hard to stay at home to be with my girls that I wasn't arriving at some tournaments until Wednesday, not even having a practice round." However, his competitive instinct remains. So sure enough, Sion now supplements weekly pro-ams with trips around Europe to play in European Club Pro Championship events. "If I didn't compete, it would do my head in," he says.

James Conteh – James took a break from Q School after 2009 and pursued some other activities including playing poker online. His card skills actually proved to be quite lucrative and even landed him a few appearances on the European Poker Tour circuit. "I made a profit every year that I played poker and it was interesting because there are a lot of similarities with golf," he says. His barman training school business also took up plenty of time as golf took a back seat and he continued to earn money helping out his friend the tiler. Still based out of Moor Park GC in Hertfordshire, he would continue to play only the odd mini tour event for a few seasons and then in 2015 he got the Q School bug one more time. "I hadn't played at all that year, but I got some money together and, on a whim, I went to First Stage at Frilford Heath." It would be nice to report a fairytale ending to the story and that James won through all the way to the European Tour, but unsurprisingly, he showed no form and withdrew after two rounds. He knows that the Q School bug is hard to kill off.

Phil Golding – There was an inevitability that Phil would walk straight onto the Senior Tour and succeed. He tried one more time at European Tour

Q School in 2008 without success (it was his 19th visit) and, after that, he became a senior golfer four years later. He was immediately competitive and it took just 12 months for him to win and he also managed the remarkable feat of scoring three straight rounds of 64, something never achieved on the any of the three main European tours. Phil has since been consistently one of the top 10 players on the European Senior Tour circuit, a situation that has allowed him to play in a number of Senior major championships. In his first four Senior seasons, he won over £500,000 in prize money.

Euan Little – Disappointments at Q School played a large part in forcing Euan off the tournament merry-go-round. In 2009 he became resident pro at Dundrum House in Tipperary, Ireland, where he found a more normal, regular lifestyle, but then a couple of years later fate led him in a quite different direction. During a return to his home in West Scotland, Euan was sitting at the bar of his home golf club in Portpatrick talking to the owner of a local hotel. The ex-pro commented about the poor state of his lunch, namely the basket of chips on offer. "Could you do any better?" came the challenge and so began a change from golf pro to catering pro. Over the next four years, Euan set up a successful catering business based on supplying potatoes and other vegetables; he was lucky to get some of the finest produce in Scotland from his uncle's nearby farm and also gain experience as a starter and dessert chef at a Portpatrick hotel. "Food's always been a hobby and even at Tipperary I would open up the kitchen and I'd make breakfasts for the members, but a full-on catering business was still a bit of a surprise," he says. Eventually, however, supplying lots of different food outlets proved too taxing and he settled for becoming the full-time caterer back at Portpatrick GC where the whole idea began. "I was working 17 hours a day including pulling stuff out of the fields at the farm, but it wasn't sustainable, so better to concentrate on one job and do it properly," says the man who has not touched a golf club since 2013 let alone thought about Q School. "It's been hard work, but life is good and I've even lost about three stones in weight. Still, you know what they say," he adds with a cheeky smile, "never trust a thin chef."

Andy Raitt – Getting married to his long-time girlfriend Lindsay and living permanently in a flat in Chelsea, central London, has helped Andy's life return to normal in recent years. No more touring as a golf pro, he settled down to a mixture of teaching and corporate days (working out of St Georges Hill GC in Surrey) along with just enough competition via the PGA regional events. "I enjoy the teaching and I play in just enough tournaments to keep me happy," he says. Andy has found some success on the PGA circuit including qualifying for the PGA Championship at Wentworth in 2010 and becoming Southern

Open champion in 2015. His injury worries have not ended – nowadays it is treatment on discs in his lower back – but his cheerfulness is undiminished and, of course, there is always the potential lure of the Seniors Tour in a few years time. "I'd quite fancy nine or 10 Seniors events, so never say never."

Martyn Thompson – Returning to life as the head pro at Parkstone Golf Club in Dorset was not a difficult adjustment for Martyn after his flirtation with Q School. He is the type of person who likes to have a lot of irons in the fire, so he has continued to dabble with various business projects while occasionally still entering various mini tour events including those on the EuroPro Tour. However, Martyn's most significant career move in the last decade was his appointment as head coach of the Dorset County Golf Union amateur team. "To work with young talent is a privilege and I hope I can pass on to them some of the skills and knowledge that I've learned over the years," he says. Martyn's mentoring duties even mean caddying for the youngsters occasionally as they try to become tournament pros. "Who knows, one of my lads from Dorset could make it onto the European Tour via Q School with me on his bag. Now that would be a story to tell."

Guy Woodman – His 2008 story and subsequent golfing achievements appear in Part Two.

The author with all seven golfers on the edge at a book launch at Hampstead Golf Club in May 2008. Clockwise from back row, far left: Martyn Thompson, James Conteh, Euan Little, Andy Raitt, Phil Golding, Guy Woodman, the author and Sion Bebb.

Pic: Richard Kendal

At one time, Phil Golding's 19 visits to Q School was an all-time record and in 2007 he managed himself to perfection around San Roque at Final Stage, using all that experience to good effect.

Pic: Richard Kendal

Sometimes worn down by the ill fortune that caused a rare injury, Andy Raitt proved to be not just a likeable subject, but also a very determined golfer who fought hard to retrieve his career and his self-belief.

Pic: The Author

Perhaps the most emotional of all the golfers on the edge, Euan Little probably talked with the most feeling about the effects of a Q School failure and has since used his skills as a chef to create a new life for himself.

Pic: Richard Kendal

Preparation time for Q School is crucial, but James Conteh (left) was forced to fill his winter down-time with money-making odd jobs outside of golf rather than practice for the tournament, while club professional Martyn Thompson (right) filled his life with so much extra work that he only entered at the very last minute.

Pic: Richard Kendal

It took 20 years as a pro before Sion Bebb made it as a full-time European Tour member. He was driven to emulate his father (a Welsh rugby great) and was always balancing ambition with the pressures of feeding his family.

Pic: Richard Kendal

After starring on American TV's *The Big Break*, the constant struggles of Guy Woodman at Q School were fascinating, especially because he was able to articulate his burning desire and his desperate disappointments.

Pic: Richard Kendal

A fresh-faced Chris Wood is flanked by his agent Stuart Cage (left) and father Richard (right). Chris was one of the favourites to progress in 2008, but his path to the Tour was filled with very dramatic twists and turns.

Pic: Richard Wood

Q School truly delivers champions - Chris Wood progressed through the School at his first attempt and here he is interviewed by the author at Hazeltine GC in Minnesota at his first ever tournament in America, the US PGA Championship in 2009.

Pic: The Author

Getting a Tour Card is a team effort. Here Ross McGowan celebrates returning to the Tour in 2015 after a four-year absence and it's all smiles with manager Ally Mellor (left) and Matthew Swales his caddie.

Pic: The Author

Coming from behind to win a Tour Card on the final day is an electrifying moment in anyone's career. Welshman Stuart Manley explains how he did it with a 6 under round in 2015 including a crucial up-and-down from a bunker on the 18th.

Pic: The Author

The 40th anniversary of the tournament produced three joint winners including, rather aptly, a 40-year-old. Veteran South African Ulrich Van Den Berg (left) missed an eight foot putt on the last and had to share the silver-plated salver with two younger men, American Daniel Im (middle) and Spaniard winner Adrian Otaegui.

Pic: The Author

PART TWO

Contrasting Journeys

There were three captivating Q School stories in 2008 about three very different people. The most noticeable tales were of two contrasting players: Guy Woodman from the Class of 2007 still fighting for a place at the golf's top table and Chris Wood, a fresh-faced, newly-minted pro tipped for stardom. Both young men started at Q School this year at First Stage in September. Their journeys would illustrate all the expectation and the fears, the anguish and the exaltation of this weird, yet wonderful, tournament that decides the careers of hundreds of professional golfers every year.

The third story was the author's. My own journey through Q School this year was another insightful one, but it was also very emotional because it's impossible to follow players closely through this kind of event and not become connected to them. Therefore, Part Two of this book is produced from the writer's perspective, the person trying to stay objective when everyone around him is close to tears of either joy or despair. It is not just professional golfers who are drawn inexorably back to this sporting torture chamber every year.

The First Easy Steps

The one huge advantage for a rookie at Q School is a lack of scar tissue from previous painful visits. Known as the white-belt brigade, the young guns or the nerveless twentysomethings, these aspiring superstars are usually taking initial steps in their pro careers when they roll up at the School for the first time. This means the natural aggressiveness of youth is yet undiluted by years of failure, disappointment and missed three footers for par. Their story, therefore, is different than that of the journeymen, but of course, no less dramatic.

Among the 2008 Q School entries are some remarkably talented rookie pros and I want to choose one of them to follow particularly closely for the section of a new book, hopefully through to Final Stage and a Tour Card. One of my potentials is the tall Bristolian Chris Wood, one of the top English amateur players who sparkled in this summer's Open Championship, finishing tied fifth and being awarded the Silver Medal as low amateur. But, as I drive up to the Oxfordshire Golf Course for day one of First Stage, I consider the other players on my list: fellow Englishman Danny Willett, who was No 1 amateur in the world; the next young Scottish hope, Callum Macaulay (playing Q School as an amateur); and Jonathan Caldwell of Northern Ireland who had been Rory McIlroy's Walker Cup partner a year earlier. However, Chris is my first choice, mostly because of his Open exploits.

The Oxfordshire is less than an hours drive from my north London home and the weather is bright and sunny without much wind, so scoring will likely be pretty low today. As I watch a few players go through practice putting drills, I ponder if Chris will provide me with a fascinating story because we had yet to meet and much will depend on his personality and whether we can strike up a working relationship. In my first Q School book, I started with more than 15 possible subjects and that number was whittled down to seven as events unfolded and as I got to know each player. Those prepared to speak from the heart were my first choices and I hoped Chris would match their honesty and authenticity. The writer/player relationship is one of trust and while I can control the in-depth questions, I cannot control the answers. Chris is not quite 21-years-old – can he express himself powerfully? Without knowing him or any of the other players before this project began, I will have to take a considerable gamble with one of them. The classic post-round-interview that fans see on TV will not be nearly enough; platitudes and a machine gun-like account of birdies or bogeys without a hint of emotion might be fine for a quick news story, but it is material for a book. I need emotionally-charged quotes, ones that provide rare insights. The value of the player to me is his eloquence and candor, how much he is prepared to explore his feelings about both the good and bad parts of the tournament, his own game and even his friends and family. Today, day one of First Stage, will give me a strong indication of whether my gamble is going to pay off. I need to gain Chris's trust early on and, if he is the intelligent young man that he appeared to be during media interviews at the Open, then all will be well. A final decision on my featured rookie cannot really wait much longer.

What I do know about Chris is that he was a keen footballer as a young boy with aspirations to play for his local team, Bristol City, but he suffered a serious knee injury and turned to golf instead. By the age 12, he had been playing at Long Ashton GC for three years and was a single-figure handicap golfer. His amateur career spotlighted him as a huge talent: he won the PING/EGU Order of Merit in 2007 and 2008 as well as the West of England, Welsh and Russian amateur titles. Then all this was capped by his performance at the Open at Royal Birkdale. Now the question is: can Chris go all the way through the School and get his Tour Card?

I choose not to talk to any of the players about my book project before they tee off and hope that a moment will arrive naturally later in the day after their rounds. I particularly hope Chris plays well because if he's in a good mood, then talk of the book will be fine; if he plays poorly then I might have to come up with another strategy.

As it turns out, Chris opens his account at Q School with a 65 and is joint leader after 18 holes. No ifs, buts or maybes there. He hunts birdies a determined predator and there is a quiet intensity about him that is impressive. Bearing in mind that Chris had not seen The Oxfordshire until two days ago, I'd say that this round confirms his pedigree; he is telling fellow Q Schoolers that he is coming through, so get out of the way.

One other factor in Chris's favour today is his caddie. His father Richard carried his golf bag at the Open, but Dad is smart enough to have consigned those duties to the past. Being a pro golfer requires a whole different level of skill and commitment from a caddie, so when Chris signed with the International Sports Management (ISM) agency, he is fixed up with a certain Gordon Faulkner as his bagman.

Luckily, I met Gordon last year when he was on Rory McIlroy's bag at the School. He is chirpy and chatty with a stinging sense of humour, plenty of funny stories and a no-holds-barred version of his own truth about the world of golf. After Chris's opening round, I say hello to Gordon while his player is signing for his score.

"How's things," I venture, shaking the caddie by the hand. "Mustn't grumble," he offers while leaning on the bag. "Played well today, he did," is the nub of his comment about Chris. Gordon has pulled out a plum of a bag and is just the right sort of fatherly figure to replace Richard; he has plenty of experience and a no-nonsense attitude to keeping his player's feet on the ground.

Knowing Gordon means that introducing myself to Chris is that much easier. When the young man emerges from the Tournament Office, I introduce myself and shake his hand. I suddenly realise just how tall Chris stands; I am 6ft 2ins, but he somehow seems much more than 3 inches taller.

Chris is immediately courteous and happy to talk. We stay pretty much on the topic of today's round and Q School in general. "I feel like the best player here comfortably really and I know I should qualify. There's obviously a bit of pressure, but I didn't feel it today because I'm more than capable of qualifying even without my 'A' game. A 65 is a massive help to that. To be honest, I think I should be on Tour now, not fighting through this. That takes a lot of pressure off mentally. It's a pretty straightforward course really; it's about placement because there's no run on the ball. Gordie has been here hundreds of times, so I don't feel I have to know the course that well. My game's suited to links golf, but the fairways here are nice and wide. I putted nicely today which I haven't done all year and didn't drop a shot."

There is not a tinge of arrogance about him, simply a matter-of-factness that is engaging. In our conversation, I illustrate my knowledge of Q School and tell him about last year's book as well as how his local paper, the Bristol Evening Post, wants me to write daily stories about him at this tournament. He offers me more telling quotes. "It gives me a lot of confidence, finishing 5th in the Open, but also the few tournaments I've played already on Tour really have helped me a lot. I didn't play well in a couple, but I only missed the cut by a shot. I also had a nice break last week and did a bit of practice, so I'm feeling alright about my game." The interview lasts no more than five or six minutes, but I feel the right connection has been made.

I push him only about one thing and that is his rivalry with other young pros coming through, particularly Danny Willett who won his First Stage Q School tournament in Germany last week. Does he want to emulate Danny and win here in England? His eyes narrow a little and the killer instinct that lives inside him, the huge desire to be a great pro golfer, flashes across his face. "Yes, I'd like to equal his achievement at least," he says and we laugh about the prospect of a Q School bet between the two of them. "No, but maybe on Tour next year," he says.

I decide at the last minute not to tell him yet of my ultimate plan to hopefully follow him on all 14 rounds; I want to get to know him a little first. But at least he is open and honest. He considers my questions carefully and gives very real answers that are short and to the point, yet still detailed. Chris is already a pro at the interview game, it seems, but his words are not those of the tired tournament veteran; there is a freshness about his whole demeanor and a pleasant thoughtfulness about the way he talks about himself and the game.

Chris is aware of what's ahead of him although has not sought much Q School advice. "Be patient" is as much as Stuart Cage of ISM has told him. Chris's view is that "it's just golf isn't it; you just have to get on with it". Of course, he would like to "do a Rory" and win enough on one of his three remaining Main Tour invites to secure a Tour Card and therefore make Q School unnecessary. But he is currently 239th on the money list and will need at least one top three finish in Birmingham, Scotland or Portugal between now and the end of October. Of course, part of me wants him to achieve one of those top threes, but another part of me hopes we can take this 14-round journey together to a Tour Card.

Of my other 'book possibles' at The Oxfordshire, Callum Macaulay starts the more confidently while Jonathan Caldwell is in the pack, but as the next three days play out, Chris is clearly the pick of the bunch. The Englishman is briefly removed from the lead on day two by three players – including Callum – after he shoots an uncomplicated 70, but Chris then returns to the top of the leaderboard on day three with a peerless 66. On day four, he knows that he will go through to Second Stage and his only problem is boredom – he waits on every single shot on the back 9 and his mood is one of barely-contained rage. Losing concentration, he drops a couple of shots and only finishes joint winner when he really could easily have taken the title on his own. Ironically, it is Jonathan with a blistering 65 who soars up the field on day four to tie with Chris while Callum finishes in the top three.

The performances of my three pre-tournament choices mean that I definitely got my forecasting right. I talk briefly to Jonathan and Callum and they would have been fine subjects, but I know now that Chris is the one I will follow. Jonathan appears to be really quite shy and lacks Chris's confident way with words. Callum has quite a bubbly personality, but he does not have the golfing high-profile that Chris achieved at the Open. I can only be in one place for Second Stage (all four tournaments take place concurrently) and the chances of all three being allocated to one venue again in two months time is infinitesimal. So my book project will now definitely rely on one man, Chris Wood.

After round four at The Oxfordshire, it is still not quite time to tell Chris of my plan. I offer quick congratulations to him and Gordon as I can see they are both desperate to start their homeward journeys and avoid the worst of the Friday night traffic. So, I make my interview short and then simply say that I will see him at Second Stage. "Not if I can help it," comes the reply from Chris without a moment's hesitation. "If I play at The Belfry next week (in the European Tour) at the British Masters like I did this week then I won't need to go to Second Stage."

I smile at his absolute confidence and sharp focus. Rory did it last year, so Chris wants to emulate him. The £1,500 cheque he receives as winner this week is of little consequence to him in the long term. The amount does not count on the Order of Merit and is loose change compared to the riches on offer on the Main Tour. So I think I could be in the presence of a remarkable golfer, just as I remember thinking the same last year with young Mr McIlroy.

~

Of the all the seven players who provided rich stories for my first Q School book in 2007, one in particular stood out. Guy Woodman is as engaging a young golfer as you can imagine and he encapsulates almost everything that Q School stands for – he loves it and hates it; part of him knows that the School has been one step too far on his pro career, yet there is an unshakeable hope that he will catch lightning in a bottle and win himself the Tour Card he so desires.

Not only does Guy's relationship with this magnificent obsession make him such an interesting topic, it is also his ability to capture his emotions about the life of a golf professional on the fringes of the elite. His generous nature allows him to answer the most delicate questions at his most raw moments, not just when he succeeds, but also when he fails. To talk at length to Guy is to understand the lifestyle of a journeyman tour pro and the torture of Q School.

Back in 2007, Guy had once again come up short at the School, so something had to change the following season, his career needed a fresh challenge. He had already decided to undertake full PGA training and take up a role as an assistant pro so that, if worst came to worst with regards his ambitions to play on Main Tour, he could become a full-time club professional and teach the game to others. Finally he has decided it is time to start the training in full and split time between his studies and his desire to be on tour.

Of course, this strategy means Guy is undermining a belief system that has driven him for more than a decade; to gain a Tour Card had been the only goal in his life for most of his adulthood. Yet, as a thirtysomething mini tour player, it would have been foolish to ignore the possibility of ultimate disappointment. To place a second bet on his future looks eminently sensible from the sidelines and both his family and friends support his PGA training decision.

Perhaps because of his more relaxed attitude to tournaments, his 2008 season brings an early highlight, he wins both the English and UK Assistant PGA Professionals titles. To his delight, Guy then breezes through First Stage of Q School at Chart Hills in September. He finishes tied 10th, a performance that includes a stunning third round 64, just one shot off the best of the week. Of course, with success comes expectation, but it is ever thus with aspiring pros like Guy.

No Place To Fall

Onto Second Stage of Q School, the acid test. This has always been Guy Woodman's stumbling block in the past; he has never made Final Stage of the tournament. But with confidence high, a top 20 place at a difficult course against a stronger field does not seem out of reach. The added bonus is that

Montenmedio Golf Club in southern Spain is not a bomber's course (Guy has never the longest off the tee) and pre-tournament heavy rain makes it even more of a place for the strategy over power.

I am at Montenmedio to see Guy and I wonder if my attention will be an added burden or a welcome distraction. On arrival, I think: "Let him get on with his dream of a Final Stage place without me hanging around." I have other players to watch, plus Guy has an experienced Main Tour caddie this year, Barry Cornwall, who also happens to be an ex-policeman, so this is a bagman who can handle himself and his player.

But as happens so often in sport, well-laid plans are scrapped. Guy opens his account with a 67 and is joint leader; I am suddenly unable to help myself from becoming a cheerleader. We meet up after the round and I beam a smile at him. The player is happy, yet cautious, so I join the mood and utter some low-key platitudes. "It's early days yet," I say. "Long way to go." Guy and Barry seem relaxed together and with me, so I decide to do an about-turn and follow them on day two.

The field at Montenmedio is only 78 players and the facilities cosy, so it is easy to find them the next morning. Guy is still taking plenty of 'well done' handshakes on the far end of the range due to yesterday's performance, but leading Q School is new territory for him and his main task from now on is to control an Achilles' heel: his paper-thin confidence. Golf fans sometimes forget that the pros are people too, they can be told to be confident, even trained to be that way, but for some it is just not natural. Guy is such a player – if his self-belief matched his talent, then Q School would not be on his season schedule every year.

His day one round means he was obviously striking the ball well and it places him in pole position to make Final Stage for the first time ever, but one bad shot, even one bad hole and the wheels on his bus could start to wobble.

However, I hear Guy's distinctive laugh as he and Barry approach the first tee. All seems well. The laugh is a low, "hur, hur" sound that begins deep in his stomach and lights up his face. He looks completely carefree as he powers his opening drive down the middle of the fairway, while a lovely second shot is just 15ft short of the pin. The birds are singing, the sun is shining and Guy is already putting for birdie. But Q School is never that simple – his first putt passes the hole and settles three and a half feet away. Just when he wants a nerve-settling tap-in, he gives himself a nerve-tingler.

So here we are, the very first hole of day two and I fear the worst. But there is no need. Guy strokes the ball in for a solid par. I raise my eyebrows towards Barry. "That putt would've phased him last year, but he's getting them now. That's the difference," says the caddie. I nod in agreement.

The openness of the course allows me to move ahead and watch both Guy's threeball group and other players at the same time. I decide to view from afar and check in with Barry occasionally to hopefully get a few thumbs-up signs.

The strategy works a treat for everyone: I see Guy swinging smoothly and holing a few putts from a respectable distance on his way to a 68 without overcrowding him. He stands at 9 under and in the lead on his own.

By now I am almost twitching with excitement for him and there is more backslapping as we meet up at the end of the day. However, there is also a realisation that the outcome will now be decided by Guy's mental strength and not just his physical capabilities. This will be an illustration of the difficulties of golf at every level – the ability to play under pressure separates the champions from the also-rans in golf and Guy has 36 holes to prove that he has the mindset of a winner.

On the morning of day three, I catch up with Guy and Barry again on the range. Tee-off times have been re-organised into a looped draw so that the leaders will start at the 1st hole and set off last; the range was clearing out as I say: "No congrats until day four." As I walk up to the duo, Barry agrees and Guy just chuckles before scorching another practice shot straight and true. "We need to keep it going," says Barry, "and we don't want any quiet periods. We had one yesterday, but we don't want any more." I look at Guy and ask what this means. "When Barry goes quiet, you know something's wrong," says the player with a knowing smile. These are two friends battling together for a memorable success, teasing each other during the crucial warm-up. It's another good sign.

However, golf is a wicked companion and as surely as you think the road ahead is clear, an unseen pothole emerges to cause a stumble. Guy's pothole is the third round. A couple of early errant drives and he is fighting to maintain par; he is worried about his driver. It feels like the alignment of the clubhead is slightly out of sync; the face looks closed which is causing him to hook his tee shots. There is nothing he can do about it during the round, but there is a niggling question in his mind. For someone who is relatively thin-skinned when it comes to self-belief, this is a crucial problem. Barry works some caddie magic and suggests the 3-wood on a few occasions, but Guy can only limit the damage. He manages a stuttering 4 over par 76 that moves him down to a tie for 7th and five shots behind the new leader, Paraguay's Fabrizio Zanotti.

The psychological re-building starts immediately Guy signs for his score. "Look, if you'd been offered 5 under and tied 7th at the start of the week, you'd've jumped at it," I say. This is re-affirming the mantra according to Barry. "You're still in a great position," says the caddie.

All these words are delivered towards a player with a face that is drained of colour. Guy has been in a self-deprecating mood all week – telling everyone that he is not hitting the ball that well – and now his words have become a self-fulfilling prophecy. Both player and caddie hang around the practice area, Guy hitting endless chips and Barry deep in thought. The player is desperately trying to clear his mind of what went wrong earlier and the consequences of another similar round tomorrow that will almost certainly put him out of Q School at Second Stage yet again.

Like so many players, Guy struggles to manage the mind games and so I decide to stay clear that evening. He has Barry at his side and he will phone his coach back in England; the last thing he needs is me blathering away. So I return to my hotel and worry there. Tomorrow will be the biggest challenge in Guy's career. Yes, he has won on the EuroPro Tour and the PGA Assistants titles, but those fields were weaker and the pressure less intense. He will need to dig deep on day four, maybe deeper than he has ever dug before.

The draw for the final day hides Guy in a threeball with Spain's Carlos del Moral and Scottish amateur Wallace Booth. He is in the third last group and just four shots inside 20th place; he needs a score of around par to bring about his dream of progress to Final Stage; that would be a splendid performance after yesterday's disappointment.

However, there is drama before Guy even hits a ball. Early morning fog causes another delay and the players are left hanging around for more than an hour waiting for the sun to burn through and allow clear views around the course. The original start time of 9.00 for the first groups becomes 10.30 and Guy will not actually tee off until 12.10.

How do players cope with delays? Well, they practice a bit more and they chat a bit more than usual. Guy's uncertainty about his driver is a hot topic for him; after all, he is training to be a PGA pro and keeping golf equipment in prime condition is part of his learning. He suspects the problem is in the hosel, the part of the club that attaches the shaft to the clubhead; he thinks some glue in the hosel needs replacing because the clubhead and the shaft connection feel loose. He mentions this to a friend, Jason Levermore, as the two of them stand by the putting green. Jason is a fully-trained PGA pro himself and he takes a look; he believes Guy may be right, the clubface might be a tiny bit out of alignment. Sometimes a tiny tweak is all that is needed, so Jason holds the clubhead between his feet, takes the grip in his hands and gently twists the shaft.

What happens next is be enough for any player to faint in horror. There is a small clicking noise and the clubhead snaps away from the shaft. To Guy, it sounds like the loudest clap of thunder. It is less than a couple of hours before he is due to hit that very club on the 1st tee and suddenly it's in two pieces. It is an unfortunate accident, Jason was only trying to help his friend, but Guy is dumbstruck.

The first instinct is to repair the club, but Montenmedio does not contain any kind of golf workshop, the sort that exists in almost every golf club in Britain. No workbench, no vice, no saw, no glue, no nothing for Guy to put his PGA training to the ultimate test.

Finally, Barry takes charge and removes the broken club to the car to eliminate it from Guy's mind and stop him wasting more time thinking of impossible ways to fix it. I try to calm Guy and agree with Barry that extra use of his trusted 3-wood will be enough. "You hit that fine. Just calm down and use the club that you know," says Barry, with me nodding by his side. Guy, however, is desperate to place a driver in his bag.

The clock is ticking down to Guy's tee-off time. Not surprisingly, Jason offers Guy a couple of his spare drivers and other players also step forward with clubs for him to try on the range. There are Pings and Callaways, but no TaylorMade drivers like the broken one now in Barry's car.

Finally, Guy chooses a replacement driver, a Ping G5 belonging to Simon Robinson (who actually shares the same coach as Guy). It is not a perfect solution, but any kind of driver in his bag seems better than none. This decision could make Guy an all-out hero by this evening or consign his dreams to the dustbin for another year.

Guy has hit only a dozen or so shots with the borrowed club, so the confident player of yesterday is now close to a nervous wreck. He was swinging wonderfully at the start of this week, but that is all forgotten as his round begins. Rather sensibly, he errs on the side of caution with his opening drive and choses his 3-wood.

It is a mark of Guy's professional ability that his first shot today lands on the fairway and leads to a birdie. The one player in the field with a last-minute borrowed driver is suddenly surprisingly calm. Another birdie on the par 5 3rd and I get a thumbs-up from Barry. Perhaps the drama of the broken club would be a story to laugh about at the end of the day.

I decide to once again keep tabs on Guy from afar, walking ahead and keeping my distance around the greens. The new driver eventually appears on the 5th hole and sends the ball straight and true; Guy was in control and has three birdies by the 7th. I even hear Guy's distinctive laugh from a distance and see him chatting animatedly with one of his playing partners. Surely, from here he is safe, I think to myself.

There is a little stumble on the back 9 as Guy begins to realise the enormity of his potential achievement, but three dropped shots do no huge damage and he crosses the line with a level par round to finish the tournament tied 10th, three shots inside the mark and off to Final Stage of Q School for the very first time.

Guy and Barry are both wearing the broadest of smiles as they walk from the 18th green to the Tournament Office. I shake both their hands and return the smile. "Just sign for it; no mistakes now," I say as Guy goes to sit at the scorer's table. Meantime, an admiring caddie emphasises Guy's achievement. "He had no worries really. He just doesn't know how good he is," says Barry who has been chief cheerleader all day.

A few minutes pass and Guy has not emerged from the scorer's tent. Surely, nothing is wrong. I poke my nose through the door and find him reading a 12-page, A5-sized photo-copied booklet with the words '2008 Qualifying School Final Stage' on the front. Guy might have been reading the 10 Commandments on the original tablets of stone – he is totally transfixed by the arrangements for hotels in Catalunya, the practice facilities at Final Stage, the details of the tournament that is one step removed from his dream of a regular place on the Main Tour. He looks about as happy as if he'd won the lottery.

The latest Final Stage Q School qualifier walks back into the sunlit outdoors I formally congratulate him by putting an arm around his shoulders and slapping him on the back. "I've wanted to get to Final Stage all my life," is about all he can utter, still overwhelmed. Unable to fully comprehend what has happened, he goes into practical mode and starts talking about next week. "Hang on," I say, "just enjoy this moment. You've done a magnificent job. You led the whole thing until the problem with the driver and then you coped with today so well." Eventually, I run out of words to tell Guy how impressive his performance has been over the last five hours.

Then his golf buddies come over to talk "shop", that means discussing the best way to Catalunya? Has anyone played there before and what are the greens like? Typical of the moment of triumph in professional golf, players' minds soon return to the job in order to take the emotion out of the situation. A golfer's season or his career is always a work in progress. Don't look back when there are so many reasons to look forward.

After half an hour, Guy does finally start to congratulate himself and acknowledge his own achievement. "If you want to see some good karaoke tonight then you'd better come with us," he tells everyone. He is buzzing, but it will be a very tired celebration for both player and caddie.

I do not join the victorious duo that night, but they collect me on their way to the airport the next day after I play my own round of golf at Montenmedio to get a sense of what the players had faced. The white-hot euphoria of Team Woodman from yesterday is now more of a warm glow as we joke our way to Jerez Airport in a hire car. I repeatedly boast how I parred the first two holes of my round earlier that day and Barry re-plays the tape in his mind's eye of Guy's face when the driver head broke off. Guy sits and listens, his deep laughter filling the car on regular occasions, his mind already wandering to the task ahead and a hectic schedule.

The next couple of days for Guy and Barry in particular will be a whirlwind. This is Sunday and arrival back at Stansted is not until very late in the evening; by the time they both walk through their front doors it will be well past midnight. Monday is only good for washing clothes and re-packing in time for the first flight out to Catalunya early on Tuesday morning. The rest of Tuesday will be taken up by a walk-round one of the courses plus a few holes of practice; on Wednesday there will be time for a full, 18-hole practice round; and the tournament will start on Thursday.

In anyone's world, that is a punishing timetable, although in truth, that is often the life of the modern professional tournament golfer. The problem for Guy, however, is that he had never actually planned getting through Second Stage. After his success at Montenmedio, his first thought is to change his travel arrangements and stay in Spain, but the stress of cancelling and re-booking the flights, the car, the hotel and goodness knows what else is an unattractive option; best to return home for a day and book flights to Catalunya for Tuesday. So, he drags his luggage, his golf bag and his tired body all the way back to Berkshire for little more than 36 hours before embarking on the latest, most important tournament of his life: Q School Final Stage. After passing through baggage collection at Stansted, I wish the pair of them good luck and give Guy the best and shortest pep talk-cum-congratulations speech that I could muster before we part.

My own turnaround time is slightly less onerous because I will be back in Spain on Thursday rather than Tuesday like all the players. For two days I work at my desk, write a Q School preview for a newspaper plus I transcribe a few notes from Second Stage, attend a couple of meetings and wonder what Guy and Barry are doing in Catalunya. On Wednesday, I send Guy a text message wishing him more good luck and he gets back to me with his usual "Cheers, Big Man" reply. He seems fine, however, I know him quite well by now and just hope that his mind can cope with the extra pressure coming his way this week.

~

It turns out that neither the British Masters nor the Alfred Dunhill Links Championship are great European Tour experiences for Chris Wood in between First and Second Stages of the School. Each decent round is accompanied by a terrible one and he misses the cut both times. However, in Portugal (the last of his seven regulation Tour invitations), his true form emerges and he improves each day, finishes with a 65 and secures 10th place. Every player in the top 10 of a European Tour event is automatically given a place in the tournament the following week, so Chris gets an eighth tournament and another chance to perform the near-miracle of winning a Tour Card without resorting to Q School.

He flies to the Castello Masters near Valencia in Spain knowing he has to attack the course to achieve a top 3 finish at least. A 68 on day one is still four behind Soren Kjeldsen in the lead and three back from Sergio Garcia in second place. This is a very classy field and, although all four of Chris's rounds are par or better, he can only finish tied 29th. This leaves Chris 162nd

Jet2.com Boarding Pass

Date of travel: 11 Aug 2016	**Name:** Mr Michael Crawford
Flight Number: LS858	**From:** Malaga AGP
Gate Closes: 20:25 **Flight Departs:** 20:55	**To:** EDINBURGH
Seat: 17C (rear steps) **Baggage:** 1 bag (22kgs allowance)	**Your Booking Ref:** 2PPFJD **Passport/Document No:** 522328680

✓

B

Seq No: 145

CHECK OUT OUR LATEST OFFERS!

Sandwich or Toastie £3.95 only onboard

ONE TA... PRIC...

With a FREE packet of Seabrook Crisps

Please fold here

in the Order of Merit with nearly €100,000 in his bank account; it is not enough to avoid Q School Second Stage. So when we meet in Montenmedio south of Jerez a few weeks later, the pressure is now on.

Chris has already faced his first few problems as a pro – the two missed cuts were unexpected – and this week, somewhere in the back of his brain, he realises for the first time that to miss out at Q School will send his career back to square one. No Tour Card and he will be relying on Main Tour invites again in 2009; he might even have to spend a year in Asia or on the Challenge Tour. Such diversions from his chosen path can hardly be countenanced. He is good enough for the Main Tour, so playing anywhere else will be a huge setback. However, plenty of young golfers with potential never make it to the Main Tour, so there are no guarantees for Chris; it is only within his power to be the best he can be. To make a stumbling start is a dark, unspoken fear for him. Q School will test his mettle, for sure.

And, having said all that, Second Stage can actually prove to be the most difficult test of the three Q School steps. First Stage events are not that strong so a player like Chris is rarely troubled and, perversely, Final Stage is a six-round event and long enough so that the cream will rise to the top. Good players see the low, first obstacle and leap it easily; then at Final Stage they rely on their class to cope with the intensity. But Second Stage is that odd middle hurdle and, for a player like Chris, it is fraught with tragic possibility: just four rounds, no safety net and so even the best players feel exposed to an unexpected tumble. Just 20 golfers will proceed from Montenmedio, so it will only take a couple of unfortunate miscues or one day when the swing goes missing to send even the best ones back to the drawing board. These are the unsaid words in Chris's mind as he settles into this tournament.

The good news is that his father, Richard, has traveled with him although only in support; Gordon Faulkner is still Chris's caddie. Richard's presence will calm his son, I have no doubt and it makes me happy to be able to meet Richard and talk about his remarkable son. However, I decide to stay in the background on day one and let everyone relax into their various routines. Chris puts together a respectable 2 under par 70 that is already good enough for tied 9th and, although it is not the blistering start he enjoyed at First Stage, it is certainly within his comfort zone. Four rounds of 70 will see him through with ease, according to my calculations. High winds had caused problems for some players on the opening day and Chris knew that it was important to get off to a solid start; it is even something he has been working on with a psychologist.

"I've had two days of practice here and I'm not nervous, my experiences on the European Tour this year are standing me in good stead. I've struggled in the first rounds of tournaments before and I didn't want to do it here because it's such an important week." For the first time Chris set himself a first round target to help him focus. "It's normal to set targets to make the cut after the second round of a pro tournament and then to set new ones over the weekend. I've just never done it for a first round. It's something I've had to learn."

After interviewing Chris, I introduce myself to Richard. All three of us are staying in the on-site hotel, so we will be tripping over each other at this rate. Richard is an agreeable fellow and in no way the kind of father to tell his son what to do in a situation like this. Having seen Chris turn professional, sign with a top management company and employ an experienced caddie, Richard has returned to being a dad who has a loving interest, but knows that his son needs to grow up by himself. It will be a very interesting week walking the course with Richard, especially because I will hear stories about Chris and his early life directly from his father. I'm soon pretty sure that Richard – who clearly loves and also admires his son very much – is a great option to deliver some early golfing information about this 20-year-old newly-minted pro.

Day two dawns and fog causes a slight delay. I hang around the practice areas watching Chris go through his warm-up; I want to give him my full attention today. The longer Q School goes on, the more the pressure is likely to tell, so today will answer some more questions about his temperament. I say hello and find Chris in a calm state, but Gordon is upset about yesterday's round. "Coulda shot 63 yesterday," is his verdict and both of them are already complaining about the state of the greens. It is the first time Montenmedio has host a European Tour event of any kind, so the demands on the greenkeepers are higher than ever. The heavy recent rain has left the surfaces too soft for top pro's standards and heel marks as well as the normal damage done by golf shoe spikes are causing everyone grief. The course manager is doing his best, but pros in general shout loudly when conditions are not to their absolute liking and too many unhappy players means events do not return to certain courses. Montenmedio does not want to be such a course.

Chris starts round two in a threeball with Fabrizio Zanotti of Paraguay who shot a 4 under 68 on day one and Mark Tullo of Chile who is on level par. Being a late-starting means they face the effects of slow play ahead of them; it could be a difficult day for Chris who hates waiting around.

Although he begins with two pars, there is already a kind of impatience about his manner; he is always keen to walk on ahead of his two playing partners to keep their pace fast. At times, it appears he is almost playing on his own.

Chris is hitting as many 2-irons off the tee as possible to maintain his accuracy and a tap-in birdie on the par 5 3rd hole is the reward. But after hitting his driver on the 4th, his ball finds a scrubby trench and his lay-up is imperfect; he is blocked by some olive trees with no shot to the green. Or at least that's how this amateur sees the situation. Instead, Chris manages a punch shot with a long iron that has such a low trajectory it is almost unbelievable. The ball comes to rest on the fringe at the back of the green and he up-and-downs for another par.

This is impressive and Chris continues with pars on the 5th and 6th before the slow play starts to upset him. "We're behind; we should push on a bit," he says as they walk from the tee. Gordon has already been glaring at his watch while their playing partners take overly long to line up putts. There is a distinct "them and us" atmosphere in the group: two who want to dawdle and one who does not.

Sure enough, the delays cause Chris to lose his concentration; he misses a tiddler of a putt on the 7th to drop him back to level par. The rest of the round becomes one of frustration: if it's not the pace of play then it's the bumpiness of the greens. Chris is struggling for the first time in six Q School rounds. He hits a bad tee shot off the par 5 11th for double bogey and, try as he might, not a single birdie putt drops in the next seven holes. A 74 is perhaps not what he deserved, but it is what he now has to deal with; he is now tied 21st and Q School just got real.

"The miss on the 7th was a bit a lack of concentration," he confirms afterwards. "I was trying my nuts off and nothing happened. I can't remember the last round when I had only one birdie." He is far from disconsolate, but two more rounds like this and it's curtains.

It has not been pleasant to watch Chris struggle, but it has given me a close-up view of how tough it is for a father in this situation. I have been able to speak at length to Richard Wood as we walked the fairways together and swapped family and golf stories. Richard is a structural engineer, Bristol born and bred with the accent to prove it. He is tall (although dwarfed by his son) and slim and has passed on many of his facial features to Chris. On the course, his demeanour can probably be best described as in a state of controlled nervousness. He marches ahead before each drive in case of an errant shot and stays well in the background on the greens to avoid unnecessary eye contact with Chris. It is a hugely difficult position to be in – wanting to help, but knowing you must not – yet I'm pretty sure Chris is glad his dad is around and it is all made right by Richard's intelligent reading of the big picture.

"The Open was a dream that just kept getting better and better," he said at one point as we wait for Chris to march up the fairway towards us. "It was wonderful for me (his caddie), let alone Chris. But afterwards, he needed another person on his bag, he needed to grow up, be his own man. The first few pro events were a bit of a whirlwind for him, but he's learned to relax. The amateur tournaments seemed important at the time and they were, but he's a pro now and this is his job. He's learned that already and I've noticed a difference in him, even at home around the house, particularly after Portugal (the penultimate tournament of the season for Chris where he finished 10th).

The good news is that he's a better player already for having turned pro."

I have met a few fathers-of-golfers during Q School, but there is no sign at all of this one living his dream vicariously via his son. Richard was a caddie as a young boy of 7 or 8 and hated it; he didn't play golf as a young lad and only changed his mind when he met his wife-to-be whose father happened to play. Suddenly he found himself falling for both the woman and the sport. With a new love of the links, Richard progressed to a single figure standard after a few years and still plays off a 4 handicap. He now describes golf as "an obsession that I enjoy".

The love of golf is something that Richard passed on to his son. It started when Chris was a toddler. By age four, Richard's only son had been bought a plastic set of golf clubs and balls from The Early Learning Centre and nothing could stop the youngster from practicing his swing, even inadvertently one day smashing a clubhead into the face of his sister Abi and bloodying her nose with an impressive follow-through. By age eight, the son was caddying for the father at Long Ashton Golf Club where Richard was a member. By the time Chris turned nine, the boy was playing a little on-course golf, but football seemed to be his first love. Then, much to Richard's delight, events took a different turn. "Chris came up to the club one beautiful summer evening and we headed down the 1st hole together. We'd done this many times before, but the course was particularly immaculate that evening, very lush and green. I can still recall the moment vividly. We got to the green and Chris suddenly noticed all the lushness around him and I saw his eyes light up in wonder. It was as if he'd seen heaven and, from that moment on, he was hooked on the game."

By age 12, Chris's handicap was into single figures and he began making a name for himself in local events around Bristol. Then there was the serious knee injury that ended any nascent football career (Bristol City had shown some interest in him, signing him to their academy at one point), so Chris could devote himself to golf. Under the guidance of local golf pro Paul Mitchell, there followed some amateur glory. Richard has plenty of stories about Chris marching through the local amateur ranks and, the older he got, the more obvious it became to Richard that his son might just be something special. It all climaxed in winning the Open Championship Silver Medal, but it passed by in a blur for the whole family, according to Richard.

Now reality has set in: on day two of Second Stage of Q School, Chris is far from his amateur glory days and in Nowheresville as a pro golfer. This is the beginning of Chris's understanding of the business end of golf; the carefree amateur has to be replaced by the grinding professional.

As Team Wood walk away from the course after this dodgy second round, I believe that this trio of minds will work things out. "Chris is very determined," I remember Richard saying to me earlier in the day; he knows the mental strength of the pros is so often their strongest weapon. There are no panic stations here. "I didn't get my share of birdies today," is how Chris signs off our conversation. "I'm due some in the next couple of days." I think he's right.

It's the crucial third round when the cavalry charge for a place at Final Stage will begin. Those in the top 20 at the moment cannot settle for par golf because those just behind them will be pressing for birdies. Every chance needs to be taken and, on this day, a bogey will feel like a double while three-putting will be almost unforgiveable.

Chris – on level par after two rounds – is just a single shot out of the crucial 20th place, but another seven players are on the same score with seven more just a shot behind. The field is bunching around par, so only the strong will survive. I decide to lock onto watching the whole of Chris's crucial round on another sunny day, this time with no early fog delays.

Meanwhile, Gordon is in a chirpy mood today. He wants to talk about the standard of Asian Tour players who are playing increasing more European Tour events. "Some of those Asian Tour players who win the co-sanctioned events – they wouldn't win on the EuroPro Tour over here," he ventures. You rarely receive half-opinions from an experienced Tour caddie and Gordon is no exception. For Faulker, substitute Forthright. Luckily for everyone, no Asian Tour player is in Chris's threeball; instead, it's England's James Hepworth and France's Victor Riu.

On the 1st tee, Gordon hands Chris the driver and off we go in search of better luck and more birdies than yesterday. Richard and I hurry ahead as has become the routine. An opening par is fine, but then Victor chips in for a birdie on the 2nd to snatch away some of the luck that Chris is hoping for. Golf continues to be cruel to the young Englishman as he blasts his approach putt 4ft past on the 2nd green. The return putt is the kind of early tester that the best pros drop into the cup; Chris drains it, but the grinding has begun. This situation is endorsed when a 3ft birdie putt at the 3rd misses, never even touching the hole on its way past. Well, at least Chris does better than playing partner James who is on the 3rd green in two and putting for eagle only to walk off with a bogey six thanks to a very careless missed tap-in.

If Chris registers James's disaster, he does not show it. However, when another birdie chance slides by on the 4th, he lets out a sigh; four pars would be OK on many days, but Chris is searching for momentum and it is eluding him. Richard is silently aggravated while Gordon is trying to keep his charge in a buoyant mood.

The 5th is where Chris showed so much class yesterday, but this time, he booms a straight drive only to then slightly block his approach shot leaving himself another incredibly difficult shot. He has to chip low under some tree branches, but if he dribbles the ball 6ft past the hole, it will catch a bank and shoot another 20ft further away. This chip requires tremendously soft hands and great touch; Chris has both and drops the ball to 4ft before holing for that first birdie. Smiles all around.

The course seems there for the taking as Chris sets up chance after chance over the next four holes, yet he walks away with only a par each time. He is not quite hitting his approaches close enough and a lack of confidence in the greens is confusing him. Or, as he says, "this is doing my head in".

Although his 1 under score for the day at the turn is not a disgrace, it is certainly not a reflection of Chris's skills and talent. He now has little margin for error as he approaches the toughest part of the course. The 10th is probably the hardest hole at Montenmedio: a 446yd par 4 with a very narrow fairway and a horseshoe-shaped water hazard around the back and two sides of the green. Chris's drive is fine, but his 7-iron approach is pulled and heading for water. He doesn't see a splash, but walks to the green fearing the worst. Somehow, the ball has stopped six inches from the water's edge. Surely, this is the luck he has been hoping for; he might not receive it on the greens, but he is happy to have it prevent a probable double bogey that would send him back over par.

Instead of a disaster, Chris turns the 10th into another par and performs the same feat on the tricky 11th before a 3ft birdie putt on the 12th. He is 2 under now and pushing for home. Richard is walking faster, Gordon's bag feels lighter and Chris can smell more birdies.

Sure enough, his instincts are correct on the 13th and he allows himself the smallest of fist pumps to celebrate moving to 3 under. If Chris can secure another of those birdies he feels he is owed then he will roar into the top 10 to take away many of his concerns about reaching Final Stage. If only Q School was so simple.

Chris pars the 14th, but drives too far left on the 15th and is stuck behind a tree. After much deliberation, he chooses to cut his approach with a left-to-right curl on the ball. It comes up well short and his pitch shot does the same thing. He has an 8-footer for par. He misses it to the left and smacks the putter face with the palm of his left hand. This is a maddening game and an even more maddening bogey.

Happily, there are no more dramas and he signs for another 70, just like day one. Chris is 2 under for the tournament and tied 15th. It is progress, but eight players are one shot behind him and Second Stage, as he now knows, is where playoffs come into the Q School mix. No one wants to finish right on the mark and play in one of those crap-shoots, as the Americans would say.

Chris is looking a little strained and Richard is working hard to hide his own nervousness. The son is bewildered by another bunch of opportunities that passed him by. The father tells him that this is about learning to be a pro. It's a tough thing for a 20-year-old to hear when he knows he is playing so much better than he is scoring. "I gave myself enough chances, but I just can't get anything going. It's the story of all three days. The key is patience and having Gordon remind me of all the time helps, but I'm still very frustrated."

There is no fear in his voice and he is quick to see that he has at least progressed up the field, but if he trips up here then he will only get those seven European Tour invitations plus a return trip to the Open next season. What he wants is full membership on the Main Tour with a schedule of around 25 tournaments and all the glamour that comes with them. "It's still massive for me (to make the Tour). It's why I get up in the morning," he says. "I still feel a buzz even here because there's so much on it."

Rather than the greens, Chris believes his pitching is letting him down and is off to practice. "I can birdie the first six holes, the eighth as well. I could make a really good score on the front nine, but I haven't been doing that." I love his attitude and watch caddie and father follow him to the range.

Although his position is still precarious, I note that no one has shot better than 67 (5 under) yet in three full days of play, so birdies are not that easy to come by. I am sure that any score under par will be good enough tomorrow; tension will make low scoring very difficult. I'm convinced Chris will overcome all the problems, but golf is not always predictable and talent does not always get its just reward.

As the final round begins for Chris, there are 11 players on 4 under or better and they would have to crumble to miss out, so (at 2 under) he is realistically fighting for one of the other nine places at Final Stage along with at least two dozen other golfers who are in contention. Someone is bound to burst out from the pack while, just as certainly, at least one luckless player will have a nightmare and miss out. I doubt Chris is fully aware of all this, but it is a sobering thought. There must be no drop in concentration levels and no getting irritated by the slowness of others; Chris simply needs to be the consummate professional, take care of his own business and let others do what they do.

A representative from his ISM agency, Stuart Cage, is on hand and walks the course with Richard and me. This almost constitutes a crowd for Second Stage of Q School and we will also be watching Andreas Högberg of Sweden and another Englishman, Gary Marks, both on 3 under.

We three spectators begin our routine of charging ahead down the 1st fairway and chatting at the same time. Stuart is a welcome addition to our duo as he is not only a sharp-minded Yorkshireman with strong opinions that he doesn't mind sharing, but he is also an extremely capable ex-Tour player. Stuart has a been-there-done-that attitude that stems from 15 years as a tournament pro that included one win on the Main Tour and no less than nine visits to Q School. He is enjoying being an agent at the School rather than a player because it was a tournament that defeated him. His stint on the Main Tour was a result of an 8th place on the Challenge Tour order of merit rather than from the School system. "It's not a nice place for most players, the School. I missed (getting a Tour Card) by one shot three times," Stuart tells me. Yes, he's been there and got this T-shirt for sure.

Stuart's presence here proves the potential of Chris. ISM has a track record of taking young players to the top; Rory McIlroy is proof of that. Stuart admires Chris's game and says that a Tour Card is well within his grasp, but nothing is guaranteed. We carry on with our conversation as Chris's opening drive twitches slightly left and as his approach rolls just 10ft from the pin. The game at this level is all about putting; an early birdie would settle Chris's nerves for sure.

He and Gordon again go to great lengths to see the line of the putt and the ball is tapped confidently forward, but it has too much pace, missing the hole to the left and leaving Chris with a nasty three-footer. He takes his time and taps it again with assuredness, yet it horseshoes out. We all stand frozen for a couple of seconds. Surely not. Chris might not have been holing his birdie chances over the last three days, but he has holed out very well all week. Yet today is different, his pro career is on the line.

"My God, he's going to miss out," is my immediate thought. Of course, that's just how most amateur hackers think after every mistake; we lack the resilience of the pros. I tell myself off for thinking such a thing. Chris simply pulls a bit of a face, taps in for a bogey and walks away. Gordon moves even quicker. The pair of them want to put this mistake behind them as soon as possible and get on with the job. One hole and one bogey, but 17 more to make up for it; I know that's what Stuart is thinking and Chris as well. Richard is probably somewhere in between, but the father is also off like a rocket down the next fairway. It will obviously be an emotional day.

The 2nd is a standard par for Chris, but the par 5 3rd has been a birdie chance all week. Chris hits two good shots to leave him an 18ft putt from an eagle; eventually, he settles for a birdie and the first hole damage is repaired. Then a wedge on the 4th is all over the pin and Chris gets a second consecutive birdie. This is a pro taking control of his round after a bit of early bad luck. I am full of respect for him.

However, fate respects no one and a bold 3-wood from the fairway on the par 5 5th sees the ball finish in a difficult spot in the front of a bunker short of the green. Chris needs a good wedge. "Get your thoughts back for this shot," warns Gordon. "Don't think about what's just happened."

Chris makes a decent fist of a tough shot, but is 45ft from the flag in three with a difficult two-putt to come. He doesn't make it and drops his second shot of the day to return to level par for this round. He consolidates with a par on the 6th and then his playing partner Andreas hits his tee shot on the par 3 7th into a bush, causing a long delay. Referees converge on the group to try and hurry it along, because more fog pushed the start times back again today and they are worried about everyone finishing on time. Chris is unaffected and manages a par, but then misses a four-footer for birdie on the next. Richard and I are definitely on edge. "At least he's playing aggressive" is Richard's comment, "but he needs a bit of luck." I am in total agreement.

The 9th hole has a tree slap bang in the middle of the fairway, but Chris takes his trusty 2-iron and fires a very decent drive well wide of it. Again, he can attack the flag. However, the pin is tantalisingly near the back of the green and Chris's 8-iron is about 5 yards too long; rather than screwing back near the hole, it rests in the fringe grass.

Every hole now seems like a test of Chris's ability to become a Tour pro. This test is failed; he fluffs the chip and misses a 12ft putt for par. Three bogeys and yet he has not played badly in any way; he is 1 over par for the round and suddenly looking over the precipice. There are no scoreboards to tell Chris how his rivals are performing, but instinctively he knows that an over par score will result in him leaving Q School. "There's always a story with Chris," says Richard who is holding onto his poise with remarkable strength. If this was my son, I'd be in bits.

All my thoughts about how this could be the making of Chris are kept to myself; if he can just remain calm, then he should make the required couple of birdies in the next nine holes. However, it is at this precise moment that the golfing gods look down on the situation and generate a situation to test Chris to the limit.

The walk from the 9th green to the 10th tee is a short one, but Richard, Stuart and I still manage to place ourselves down the fairway in time to see another of Chris's 2-iron drives fly straight-and-true. The ball lands in the middle of the tight fairway; this is a great start to "the hardest hole by a mile", according to Chris. He and Gordon march confidently to their ball and begin the normal process of checking the yardage and the wind direction; at just under 200 yards from the flag, it looks like a 6-iron shot. But something is wrong. Richard, Stuart and I are all at the greenside watching Gordon ferreting around in his bag. Richard is the one who guesses what's going on; he thinks the 6-iron is not there. As the man who caddied for Chris at so many amateur events, Richard has a sixth sense and he is right. Somehow, amid all the tension that Q School delivers, Gordon has left the 6-iron back on the 7th tee.

There some occasions (not many, I grant you) when a pro would see the funny side of such a mistake; after all, no one is perfect. In fact, Richard even remembered mislaying his son's sand wedge once during the South of England Amateur Championship at Walton Heath. Luckily, on that occasion, Chris's mum Sara retrieved the club and the incident became part of the Wood family folklore, something still talked about with mild amusement (and embarrassment for Richard) because no damage was done. This, however, is not a mid-level amateur event, but the launching of Chris's professional career. Had it been an early round, then it would not look so significant, but as Chris stands on the 10th fairway, his round is in the balance and his club of choice is not available. He cannot afford another mistake and a tough shot onto a water-guarded green just got tougher. If Chris loses his cool or drops a shot now then any chance of catch-up birdies will be slim and a Tour Card will disappear as well.

So it is to Chris's immense credit that he takes an extra breath, remains calm and chooses to hit a soft 5-iron rather than a full 6. He finds the green and eventually holes a tricky 3ft putt for par. As his threeball makes its way to the 11th tee, Chris walks alone pouring over his yardage book in deep concentration; he needs to focus on each forthcoming hole and completely forget about the missing club. This is a good sign and Gordon is experienced enough to give him the required space. The caddie has sent word via an official in a nearby buggy that a club has gone missing and the 6-iron is duly handed back to Gordon on the 11th fairway.

For golfers of every standard, the game is a series of small tests to either pass or fail. Sometimes, you miss an early 4-footer and seem to face the same putt again and again. Other times the test can be something more subtle, the temporary loss of a club (I've done it on several occasions myself). The point is that here at Second Stage of Q School, the tests are large ones. Chris could easily have berated Gordon, lost his temper and stomped around for 10 minutes at a crucial point in his round. The fact that he coped so decisively says a great deal about him.

Back on the 11th hole, not only does Chris get a club back, but he also gets a shot back: a short drive, excellent second to the back of the green, a chip to 5ft and a solid putt. At level par again with another par 5 coming up next, Chris shows his class at the 12th by holing from 5ft for another birdie. This is an uplifting moment. Everyone is smiling: Richard and I for sure, even Stuart who is much harder to please (as the seasoned pro/agent should be). No more crises, please Chris, is in all our heads and on the 13th he holes a 3ft squeaker for par to settle our pulses.

His round is more than two thirds completed and at 1 under, I am sure he is inside the top 20. Unfortunately, there is no way of knowing. There are no temporary scoreboards around the course, so we can only hope. It is the worst feeling to think that Chris is doing well when we all might later find out it was not enough. There is only solace in the knowledge that no one else knows either.

The 14th hole – a 469yd par 4 – is an innocuous one at first sight. Its distinctiveness is down to an equestrian area that lies at the corner of a dogleg to the right of the fairway, about 30ft or more from the mown grass. I have walked through the blue and yellow fences on each day, but never taken much notice of them. However, when Chris's drive lands right in the middle of this area, close to one of the structures, Richard, Stuart and I wonder whether or not this is out of bounds because there are white lines everywhere. When Chris and Gordon arrive and also confess a lack of knowledge, our smiles of two holes ago are replaced by wide-eyed expressions of horror.

After several awkward minutes, referee and tournament director Miguel Vidaor is on hand. There is no question: the equestrian obstacles are immovable obstructions that have been marked as such and players can get normal relief plus one club length.

The panic is over. I realise that my jaw is locked tight and I finally relax while Richard lets out a sigh. Even Stuart, who played pro tournaments for 15 years and knows more about the rules than both of us put together, was fearing the worst. "My heart went past here," says the ex-pro indicating his mouth, "and up to here." Stuart is pointing to a place well above his head. We laugh to release the tension.

In the end, the 14th is just another par on the scorecard; the same goes for the 15th and 16th. Two more holes and Chris is still 1 under for today. He is surely good enough to make it from here, I think; he just needs two more pars and Final Stage of Q School will be his next destination.

On the 17th, Chris hits another solid drive and has a slight downhill lie for his second; it looks like a tough shot, yet he stiffs his approach to 6ft and then holes the putt for another birdie, his third of the back 9. That's it, only the little par 3 18th to navigate and anywhere on the green will do. Chris fires his long iron into a patch of rough just next to a bunker; he hits a magnificent chip to 2ft and taps in for a par and a score of 70. He blows out his cheeks and shakes hands with Gordon. "Chris looks relieved," says Richard. He's not the only one. I think we're all off to Final Stage.

The day has been a long one and filled with classic Q School drama, yet its ultimate significance is still to be decided. If Chris goes on to be a Tour champion like so many people are predicting, this 18 holes at Second Stage will be a fairly forgettable moment in his career. However, if somehow today's round was not enough and he has to return to Q School, then the memory is worth keeping.

We three amigos who trailed around watching Chris are hoping for the best. "I knew he'd do it, but I've never been so nervous," says Richard as we walk to the scorer's tent. Stuart is one happy agent as well. He has been texting Chubby Chandler, his boss, throughout the afternoon with the scores and was making plane reservations to Final Stage almost before Chris tapped in his last putt. He's certain Chris has done enough. "He's learned a lot about himself since the 9th," Stuart says. These are the words of truth from a pro who knows. I write them down in my notebook with alacrity,

Sure enough, Chris comes from the Tournament Office with confirmation that his 4 under finish is good enough for 11th place. I give

Chris a firm handshake of congratulations. I was right in my forecast that anything under par for him today was good enough, but it was incredibly tight in the end. Twenty players finished on 2 under or better to make Final Stage and 2 under was where Chris started the day.

I realise that he was 1 over for the day after 9 holes and out of the top 20 at that moment. Knowing what I know now, it makes his three birdies on the back 9 look even more impressive.

And then, of course, there was the lost club. Afterwards, Gordon says: "I've been a caddie for 20 years and 99% of players would've gone ape-shit and it would've messed up the rest of the round for them." Although, Chris makes nothing of it when I interview him later, his father recognises that this was a significant moment on many levels for his son. "That was one of the proudest moments of Q School for me. I will always remember it," Richard said later.

The atmosphere around the Tournament Office when all cards are signed is mixed – there is excitement among the successful and beer-induced commiserations for those who stumbled. The bar is doing good business, so I take Chris away from this area to speak privately. He is definitely breathing more easily. "It's a massive relief to get through especially as I wasn't on my best game. Now I can see my coach on Sunday and hopefully come back a bit better next week."

It seems like a long time since his opening hole bogey and I remind him of that moment. I say to him that, as an amateur, I'd've been thinking: "Oh, ****!" Even though Chris looked calm then, he now confesses that he wasn't. "Yeh, I thought the same really. I'd already missed two other really short putts this week and I'm blaming the greens. I've holed absolutely nothing of any length all week plus I struggled with the pace today. My confidence wasn't there with my putting and I'm looking forward to getting on decent greens. What have I learned? That Q School is not the place to be. It's been horrible this week; it's nice when you get through, but it's been a grind. People have said to me about the prize money here, but once you get on Tour £1,500 is not an issue, so it's not about that, it's just a case of getting through. The key is thinking about birdies, not bogeys, but I also stayed patient. It was a good sign that I shot three birdies on the back 9 when I was under the cosh," he says.

Second Stage has been another hugely spectacular event for my book project because Chris has proved to be such a great subject. He is eight rounds into the tournament's total of 14 and only one of these has been played over par. He has played pretty well, but still managed to feel the torture of Q School. For a 20-year-old, he's remarkably poised.

Final Stage is four days away, so we all have little time to draw breath. We say our goodbyes and I think maybe the Open Silver Medallist is over the worst of Q School. Will a Tour Card in nine days time mean more than that wonderful 5th place at Royal Birkdale just four months ago? I suspect it will, but even Chris doesn't know the answer to that question just yet.

A Final Triumph Or Tragedy

My arrival at PGA Catalunya for Final Stage is timed so that I can see a few players start the tournament on opening day and catch everyone after their rounds are complete. The draw does Guy Woodman no favours; instead of a late start on day one to give him at least a few more hours of rest after his hectic return to England, he is teeing off in the very first threeball of the day on the tough Green Course (later re-titled the Stadium Course) at 9.00am along with Swede Johan Wahlqvist and Dennis Kupper of Germany.

There is a slight fog delay on that first morning, but conditions are favourable for golf in November. A little after lunchtime I see Guy and Barry pacing towards to the Tournament Office after their opening 18 holes. Their mood looks dark, a sharp contrast to the last time I had seen them. Guy is one of the easiest golfers to read in terms of his facial expression and body language; he is clearly distraught.

It turns out that nerves did indeed grabb hold of him from the very first shot, his opening drive on the 10th tee. "The 10th to 12th are the three easiest holes on the course," he says, "but I virtually shanked my tee shots and then I three-putted on the greens including missing a real short one." The thin skin of confidence he wore at Montenmedio had been ripped off his back.

"My technique just doesn't hold up. My brain just doesn't hold up. I holed nothing inside 20ft. I even bogeyed the last. I played like shit," he says, unburdening himself of all the negative feeling. This is both incredibly sad, but also incredibly revealing: these are the raw feelings of a golfer in poor form, not the saccharine-coated TV interview that most golf fans see. Two double bogeys at the opening two holes are about as bad a start as anyone suffered today and Guy's final score on day one is 5 over par, a 77 that leaves him well behind the leaders. The remarkable thing about his round, however, is that, after dropping four early shots, he recovered really well and was only 1 over for the next 16. I tell him this, but the bruised golfer is still licking his wounds. Barry clearly had his hands full today and worked hard to keep Guy's chin up after those early holes. He admires his player's guts: "He did ever so well to keep it to 77. If he'd holed a couple of putts, it would've helped him a lot."

After sitting for a moment, Guy begins to recover his composure and thinks of how to recover his tournament. "I suppose you have to be here in order to learn how to play at this level," he says with a resigned tone. He wants to telephone his coach back in England.

Now is the time for me to speak. "Take a deep breath. There's still a lot of golf left and tomorrow is the Red Course (later renamed the Tour Course), it's a bit easier." Guy absorbs the words and marches off to make his call.

There are only four players who shot scores worse than Guy's 77 that day, so he really is at the back end of the field. I wonder if he can find the confidence of last week; how come it disappeared so quickly? So few golfers have the answer to this conundrum: why does knowing the reason for your troubles not always mean you can administer the cure?

Despite an evening and a night of deep thought and reflection, Guy's second round does not turn out to be the one that he dreamed of. Although his ball striking problems are ironed out, it is a frustrating time on the greens on day two; his putts inside 20ft again do not drop. A 71 is level par, but there are over two dozen rounds in the 60s on the Red Course today and so Guy's progress is minimal, he moved up to tied 134th in the overall field, still way off the pace. However, he manages a smile when I see him after his round. Thirty six holes left to make the four-round cut; only then will he truly be fighting for that Tour Card. He is five shots off the mark and hope remains.

At the back of his mind all the time is the question about whether he is good enough. Again, it is a question shared by many golfers at every level. This is a moment on my own Q School journey when I realise that what I feel as a struggling hacker is very similar to what is going on with the pros. The difference, of course, is that the stakes are higher for them than for me. I remember getting my handicap down to 9.1 in the autumn of 2006, the first time I'd reached single figures. This was the finest achievement in my golfing career and yet almost immediately I felt unworthy of the low number, frozen by a lack of self-belief when I played with other single figure handicappers. Guy's torment is not that much different, but sharing my story with him isn't going to help, so I keep my thoughts to myself.

On day three, the threeballs are re-arranged and Guy finds himself back on the tougher Green Course with two new partners. He again starts his round on the 10th, however, there is no repeat performance of the shanks from two days ago. Instead, Guy Woodman finally comes to the Q School Final Stage party with a 3 under 69 despite a difficult wind. Only a handful of players score better on that course today and afterwards he explains his best round of the week so far: "It's strange because I struggled on the range to start with, but found something at the very end before I teed off. My driver was still awful, but my 3-wood was good and I hit some fantastic iron shots – which is hard for me to say, but I did. I want to see those shots more often, but it's good to see I can produce them under pressure. I didn't hole much on the greens that was long, but I was good with anything from 6ft. I'm really chuffed."

I feel an enormous sense of pride as I consider myself to be a small part of Team Woodman. I try to emphasise the best bits of his day when I interview him, forcing him to say for a second time the phrase "I hit some fantastic iron shots". I know it is a bit of faux psychology on my part, but the first time Guy said those words of self-praise, it was followed by "which is hard for me to say". I do not let him repeat and self-deprecating caveat. Maybe that will help him tomorrow.

"I stayed relaxed, walking at the same pace, keeping my breathing in control – that's the key. There was a few times I felt myself getting nervous, but then I just looked at the amazing scenery around here and it relaxed me. Tobias Dier (one of Guy's playing partners) birdied the first three holes and made it look ridiculously easy, but he struggled from then on and I felt like I was the better player. But I suppose everyone has his day. In the past, I might have gone into my shell, but I hit enough shots to know I can compete. When I start thinking about other players, I say to myself 'Let them get on with it' because I can only control my golf ball."

I nod at all these positive words and tell him how he is now in the tournament for real and as good as anyone here; his performance today underscores that. Barry is grinning, while I am telling all the other journalists around me how well Guy has done. My sense of delight is through the roof; I fell like a father handing out cigars after the birth of his first son.

"Tomorrow playing the Red Course, there are more opportunities out there. Why shouldn't I shoot another low score," says Guy as he departs for some well-earned food. He has now moved up to tied 96th and is just three shots off the cut mark. At this stage, he has every right to think "if only he hadn't double bogeyed those two opening holes on day one". But he does not and I am smart enough not to tell him that this phrase is in my own head. You see, Q School is like a worm of doubt in your head and it never seems to go away.

Another bright, sunny day dawns on day four and Guy is in the very last threeball on the Red Course, starting from the 10th. Once again I am torn between following him around for the whole 18 holes (which I feared might put him under more pressure) or simply keeping tabs on his round as I try to spread myself around to watch many different groups. I opt for the latter strategy.

As it turns out, I don't find Guy and Barry until they come to the green on the par 4 18th (his 9th). I watch Guy hit the green with his approach shot and then miss a good chance for a birdie. As they walks towards the next tee, I give Guy a fist pump for encouragement and then look to Barry. There is a grimace. "He's nervous. It's not happening right now," he says. Guy is at 1 over for tournament and that will certainly not be good enough to make the cut. He probably needs to finish on 4 under, 3 under at the very least. I catch sight of him again one more time during his back 9, but the storyline has not changed: Guy is heading out of Q School.

Finally, he arrives, shoulders slumped, at the Tournament Office with his scorecard. "Not my day," he says before going inside to sign for a 1 over par 72. It leaves him tied 99th for the tournament at 3 over par. The cut for entry to rounds five and six is 1 under. Guy has missed by four shots, the exact same number he dropped on the opening two holes on day one. So, for 70 holes, Guy was good enough, but for two holes he was not. Pro golfers' lives are determined by such margins.

Guy knew his fate halfway through the back 9 and, by the time I see him, some of the disappointment has already worked through his system. "I panicked, I think," he says. "Part of me thinks I still can't believe that I'm good enough. Plus I've not played as well as last week. It's the mind games I need to be better at."

The remarkable thing is that Guy still has to be told how much he had achieved even if he has fallen short on this one day. Despite a feeling of failure, his appearance at Final Stage means he is automatically a full member of the Challenge Tour, a position in pro tournament golf that he has never achieved before.

He is handed all the Challenge Tour information after signing for his score and I introduce him to one of the tour administrators who I know. She assures him he can plan for a dozen or so of these high-class events on his schedule next season. This is a big step forward, a chance to taste life on the Challenge Tour that is only one level away from Main Tour.

Within an hour of his round finishing, the penny starts to drop that the 2008 Q School had been a wonderful one for Guy: he made it to the Final Stage for the first time; has himself a Challenge Tour season to look forward to; and has finished ahead of far more experienced golfers and former Tour champions like Jean-Francois Remesy, Patrik Sjoland, David Carter, Edoardo Molinari, Andrew Oldcorn, Emanuele Canonica and Sven Struver. There is even a cheque for £700 to cover some of his expenses. In addition, at Second Stage, he shot a remarkable 64 and was leading on his own after two rounds before having to cope with the breaking of his driver. Plus at First Stage, he cruised through without a worry. The big picture is rather rosy.

At this point, Phil Golding comes over to see Guy. If anyone has a full understanding of Q School, it is Phil. His re-assurances that Guy has done very well are authentic and one particular sentence rings true. "I didn't get my first Tour Card until I was 31," says Phil who famously then took another 10 years to win his one and only European Tour title, the French Open in 2003.

Guy is 31 this year. A majority of pro golfers reach their full potential in their 30s, so his journey as a tournament professional is far from over and the peak perhaps still somewhere on the horizon.

As an example of a golfer on the edge of European Tour riches, Guy's is a classic case, an almost obsessive, love-hate relationship for the struggle that is the Q School. And, the truth is, he is not alone. Only 3% of Q Schoolers who enter the tournament are awarded a Tour Card every year, so the stories of Guy and the other 97% are the most common among the community of aspiring tournament pros. In one way, it is inspiring, but in another it is painfully sad – so many dream that will remain unfulfilled.

~

For his third Q School tournament of 2008, Chris Wood again is forced to play on a course that he has never seen before. It is a reasonably normal occurrence for new pros; it is a test of their talent, requiring them to perform at a high level even without real familiarity. The smart pros – and even more especially those at the very top echelon – avoid their least favourite courses wherever possible. Given a chance, they turn up at courses that suit their game; being the best gives you choice, so why not maximise it. Tiger Woods is particularly adept at this strategy: courses like Torrey Pines in California, Bay Hill in Florida, Firestone Country Club in Ohio – these are among the first places he wants to play each season because he has won there on several occasions. Meanwhile, Padraig Harrington, for example, has deliberately kept the PGA Championship at Wentworth off his schedule in the past because he hates the greens there. However, if you are a lower level pro then you have little choice – you turn up to play and make the best of every situation.

It is more the quality of the course in general and, particularly, the greens that concerns Chris. The putting surface is certainly on his mind at Catalunya especially after the problems he had at Montenmedio. The Girona course, however, has not been hit by the same devastating amount of rain as the links to the south, so Chris is happier when he finds that Catalunya, the pride of the PGA in Europe, is in tip-top shape.

The first day is not a time for heroics and Chris's opening round tactics are simply to settle himself into the tournament. I stay clear of him to ensure he is undistracted; I leave the support team of father and agent to take care of him. I see Richard and make a point of asking him about their quick trip home to Nailsea after Second Stage. He thought it was a good idea for them to make the journey even if they slept in their own beds for only one night and I agree with him.

It turns out that I miss nothing; Chris shoots a level par 72 on the harder Green Course. He reports that it consisted of three birdies matched by three bogeys. "I think six steady rounds won't be far away and it's to my advantage that the tournament is a long one. I seem to start slowly for some reason and usually get into an event more after the first round," he says. "I'm treating it like a normal golf tournament, but because I was hitting it so badly in practice this week, I'm feeling good about today's round being quite consistent, 36 out and 36 back."

But Chris is still not 100% happy with his swing. "I'm not that far away with my game, but I'm trying to sort out a couple of things with my grip. I played the toughest of the two courses today, so level par makes me pretty happy. I'm starting to putt a little better, but still didn't hole much today. We were last out and had the worst of the greens, so it should be easier tomorrow."

Chris is listed as tied 91st in the 156-man field, but this is meaningless given that he plays the easier course tomorrow; only then will he have a true idea of his position. He is among the favourites to gain a Tour Card and I wonder if he knows that the first visit to the School has been too much for even some of the great names in modern-day golf – Cabrera, Campbell, Jimenez, Poulter – who all needed more than one attempt before their careers went into orbit. It is a sobering thought.

I watch on the range as Chris puts himself through quite a few post-round hours of practice before having a quiet supper. I'm not sure practice is what he needs; by the end of the week, it will be energy.

Day two and I follow Chris's group for a full nine holes. It is arguably the most exciting threeball on display this week for the future of European golf: Chris, plus his great rival from amateur days Danny Willett and the 2006 British Amateur champion Julien Guerrier of France. Yesterday Danny shot a 70 while Julien matched Chris's 72, so the form guide says they should all be on Tour together next year.

They are playing the Red Course and start at the 10th hole. There is good news early on for Chris as he birdies the opening par 5 hole. Danny does the same and this threeball is living up to its reputation.

I take particular notice of Richard today. He is suffering like so many fathers at Q School, but those that have travelled this path with their sons should take a leaf out of Richard's book. He is smart enough to show his support for Chris when it is appropriate but he is not an overbearing presence. It is a difficult balance: to worry and yet remain emotionally in control. I hope that having someone to chat with on the course helps him express some of his less appropriate thoughts away from Chris's direct vicinity. I'm trying to keep both of them a little more sane in this crazy week.

The next two hours prove that there are some fabulous young golfers coming through England and France. We are following a threeball displaying outstanding skills in all areas of the game. Chris looks unfazed by everything and comes off his last green with a 5 under score of 66, his best performance since his opening 18 holes at First Stage. He surges through the field up to tied 17th position and the difference – in his mind as well as in reality – is the quality of the greens which have helped him rediscover some of the confidence in his putter. He did not suddenly become a bad putter last week, and simply needed this change of scenery.

"Compared to last week, I feel like these greens are as good as Augusta. I can see when the sun goes down later, it might be a bit worse, but they're a lot, lot better than last week," he says. Chris also has a very clear plan of attack for at least the first four days. "I was discussing it with Gordon and we said we needed to score on the Red and take whatever we can get on the Green. All my five birdies were tap-ins and it shows that my long game is fine. So there is still a lot of improvement to be made with my putting, but I'm in a good position even though I haven't played my best golf yet. I'm only three off the lead, but I'm going back on the range first and then do some more work on my putting." I file copy to the *Bristol Evening Post* because the number of Wood-watchers is growing all the time.

On day three, Chris gets another chance to push further under par as the field is split based on performance. The leaders (including Chris) are on the Red Course and today he partners Richard McEvoy of England and Jesus Maria Arruti of Spain, the man with a record 20 appearances at Q School.

Chris again hits lots of fairways and greens; it seems the hours of practice on the range here are paying off and not diminishing his energy levels too much. The ball, however, does not drop quite as obligingly today and after getting to 3 under at the turn for his round, he fails to push on. He has to eventually settle for a 2 under par score of 69, probably about average for the Red Course today. It is enough to slightly improve his position – he moves up to tied 15th – but the perfectionist in Chris is hugely frustrated.

"I've given myself 18 birdie chances today, but still I missed so many including two 3-footers in the last four holes. If I'd holed those, I'd be cruising. My long game is better than anyone's here, so I could be making life so much easier for myself. It's horrible, I can't take much more of this," he says.

I get the feeling that the tension of Q School plus the lack of birdies are inter-related and Chris is in the same boat as most players here. I mention the tension, but he straight-bats any possibility of it affecting him. "It's still a long way until Tuesday (the last day), but I feel pretty much in control. No one's hitting the ball better than me and I feel like I could be running away with the tournament if I'd holed my fair share of putts."

With one day to go before the four round cut, Chris is seven shots clear of that little problem and two shots inside 30th place which would mean a Tour Card. He is looking upwards towards the leaders rather than downwards. It is partly his nature, but also something of a necessary strategy at the School: on day four, every player in Chris's position should be more concerned about moving up to challenge the leaders than scrapping for the minor places.

Chris goes ahead and consolidates his position on the opening seven holes of day four's round on the Green Course and is two under par. Then he makes a wrong choice at the par 3 8th – a soft 6-iron instead of a full 7 – and pays the price. He hits long and left with the ball finishing on a cart path and he decides to play it from there; it means his first double bogey of the week. A plugged lie in a fairway bunker on the 10th leads to another bogey and he is temporarily outside the top 25. It takes a little brilliance – a chip-in on the 14th and then a birdie on the par 5 15th – to restore his equilibrium. Chris finishes with a 1 under par 71, good enough to edge up the field yet again into tied 13th. Despite this result, it has been another seriously stressful day.

"I let the double bogey effect me until the 14th, I suppose. After seven holes I felt like it was a day I could shoot 66, but I didn't press on. That's been the story all four days. I'm confident now and know there's a score out there for me. I want to push my way up to the top five and I'm due a few breaks in the next two days," he says. Perhaps the worst is over for Chris who is three shots inside the top 30 mark with two rounds to go and talking the talk, for sure. Richard is all smiles and Stuart can see his investment paying off. Everyone's sun is shining.

After all that's happened, Chris wants day five to be when he virtually secures his Card. While others are consolidating or trying to force their way back into the crucial top 30, he aims for another round under par; he is set on that top 5 finish.

However despite his positive attitude, the first few holes do not give up the kind of score Chris is expecting. He is 1 over par after the 6th, birdies the next hole and then drains a 20-footer for par on the 8th. That seems to settle him down. Three more birdies and he records a very creditable 3 under par 69. This is the mark of a future European Tour star. Only three players score better than 69 today while most are happy with par, so Chris has one hand on a Tour Card. My conversations with him, his dad and his agent are now drifting towards life beyond a Q School success. Chris sums up the situation well. "I've put a lot of pressure on myself and it's been very mentally draining, but I feel like I've played well all week. This time tomorrow it will be nice when Q School's done with." The Main Tour is beckoning and, although there is still 10% worth of caution in the air with the final day still ahead, everyone in Team Wood will sleep soundly tonight.

I make a strategic decision for the last day not to stick too closely to Chris, but follow some others much more involved in the struggle for their Cards. I will keep an eye on him, but he is tied 6th this morning and it would take a collapse of monumental proportions for him to fall now; that is not in the least bit likely. As long as his first six holes are without drama, I will just pick him towards the end of his round. Richard agrees with my plan. Having covered Final Stage now for three years, I think I have a handle on where to be and when.

A couple of hours later and I have reached the turn with my three selected groups and can check Chris's progress on the giant scoreboard near the clubhouse. It tells me that he is on track; after three holes, he already has a couple of birdies. He has been saying all week that he likes these opening few holes on the Green Course and he is finally making good. In fact, he manages four birdies in the first seven holes and goes on to shoot the second best score of the day – a 68 – to end his Q School journey on 15 under and reach 5th place overall.

It is a stunning performance to have come through all 14 rounds. Like many before him, Chris arrived at Q School amid forecasts of one day becoming a champion on Main Tour, but very few fulfill that prediction.

One bad week – even one bad shot – and all that potential can be put on hold at the School, perhaps even indefinitely. However, I feel like Chris has progressed considerably thanks to this tournament.

When I congratulate him for the last time about his Q School progress, he thanks me and then comments that he did not see me at all today. I explain that I stayed away, not wanting to jinx him. He chuckles and it is actually the first time since I met Chris two months ago that his face shows no sign of fatigue or tightness. I tell him so and he acknowledges his relief. So far in all our pre and post-round chats, I have not pushed him to tell me about that bug in the back of everyone's mind at Q School – the voice that keeps saying they might fail. Now, however, it is time.

"I woke up at 5am this morning and couldn't get back to sleep; there was a lot on my mind, I suppose, and I knew it was a big day. I was a bit nervous at the start, in fact, I was even nervous on the range. My fear? Everything comes into your mind, I think; the doubt about what I needed to shoot; what is the worst score I could shoot because it's shit or bust. It doesn't take much to fall outside the top 30 and you could miss by a shot and be on Challenge Tour. That's what it was."

Although Chris has never been close to missing out this week, the Q School takes its toll. "It's been horrible, I don't want to be here ever again. It's so long and although I've played very steady all week, I got no breaks. I've played more than 250 holes since First Stage in September and come through it all, so that's a pretty good achievement. Now I just can't wait to get started on the Main Tour. I've worked really hard for this and I feel like I deserve everything I get."

Chris has proven himself and he has shown a quality that will be of huge value in the future: he leaves his troubles behind once he steps on the 1st tee. "I'm pretty good once I get on the course and after those four birdies early on, I was cruising from there and enjoying it. I still holed nothing long and my birdies were all tap-ins again, but I'm really very happy now it's all over. It's brilliant." And he is totally right. What a great way to celebrate the start of what should be a fabulous career.

Meanwhile, Gordon is legitimately taking some of the plaudits for his job as caddie and Stuart has another client for ISM on Main Tour for next season. But it is the father who looks the happiest. Richard has been a great companion for me both this week and last, plus we have shared a few jokes as well as a few of what my mother would have called "old fashioned looks" when Chris missed the odd putt. Richard might have aged a little over the last few days, but now he is pride personified just as he was four months ago at the Open.

Another question comes into my mind for Chris – so is 5th at Q School better than 5th at the Open? "At the time on that back 9 at Royal Birkdale, the Open was as good as golf ever gets," he says, "but knowing I've got a whole year ahead of me on the European Tour, it's just as good. I'm going to relax finally. I'm celebrating my 21st birthday this Saturday with some friends and I'm going to get absolutely wasted. I can't wait to get away from golf for a while."

My feelings? Well, I have seen a lot of heartache at Q School, so it's marvelous to be associated with such a great triumph. I'm relieved that Chris has avoided all the heartache of failure and I congratulate him again. I also thank him profusely before we go our separate ways for the terrific story he has given me. Plus, it seems like a win-win-win situation: Chris has his career sorted, I have my book to write and, to paraphrase a certain movie "we'll always have Q School".

Author's Postscript

In the following seasons, I follow Chris Wood at various tournaments including his first foray to America when he qualifies for the 2009 US PGA Championship at Hazeltine. That season he is given the Sir Henry Cotton Award as the European Tour's rookie of the year and he goes on to fulfill the promise he showed at the School, racking up millions of pounds in prize money. His first win as a pro comes on the Asian Tour, then the following season he takes the Qatar Masters on the European Tour with a stunning final hole eagle. I watch live on television as he covers his face with his cap on the 72nd hole to stop anyone seeing his tears. This initial victory among his European peers is the first time I have seen such emotion from him; it is a mark of his compassionate upbringing and honest character. It reminds me of the young Bristol lad who confessed to never liking lessons or exams as a boy, but who came through golf's toughest school in autumn 2008 to become a man.

~

My friendship with Guy proved to be the strongest among the seven players who I originally wrote about in the Golf On The Edge books. I followed his progress closely after 2008 and was thrilled when he came through the Asian Tour Q School both in 2012 and 2014. In fact, this may one day be his pathway to the European Tour as be two golfing organisations are working ever more closely together, including perhaps combining their Q Schools. "I definitely haven't given up on the dream and will probably go back to the School again at some time," he says after taking a break from the European version in the last couple of years. During all this time, Guy passed his PGA exams and became a fully qualified professional who went on to teach at various clubs including East Berkshire. He also is still playing the mini tours and pro-ams around the UK and in 2015 he finished 3rd in the South

Region order of merit. He has remained a highly personable golfer with plenty of golf business ideas (including representing the Canadian clothing brand Longball) and now has a steady girlfriend. He has even returned to Q School twice as a caddie for the talented American player Dodge Kemmer. "I'm more sorted out with my life these days, but I'll never regret a moment of chasing the dream of a Tour Card."

PART THREE

40 Q Schools Year by Year

1976

The first ever Q School was officially called the PGA Tournament Players Division Qualifying School and took place on three courses with just £1,400 worth of prize money. A Tour Card in 1976 would provide membership of the Tour, but only access to the Monday Qualifiers at European Tour events rather than actually being able to tee it up in the tournament itself.

The Tour administrators needed three Q School courses to cope with the entry numbers (a total of 261) and chose the Longcross and Chertsey courses at Foxhills in Surrey and nearby Walton Heath's New Course. Foxhills had the advantage of being brand spanking new with leading PGA pro Bernard Hunt attached to the club and the owners liked the idea of a prestigious group of pros visiting for two days of practice and four days of the tournament itself.

The entrants were mostly UK and Ireland club pros or assistants given special time off to pursue their tournament ambitions. Very few continental Europeans or continental-based British-born pros decided to drive to a north European port, catch a ferry (flying would most likely be too expensive) and then stay away from their club jobs for a week in the UK with little prize money on offer.

To say that the 1st Qualifying School was low key would almost be an exaggeration. It was a 72-hole four-round event played between 8th and 11th November with a cut after 54 hole cut. The scoring, especially early on, was shockingly high. One player – who eventually retired from the event after two rounds – opened his account with a remarkable 107, 35 over par.

The summer of 1976 had seen record low levels of rain and, even by the autumn, the conditions were still dry and difficult (Longcross proved to be the biggest nightmare) while plenty of tree-lined fairways on all three courses meant recovery shots were often a sideways pitch back onto the fairway. Like almost all tournament events in those days, the Tour players and their administrators were merely guests and did set up the courses, that job was done by the resident pro, the greenkeeper and/or an experienced club secretary. The players just had to make the most of the tricky conditions.

In the end, the top 120 players and ties (a total of 127, almost half the field) received tour membership for the following season. David A Russell, a 19-year-old assistant from Mid-Kent GC, won the first prize of £270 with a winning score of 9 over par (yes, *over* par); only two rounds were recorded in the 60s (68 was the best) out of more than 850 played over the four days. David was one of several young players who saw pro tournament golf as a potential career at that time; a certain young Welsh lad named Ian Woosnam lined up alongside him.

"In the days before Q School, a young pro was only allowed to play in Tour events after he had been an apprentice for two years. I didn't fancy earning £10 a week working in the pro shop for all that time and not playing in the big events. So when my father told me about Q School, I went along and tried it. I had nothing to lose," remembers David who originally wanted to become an airline pilot.

Q School was David's very first pro event and his main accomplishment was to keep his poise despite bad weather and plenty of bogeys. Neil Coles presented him with his prize and being the answer to a golf trivia question is something David now enjoys. "I realised it was quite an achievement, but I had no idea about being a pro golfer. I was just tremendously excited." David's Q School win led to a 20-year career on Tour which peaked in 1987 when he finished 41st on the money list with £43,000.

Among the 126 other success stories were future Ryder Cup players Gordon J Brand (tied 4th) and Ian Woosnam (tied 34th) along with Ross Drummond (tied 47th) and Andrew Murray (tied 70th). Those who missed out included Derrick Cooper (later a European Tour board member) and Gary Alliss (son of Ryder Cup player and TV commentator Peter).

However, it was a sobering moment for the majority of the entrants, especially those shooting in the 80s and 90s. In fact, Tour Cards were won with an average score per round of just over 80 and the first Q School had performed its purpose: it showed that, to join the Tour, you had to be a special player even though overall scoring this time was pretty awful.

Nevertheless, glory and hefty amounts of prize money awaited the successful Q Schoolers who had witnessed Seve Ballesteros winning this year's Order of Merit with a total of £39,500. The new Tour members were now part of golf's gold rush.

1977

The early years of the Q School were a continual learning experience for the Tour especially in terms of how many players should receive Tour Cards. In this second event, played in October, the number of Cards handed out was reduced to the top 100 and ties, down from the inaugural year's 120. This kind of refinement happened continually as the European tournament golf scene began to mature: this was the year Nick Faldo emerged, while Seve Ballesteros was about to take the whole golf world by storm.

Scores at this year's School were slightly better with conditions easier as Foxhills became the sole venue (Walton Heath was dropped). Entries rose to over 300 compared to 260 last year and, while the four-round winning total was still high at 295, the players getting Tour Cards for finishing around 100th place were about nine shots better than the inaugural tournament.

"The bigger entry surprised us, but it was a nice surprise to have. We looked at having a third course, but that would mean a cut could only come after three rounds. This year, we stuck to Foxhills and the cut was made after 36 holes," says John Paramor, tournament director.

This School would also mark the first time that a true champion of the future would win the tournament. Sandy Lyle took victory by two shots and a first prize cheque of £300. "The pressure on you was the same then as it is now," says Sandy who would go on to win two major titles. "Your whole life was wrapped around those four rounds of golf. It was not easy conditions and Foxhills was a tight golf course, so there weren't a lot of great scores. It wasn't a nice week to play, in fact it was gut-wrenching. It's tougher and tighter these days because there are so many good players. Now you'll be at Q School and maybe compete against 60 other really good players whereas I was probably playing with about 15.

"Of course, I expected to get through, everybody did and still does. I played cagey golf and managed to put some half decent scores on the board early doors and didn't look back. In those days, I hit the 1-iron as often as I could off the tee because that was my safety shot; I could back off the driver and still hit the ball 250-260 yards and that was ample around Foxhills," he says.

Joining Sandy on Tour for the next season would be Denis Pugh (now a noted golf coach), David A Russell (the Q School winner 12 months earlier who was tied 79th this time) and, once again, Ian Woosnam (tied 85th, the last slot for a Card). Missing out were David Leadbetter (later to become one of the world's best-known coaches) and David Feherty (Ryder Cupper of the future).

1978

Year three saw another couple of changes as Tour mandarins were still working out how to balance the number of end-of-season Tour Cards awarded via the Order of Merit with those handed out at Q School. This year, available Q School Cards at the end of October were reduced to 80, something that caused the number of School entries to increase to 350 (up from 260 only two years earlier) and the number of courses to return to three (Downshire in Berkshire was introduced just for this year).

Other developments included a sprinkling of foreign players showing up (including some from the USA, Canada and Australia, with four grabbing Cards), while British pros based in Scandinavia also made an appearance for the first time. Even a few spectators were drawn to the growing drama of Q School.

Ian Woosnam exemplified how young pros were using the School to progress up the professional ranks. The Welshman had his best finish in three attempts – tied 4th, worth £125 in prize money – and his days as a journeyman player, sleeping in camper vans and eating baked beans to save money, were over.

1979

By year four, Q School needed another major facelift. The regular tournament season was drifting into October, so the School moved to November. However, that meant dangerously short amounts of UK daylight with which to complete the tournament and an increased threat of bad weather. Holding the event in southern Portugal was the answer, the Dom Pedro and Quinta Do Lago golf courses. Along with more daylight and sunshine, there were other benefits of the move: the Tour signed a three-year deal that saved some money and gave the event some continuity.

And because of the extra distance to travel and the higher costs for most players (still 95% of Q School players would travel from the UK), the Tour operated two separate tournaments played in consecutive weeks. Players could enter one, but not both and the top 40 and ties from each event gained their Tour Card.

The switch to continental Europe also had another effect: Q School started to get even more serious. Players traveling to Portugal were making a real statement about wanting a future as a tournament pro, while the less committed saved money and stayed at home.

John Paramor also remembers the fun of this sporting travelling circus. "We organised package deals from the UK and the pros traveled down there together to make it as cheap as possible. We even managed to include a hire car in the price to be shared by three players. These were Minis with roof racks and I did hear about a car rally being organised around one hotel, so spirits were high; it was a bit of a jolly for some of the guys, for sure. One of the Minis ended up parked in the reception of the Dom Pedro Hotel where the players were staying and another was turned over and put on its roof in the car park. It was boys being boys, I suppose."

The continental venue attracted some top continental golfers for the first time: Marc Farry of France and Torsten Gideon of Germany were among the entrants along with Spaniards, Italians, Scandinavians and a Swiss. However, overall entries were now under 300 mainly because of the cost implications of travel and accommodation for the Brits.

Prize money totaled £1,000 at each of the two tournaments, but Q School was still a tough place to play and offered no guarantees of a Tour career. Take the examples of this year's two Q School champions, club pros Charles Cox of Royal Epping Forest and Keith Williams of Sunningdale: on Tour the following season, they won just over £1,500 between them finishing 121st and 152nd respectively on the Order of Merit and found themselves right back at the School again.

The sense of failure at missing out on a Tour Card was beginning to really matter to a young pro's career. "When we had the prize giving afterwards, there were a couple of guys who needed shoulders to cry on, they were in tears because they had just missed out," said Paramor. "There was one young player who we had to disqualify after we found out he had changed his last round scorecard and another who played his final 18 with a bashed up ankle after a car crash – Q School was starting to really mean something to the players."

The desire to succeed as a European Tour pro was growing because leading Tour members like Seve Ballesteros won the Open Championship at Royal Lytham this summer and a proper European team contested the Ryder Cup for the first time. The European Tour was now truly a product of the whole continent rather than mostly the UK and Ireland and this new excitement was starting to translate into prize money. In 1976, Seve had won the money list with almost £40,000 in earnings, while this year's No 1 was Sandy Lyle with £68,000, but by 1983 Nick Faldo topped the Order of Merit with a staggering £120,000. Total prize money was also rising fast: £800,000 in 1976, almost £1.6 million this year and onto to £3.3 million by 1983.

1980

There was another cut in the number of Q School Tour Cards this year, from 40 plus ties from each event down to 35. For the first time, continental European golfers made an impact: the week two event was won by Manuel Montes of Spain – who became the first continental European winner – while fellow countryman and future Tour winner and Ryder Cup player Jose Rivero finished tied 5th. The continental Europeans were welcomed because the European Tour was trying each year to cut the number of tournament entries given to the Continental Tour Players Association (CTPA). By pushing those players towards the School each autumn, it would guarantee a better field at each Tour event. That strategy was working because nine non-Brits or Irish won through this year as opposed to just one or two in each of the first few Schools. In addition, more than 20 other players from outside Great Britain and Ireland took part including two from the Ivory Coast, one from Bermuda and one from Canada. That meant 10% of the field at Q School was already from outside the UK and Ireland.

Among the failures this year was Barry Lane (actually for the second year running), who would eventually enjoy more than 20 successful seasons on Tour. Barry missed his Tour Card by a single shot. "I was devastated. A few guys got drunk and a few cried, but getting upset won't pay the mortgage, so you have to get on with it, you have to set your goals for the next year. But Q School does make you better if you stick at it. Even when I got my Card the first time, I still couldn't afford to play until I got a sponsor. That's the kind of pressure that makes you play negative golf at Q School; it's the hardest thing, it really is. We're professional golfers, this is what we do, so we have to keep going back. I wouldn't fancy a trip to Q School these days, but if I had to go then I would.

"I had to play PGA South regional events (in 1981) and just wait all year for another chance," says Lane who was a poorly paid assistant pro in those days at Downshire GC in Berkshire. "If you're not on form for that week, then it's always hard. In those days, there was no Challenge Tour and the Q School was the only four-round tournament I would play."

1981

There were more changes in year six – prize money doubled to £2,000 per tournament and the number of available Tour Cards dropped again, this time to 30 and ties for each event. Also, the media began to notice the event because it was now recognised as a gateway to the Tour, especially as the winner in 1977 (Sandy Lyle) had won the Order of Merit two years running.

In the first week of Q School, ex-top amateurs Gordon Brand Jnr of Scotland and Roger Chapman of England were two of the new Brits receiving most of the attention and eventually finished first and second: Brand Jr shot a four-round Q School record 288 and Chapman managed the runners-up spot despite a last round 81. Both players would go on to be European Tour winners. By contrast, neither of the top two players at the week two event – Englishmen Robin Mann and Philip Morley – would make a mark on Tour, although Anders Forsbrand, Mats Lanner and Paul Way (all future Tour champions) were among those who came through successfully just behind them.

1982

This was another significant year for the development of the European Tour. Firstly, in April, the Tour calendar teed off with its first event based outside the UK, Ireland or Continental Europe: the Tunisian Open, won by Spain's Antonio Garrido and deemed a success. This tournament would be the forerunner of a vast geographical expansion of the Tour including co-sanctioned events in southern Africa, Asia and Australasia over the next few years.

In November, the Q School – still a two-tournament, two-week event – moved to Spain, the country where it remained for all but two of the next 33 years. La Manga had been the venue of the Spanish Open for much of the 1970s and its North and South courses were adjacent with each other (rather than on two sites) making practical sense for the School. Also, there was a whole sports complex to occupy the players after their rounds and plenty of villas offering reasonably-priced accommodation.

At this time, any player finishing in the top 150 at the end of the season automatically kept a Tour Card, while those below that position were on their way to La Manga where the pressure was now intensifying. The new, single venue allowed a single giant scoreboard – like those already used in normal tournament events – to be erected for the first time so that all the players and plenty of ex-pat British golf fans could follow exactly what was happening.

A total of 66 Q School Tour Cards were won this year by some highly-skilled pros. Jose Rivero of Spain won week one and Grant Turner of England finished top in week two. Italy's Costantino Rocca (later of Ryder Cup fame), England's Robert Lee (now better known for his work on Sky Sports) and Richard Boxall (another future TV golf commentator) were also among the recipients of Tour membership for the privilege of weekly Monday Qualifying the following season. The growing strength of the Tour was now evident by the fact that only 18 of the 66 Card winners this year (just 27%) would finish in the top 150 the following season and retain membership.

By now, the system of exemptions was creating stronger golfers in Europe, just what the Tour had wanted when it made the original changes back in the early 1970s. Even quality tournament pros were having to regularly return to Q School to keep their careers in tact; the event was becoming a rite of passage, the means to a potentially very lucrative end.

1983

A total of 326 players entered this year (the same as in 1982) as Q School kept the same format as the past four years. Week one was won by David Ray of England while Scotland's Andrew Oldcorn and Frederic Regard of France were joint top in week two. Well-known names were not very plentiful among the 71 Card winners, but they included Miguel Martin, Mark Mouland and Peter Mitchell. Competition was stiffer yet again as the ease of travel to La Manga and the affordable accommodation was starting to attract more players from around the world to Q School. This year over a dozen different nations were represented in the field.

The class of 1983 would be the final large group that Q School would provide to the Tour because more changes were afoot. The Players' Committee wanted to move to an all-exempt Tour – something the US PGA had already successfully introduced. This meant a category system would be adopted to create a ladder of eligibility so that the highest and lowest ranked pros would all know where they stood.

From next season, all Tour members would be ranked in lists with Category 1 players (ie the very top golfers, major champions or Order of Merit winners etc) having first dibs at every event, Category 2 players being next in line and so on. Sometimes (usually at the bigger prize money events) those pros in the lower categories would miss out on entry because there were too many other Tour members ranked above them wishing to play, but at least every tournament golfer had a clear idea of where he stood in the rankings and what his chances were of pegging it up in any particular week.

The best news of all, perhaps, was the end of the dreaded Monday Qualifying system, that was scrapped altogether. This meant that the category for Q School Tour Card winners – although one of the lower rankings – not only provided Tour membership, but also guaranteed a number of starts that could be circled in the calendar in time for the opening of the season. This was better than just a series of perilous pre-qualifying tournaments at the beginning of every week.

It was hoped that the category system would benefit Q Schoolers and give them a better chance of holding onto their hard-won cards. However, the toughness of the Tour showed otherwise as only 10 of this year's 71 Card winners would avoid returning to the School after the 1984 season; it was the worst success rate (14%) since the very first event.

1984

At the end of this season, the all-exempt tour system would come into effect. There had been 27 events on Tour with a £4 million in total prize money with some tournaments offering astonishing amounts of cash – £440,000 to share at the Open and a dozen more events with the total pot over £100,000. European greats like Ballesteros, Faldo, Langer, Woosnam and Lyle were taking on the world of golf, while television and sponsorship money was rushing in.

After the season-ending Portuguese Open in November, the top 125 players on the money list automatically retained their Tour Card (a drop from 150 the year before), while 50 Cards would be available at Q School (down from 71 in 1983). Despite the restrictions, more pros wanted to play on the Tour and Q School entries are up from 326 last year to 388. Pros noted that the very top player earnings were now into six figures (Bernhard Langer, Sam Torrance and Howard Clark all took home over £100,000 in 1984). The gold rush had really begun.

Q School Tour Cards were refined in another way: each one was given its own ranking, so winning the School would give a player the No 1 status in the Q School Tour Card category and probably allow him entry to 23 of the 26 Tour events. However, the value of the Tour for someone finishing 50th at Q School meant a ranking position further down the entry list of all events, so that player could expect less than 20 starts. Again, the Tour was trying to reward the best players and, in the new meritocracy, there was no reason why the Q School winner should not receive some kind of benefit, so access to more tournaments seemed most appropriate.

The School stayed at La Manga, but was limited to a single event and, in another innovation, the event was staged over six-rounds rather than four. This was another way to ensure that the best players would emerge from Q School: there would even be a four-round cut.

However, there were also some unexpected consequences to all these Tour and Q School improvements. The opportunity of playing on such a lucrative Tour attracted more non-European talent. Although that was part of the plan, a flood of North Americans was not expected. Starting this year, dozens of US players used the European Q School as an insurance against failure in their own Tour's qualifying event. Jeff Sluman (who would go on to win a major – the US PGA – four years later) was among the Americans who played in Q Schools on both sides of the Atlantic in 1984. He finished second at La Manga to another American Robert Wrenn Jnr. However, both men subsequently won Tour Cards in America a few weeks later and did not play in a single European Tour event in 1985.

The Americans had simply taken advantage of the fact that the Q Schools on each side of the Atlantic were staged on different weeks in

November. It was not a happy situation for the pros supporting European golf because winning a Card in this way and then not playing on the Tour was in defiance of the system and did not promote loyalty to either Tour. Although the European Tour organisers never deliberately moved their Q School directly opposite the American version, there were no tears in Europe a few seasons later when the dates of the two Schools clashed for the first time. That put a stop to the "Sluman effect".

European talent coming through Q School in 1983 included Andrew "Chubby" Chandler (later the boss of the ISM agency and manager to pros including Lee Westwood and Darren Clarke) and Mark Roe (now a Sky Sports pundit).

The most surprising Q School success story, however, was that of another American, a certain Nathaniel Crosby, son of the king of the crooners Bing Crosby. Nathaniel won the 22nd Tour Card and would go on to finish 87th in the Order of Merit the next season winning just over £9,000 in prize money.

1985

European Tour Q School celebrated its 10th anniversary this year and was settling into a recognised format as inaugural tournament director John Paramor moved on to become Director of Tour Operations (he would become Chief Referee a few years later) and leave Andy McFee as Q School Director. At age 27, Andy had golf in his blood and would retain the job into the 21st century.

Q School was now anchored in November and the number of Tour Cards was to remain at 50 for at least the next few seasons as the all-exempt Tour mechanics bedded down. The entry field was once again a record this year as the number of pros involved broke the 400 mark for the first time. The strength of international golf was becoming evident because despite the vast majority of the total entries coming from the UK and Ireland, just 13 'home nations' players won Tour Cards while only a further eight were from other parts of Europe.

Leading the way was this season's undoubted star of the tournament, Jose Maria Olazabal – the winner of the British Boys, Youth and Amateur championships. At just 19 years old, Olazabal opened with a 66 and led for all six days, pulling his own trolley around the links in the most unassuming of ways. Looking back, Olazabal remembers the tension: "It was very windy and it was a large field of players, so I was very nervous especially at the beginning of the final round. But I managed to settle the nerves and down the stretch, I was really happy. Getting the best Card meant I was guaranteed a lot of tournaments." With the best Tour Card in his pocket, the young Spaniard would go on to finish in 2nd place in the Order of Merit the following season.

Also picking up Cards were Greg Turner and Frank Nobilo from New Zealand and Mike Harwood of Australia. The problem was that many of the non-European players winning Cards (31 of them) only played a handful of events in the following season. The integrity of the Tour was being threatened, but as the Q School grew in prestige, so these issues would eventually have to be addressed.

1986

Into its second decade and Q School entries were now so large that pre-qualifying events had to be staged. PQ1 was staged in September at Foxhills and Silvermere GCs in England and PQ2 took place in November at El Saler and Escorpion GCs in Spain. All these events were played over 36 holes and players failing at PQ1 could still enter PQ2.

The now-titled Final Stage of the School was still at La Manga and saw particularly windy weather this year that suited the stronger players. More European talent came more to the fore including Steen Tinning, Andrew Sherbourne, Jamie Spence, Ross McFarlane, Costantino Rocca and David Gilford – all Tour Card winners.

However, despite the School becoming ever tougher and sorting out the better players, just eight of the 50 Card-winning players from this year (16%) kept their Cards via the Order of Merit the following season.

1987

There was another large entry this year as Main Tour prize money became evermore alluring: finish inside the top 50 now on Tour and your earnings would be around £40,000, more than the amount that won the Order of Merit just over a decade earlier. There were now well over 20 events available for successful Q Schoolers to enter and even the very smallest tournaments boasted total prize money of over £100,000.

The most notable name among this year's Q School Card winners was a tall, young Scot named Colin Montgomerie who had won his PQ event at Foxhills to make it to La Manga where he finished only 28th. Monty remembers: "I only went once to the School and thank goodness, I wouldn't like to do it now. My mom was my chef for the week and it was great, but anyone who goes through that knows it's hell. It was your job, your career on the line for six rounds of golf. If you can play the back 9 under par to get your Card then you can handle anything. I respect anyone who can do that."

At one point, a stomach-settling potion was brought onto the course for Monty. "The stresses and strains of finishing first or second in a tournament are nothing compared to battling for 120th place on the Order of Merit or for your Tour Card," says the Scot. "Q School is the most stressful time for golfers, it's horrific."

Monty would go on to play in 11 events in the 1988 season and achieve 52nd place in the 1988 Order of Merit. Also in the Tour Card winners' circle were well-known names such as Craig Parry, Eduardo Romero, Peter Mitchell and David Gilford.

1988

The very best players don't have to win Q School to go on to great things, but sometimes they cannot help it. This year saw the strongest ever 1-2 finishers: Jesper Parnevik of Sweden took the winner's cheque ahead of Fiji's Vijay Singh. Both would win events all over the globe and Singh would win three majors as well as reach the No 1 ranking position in the world. Proof that Q School was no breeze comes from the fact that both Parnevik and Singh had failed to win a Tour Card at the School the year before.

The class of 1988 was full of exceptional players and future Tour winners and Ryder Cup players included Miguel Angel Jimenez who finished 6th (this was his fourth attempt and his first success; he has not returned); Paul Broadhurst at 18th (the six-time Tour winner would have to return to Q School 13 years later); Jean Van de Velde (on his second and final attempt so far); Marc Farry (his first success in four attempts); and Paraguay's Carlos Franco who did not play in Europe the following season but would go on to earn millions of American dollars on the US PGA Tour.

1989

The growing popularity of Q School meant that the number of PQ1 and PQ2 tournaments rose to seven, up from four. At Final Stage, another very strong field of players turned up in southern Spain and among those with fond Tour Card memories of this year's event are Greg Turner, Joakim Haeggman, Jamie Spence, John Hawksworth, Russell Claydon, Peter Hedblom, Stephen Richardson and Santiago Luna.

But this would be the final year for La Manga as the venue of the School. By now, the influx of money into European professional golf and the increasing TV audiences meant that courses in Europe and elsewhere were approaching the Tour with special financial deals (including sponsorships) that allowed more tournaments to turn a profit while still increasing prize money.

Although the Q School would remain unsponsored, the Tour had a brand that it could "sell" to any course that wished to be part of its success.

It was time to look at other venues in southern Europe that were in equally good condition, where the larger entry (now up to 497 in total, but set to rise substantially again next year) could still be accommodated and where the deal was sweeter.

The Tour bosses did talk of staying at La Manga with its uniquely intense atmosphere, large amounts of on-site housing and its legacy of being loved by the players. In fact for some people, the memorable off-course antics were a potential reason to stay in this part of southern Spain. However, with players together all day, both on the course or driving range and then in the main bar and restaurant in the evening, tempers sometimes flared and the odd bar room fight broke out.

Andy McFee remembers: "It was pretty severe at La Manga. I remember a couple of players coming off the course and walking straight into the nearest swimming pool, clubs and all, some with relief at getting a Card and some as a punishment. These were the days of the Tour without driving range balls or courtesy cars and it was tough. Golfers were learning to live in this difficult environment and they were all doing their best, but some of them could only see all the money disappearing from their bank account. There were floods tears, there were huge disappointments and there were lots of distraught young men. For intensity, there was nothing like La Manga."

The stories from La Manga are both funny and tragic, but they speak volumes for how the Q School is a unique caldron of emotions that can destroy good golfers. Andy's favourite tale revolves around a regular visitor to the School at this time, American Danny Goodman, who was taking such a pounding from the course one year that he simply lay down on a fairway and started sunbathing. Andy was called to investigate.

"Danny was a nice lad, but a bit of a fruitcake and one year I was called out to the 11th hole for what I thought was a ruling. I found Danny lying down in the middle of the fairway so I asked him what he was doing. 'I've had it, man, this game has done me in' he told me in this fabulous southern drawl. 'I'm going to lie here and soak a few rays,' he said. I told him he really had to move because the guys behind wanted to keep playing. And he quit the tournament right there. He never came to our Q School again."

Eventually, negotiations with the owners of La Manga proved fruitless and Q School moved on. It was definitely the end of an era.

1990

This was the first year of the Challenge Tour, the secondary feeder circuit for the European Tour that had been in the planning stage for almost a decade. Challenge Tour would also offer end-of-season Tour Cards, so now there were two entry points for full European Tour membership.

Now the School had to develop as well: there would be a reduction in the number of Q School Tour Cards from 50 to 40 with the Challenge Tour delivering 10 players to the Main Tour from its own Order of Merit at the end of its season.

Despite the change, entries to the School still rose, this time to 542 as pre-qualifying was extended and two new venues for the Final Stage were used, La Grande Motte and Massane in France. This was an upgrade in terms of quality of courses, but the two clubs were about 10 miles apart; it was suddenly not easy for the players to wander from one course to the other in a borrowed golf cart like at La Manga. The other problem this year was weather; the sun failed to shine in southern France.

Nevertheless, the School still unearthed real talent for the Tour. Among this year's happy Q Schoolers were Swedes Per-Ulrik Johansson and Robert Karlsson, Australia's Peter Lonard, Darren Clarke of Northern Ireland, Jose Coceres of Argentina and Thomas Levet of France.

1991

A record entry of 554 players chased just 40 places at this School; there was now only a one in 14 chance of a Q School entrant gaining a Tour Card. Nevertheless, the cream was rising to the top and Q School's reputation as a furnace in which good players were forged was being underlined. Coceres, Levet and Lonard were among those who returned to gain another Card for a second year running, but others who triumphed included Paul McGinley, Gary Evans, Steen Tinning, Paul Lawrie, Philip Parkin and Jim Payne.

The 21-year-old Payne from the small town of Louth in Lincolnshire would become a classic Q School story. He managed only the 33rd Card in this year's event; it was his initial year as a pro and his first attempt at Q School. Then, the following season Payne won £148,000 on Tour to finish 32nd in the Order of Merit and take the Henry Cotton Rookie of the Year award. Q School advocates always look at stories like Payne's, men who just scrape a Tour Card yet go on to much larger successes. Unfortunately, a back injury did much to shorten Jim's career and although he won on Tour in 1993 and finished as high as 27th in the Order of Merit in 1996, his career as a top tournament pro was a short one.

1992

This year, an eighth PQ tournament was added as entries rose to 634 (easily a new record). Meanwhile at Finals, South Africa's Retief Goosen won the event to become the third future Major winner to launch his career by winning this title. His "classmates" in the winners' circle included several other outstanding pros: Stephen Ames, Andrew Oldcorn, Andrew Coltart, Garry Orr, Bill Longmuir and Peter Lonard.

By now, the European Tour season that had once taken place from late spring to early autumn started in January and carried on until early November. A Q School Tour Card qualified a player for plenty of tournaments with as many as three dozen events now to choose from. With more Q Schoolers seeming to retain their Cards every season, this was a prime time to enter PQ1 or 2.

1993

The eight PQ tournaments this year moved from being 36 to 54-hole events, but the extra 18-holes did not deter players from attempting to jump this golfing hurdle, especially those from outside of the UK and Ireland, the original power bases of the European Tour. In fact, in the previous nine years, only one Brit (Andrew Hare in 1991) had won the event.

Rather than players from the home nations, Q School had been won in recent years by a Swede, a South African, a Spaniard, a Portuguese, a German, an Australian and a couple of Americans. This year another American, the surprising Brian Nelson, took the top spot, but it was the presence of only 19 British players among the Q School Card winners that caught the eye, while, Sweden provided no less than five of the 40 Card-winning players.

Two men – both English, however – stand out from this year's field. Phil Golding won through for the first time in 10 attempts and would go on to be one of the most prolific returnees to Q School, while Lee Westwood would become the most successful of this year's Card winners after finishing 5th. Lee, who was in his first year as a pro, now says that he never realised how much a successful Q School would mean to his career. Of those who truly become great Tour players, Lee's words about the School are a good example of what a brief but significant stepping stone the event had become. "I didn't find it that stressful really because I was playing well going into the tournament. I didn't have nerves really, I was comfortable. I was in the top 10 all week and went into it just believing I was going to get a Card. You can't think of the future and that's what separates the journeyman from the better players."

1994

Despite this originally being planned as another two-venue Q School Final Stage in France, Massane actually staged the event on its own because of huge weather problems. Play actually began at La Grande Motte on the opening day but was then halted; the rain was so severe that the tournament officers believed day two was going to be a washout as well and that would mean only half the field would play their opening rounds at this course. Tournament Director Andy McFee had one of his most difficult decisions to make.

"It's necessary for players at Q School to all be treated the same so that their like-for-like scores will fairly determine who gets a Card. So we were forced to scrap all the opening round scores at La Grande Motte because half the field couldn't play the course. It was a very controversial decision to some players – although blindingly obvious to me and my colleagues. Those players who scored well on that cancelled round complained bitterly, of course, and those who scored badly rejoiced. But no one could come up with a viable alternative, so half the field played a second first round."

In the end, La Grande Motte was not used at all for Q School this year and Tour Cards were distributed after only four rounds (rather than the normal six), all played at Massane. Christan Cévaer almost brought a home win, but he eventually finished second to David Carter of England. Another fascinating group of pros also won through including Golding (again), Carl Suneson (also his second time running), Freddie Jacobson, Stephen Dodd, Emanuele Canonica, Gary Emerson and Dean Robertson.

The 40th and very final Card went to Spain's Jose Maria Arruti whose relationship with Q School has become the longest and most persistent of any player. This year was already his sixth attempt, but his first Tour Card. By the 2010 tournament, Arruti would hold the record of 22 appearances at Q School, with just five successes.

The Challenge Tour effects were also being felt. The secondary Tour had been running since 1990 and many more young Europeans were learning how to construct 72-hole scores (something previously more available to players from countries like America and Australia). The Challenge Tour helped European natives win 39 of the 40 Tour Cards on offer this year, a ratio that had never been close to being achieved before.

1995

The Q School moved back to southern Spain this year, San Roque and Guadalmina shared the Finals Stage tournament. There was also another significant change: no longer was the number of Tour Cards set at exactly 40, something that required heartbreaking playoffs. Instead, 40th position and ties would receive Cards and avoid the unfairness of sudden death in this already excruciatingly tough event.

Steve Webster won this year along with Stephen Gallacher, Patrik Sjoland, Raymond Russell, David Howell, Miles Tunnicliff, Greg Owen,

Daniel Chopra and Anders Hansen (who won the very last – the 41st – Card), while two future major winners also sneaked onto the Tour at this year's Q School. Padraig Harrington had turned pro only a few months earlier and finished 16th while Argentina's Angel Cabrera finally made it through at his fourth attempt; he won the 18th Card. Angel's determination to make it on Tour via the School is another fine example that everything is possible once you secure a Card and players do not all have to fly through the School at the first attempt to become major winners.

1996

A ninth PQ1 event was added this year as Q School fields grew ever larger and stronger. Very few poor players could now survive the test, while even those who were set for solid Tour careers often had to return more than once. Niclas Fasth became the second Swede to win the event this year (based at San Roque and Sotogrande) with England's Brian Davis a close second.

Steve Webster had to come back despite winning last year, but he was successful along with Jean-Francois Remesy, Warren Bennett, Phil Golding, Anders Hansen, John Bickerton, Stephen Gallacher, American Bob May (who would one day take Tiger Woods to a playoff for the US PGA title), Ariel Canete of Argentina, Mark Foster, Gordon J Brand, Rafael Jacquelin and Anthony Wall.

A total of 45 Cards were handed out, but among those who failed was a young assistant from Hertfordshire, Ian Poulter, who would need another three attempts before gaining a Tour Card in 1999.

Also, interestingly, Challenge Tour finishers from 11 to 15 also gained Tour Cards for the first time this year rather than just the top 10 as the Tour grandees put more emphasis on the season-long efforts of players.

1997

Entries this year totaled an astonishing 750 as heavy rain cut Final Stage rounds from six to five and another future major champion cut his competitive teeth at the School this year. New Zealand's Michael Campbell had tried Q School four years earlier during his first year as a pro, but he failed to make the grade. This time, at his second attempt, he finished 5th. More future Tour winners emerged along with him including Robert-Jan Derksen and Jeev Milka Singh. Also through in 21st place was Gary Nicklaus, son of Jack.

1998

The influence of the Challenge Tour was felt again this year at Q School as, once again, the number of Tour Cards on offer at Finals was reduced; this time it fell from those tied 40th to those tied 35th. The change reflected the 1996 increase – by five to 15 – of Challenge Tour Cards.

Just 38 players would succeed in winning Cards this year including Ross Drummond of Scotland who finished who top of the class and first-year pro Geoff Ogilvy from Australia. Fellow Aussie Nick O'Hern joined Ogilvy in the top 35 as did Mac O'Grady, an American pro who would become one of the sport's most flamboyant coaches.

The golfing year, however, had been highlighted by the performance of a young Justin Rose at the Open Championship at Royal Birkdale. Rose immediately turned pro, but did not make a cut for the rest of the season and ended up also failing at this year's Q School. Justin would have to return two more times – in 1999 and 2000 when he gained Tour Cards each time – before his career was fully on track.

1999

Another major structural change to Q School occurred with the creation of three stages. The most inexperienced players began at First Stage where five tournaments containing a total of 491 players weeded out the best with almost one third (149) moving on. They qualified for Second Stage and were joined by 93 players who had been given an exemption to miss the initial events. That meant 243 players battled at three different venues with a total of 95 progressing to Final Stage where they were joined by 73 exempt players. So the climax of the three stages featured 168 players (it has since been reduced to 156) and the structure of Q School as we know it today had been set.

A huge glut of 42 players managed to win Cards this year. Alastair Forsyth of Scotland won the tournament from Niclas Fasth who was returning for the fourth time. Justin Rose and Ian Poulter – at his fourth attempt – were also successful this year. Poulter commented years later: "I was very inexperienced in the early Schools and if I'd made my Card earlier, it would probably have been a mistake for me. Basically, it's horrible, horrible. You have a few rounds of golf and can't make a mistake. You can't afford too many bad holes, but there are enough rounds for the best players to get through. You have to be patient and don't panic if you have a few bad holes."

Others to receive Tour Cards this year were Philip Archer (his first Card in six visits), Simon Wakefield, Peter Fowler of Australia, Gary Murphy of Ireland and England's Andrew Raitt (his fifth visit and second Card). Total prize money over all three stages was £90,000 with the Final Stage winner picking up a cheque for £10,000.

2000

By now, co-sanctioned events in South Africa were established on the Main Tour and plenty of African golfers would come through Q School. Four South Africans were successful this year, the most ever. Another strong field of Card winners included Brett Rumford, Graeme Storm, Peter Hanson, Carl Petterson, Gregory Havret, Kenneth Ferrie, Hennie Otto, Stephen Richardson and Simon Dyson who won the 33rd of 35 Cards.

Dyson had failed at Second Stage the previous year, but went onto the Asian Tour for a season to toughen up his game. However, despite his Asia experiences, Q School was far from plain sailing. "In the third round, I shot 81 and so I was looking on the internet checking on my flight back home. I was miles off. Then suddenly I shot 63 in the fourth round, finished it off with a couple of 69s and got my Card. It's always the same: never give in. When I hit the 81, I was thinking of going back to Asia; it wasn't so bad to have that to fall back on and it relaxed me. I don't even know what I did to change my game after the 81, maybe it was a couple of beers. It was weird, but something just went well.

"I don't remember the 81 now, but I remember the 63; anything inside 15ft I was knocking it in. I started off steady, but then I birdied six on the bounce and parred the 9th; I remember thinking that I just hope it makes the cut and it did, easily. Eighteen shots different and I didn't do anything different. One day I felt terrible and the next day, the hole was the size of a bucket. I remember the 12-footer I holed on the last day to get a Card and that was a nice feeling. I was still on the bubble on the last day, but I felt no nerves even then. It is a crazy tournament and I don't want to do it again," Simon says.

This event also marked the end of Andy McFee as tournament director after 16 years in charge. "The quality level has gone up so much since I started and the process was now hardening the players. It might take two, three four visits to Q School, but if they are determined then they will make it. Some players take time to find their feet, but Q School is a hard system because we want to turn out high quality players."

Andy McFee had been promoted within the Main Tour's refereeing structure in 1997 and that role did not sit well with running Q School, so he needed to move on. "It was time for me to stop running the School, but I will always believe there is a place for it on the European Tour. There was an argument about taking Q School away and giving all the Tour Cards to the Challenge Tour Order of Merit finishers at one time. But I think there is a place for Cards being given via both systems. Look at all the players who have gone through Q School and then made a huge success on Main Tour. You can't postpone the dreams of players and, if they're good enough, then we should get them on Tour as soon as possible. I will always think that."

2001

Mike Stewart took charge of Q School this year. Mike had been working on events at the European Tour for 15 years and was the obvious choice to take over from Andy McFee. Mike had learned the tournament trade in the PGA's Scottish region under the keen eye of Sandy Jones, now chief executive of the British PGA. Apart from Mike's CV, his own golf pedigree was helpful in knowing what players needed; his sister Gillian was a long-time top amateur (including playing in the Curtis Cup) while second cousin Murray Urquhart was a tournament pro and multiple Q Schooler.

Mike's first Q School this year included a group of players fresh from the Walker Cup including England's Nick Dougherty who breezed through finishing 3rd. Other Card winners were David Drysdale, David Park, Arjun Atwal, Iain Pyman, Simon Khan and Marcel Siem.

This was quite a classy group of qualifiers, but Dougherty was the pick of them with a big spotlight on him. Mentored as a teenager by Nick Faldo, the cheeky 19-year-old from Liverpool had the kind of Q School experience that all young players dream about. "It wasn't bad for me. I played well and was never under real stress. But I can see now that Q School is a huge amount of pressure. There is enough golf (at Q School) to separate the guys who have consistency and those who haven't, but the nerves you deal with there are what you do on Tour. It makes you a better golfer to get through it."

During this Q School visit, Nick had to pass through all three stages because as a new professional he had no ranking, no status. Even so, he could recognise the gulf in quality between golfers he saw at each stage. "There are certain people who won't get through Q School. A lot of people at First Stage are just not good enough or they have a full-time job in a pro shop or other golf or life aspirations. But if you dedicate your life to golf then (getting past Q School) can happen. The people who are passionate about it and who give it the time, they are the ones who should keep trying at the School."

To play with a level of brashness and certainty about your ability is what the modern young pro needs. Nick certainly had it. "When I went to Q School, the first thing I looked at was how much the prize money was. That is the best way to look at it for me and the good players naturally do that. There was a certain amount of relief (when I got through) because I'd been and done it. But I knew I could do it, and to get it done was great."

But then there was the nervousness, something felt by others and not Nick. "I remember Graham Rankin coming up to me on the putting green; I was having a laugh with Kenneth Ferrie. I'll never forget it. He asked me why was I laughing? There is nothing to be happy about at Q School, he said, because if you're here, life's crap. I didn't see it that way; it was just a stepping stone for me. It was part of the process and I cherished the opportunity. That attitude is worth five shots, a fortune. The enormity of what it means is what holds people back. I see that now. It's an opportunity for your life to completely change. I didn't feel the nerves at all; it doesn't make sense. I went in with a great attitude. You have to do your own thing; you have to play 'me'. If you leave it all out there and it's not good enough, then fair enough. I was just very fortunate. If I went back I'd feel the nerves more because I'd understand the consequences better."

Nick might have been just a teenager at Q School, but he is refreshingly frank both about what it takes to be a pro these days and what it means. "For most people, their boss might one day come up to them and give them a promotion and a bit more money, but if you get through Q School it's like moving from being an intern to the vice-president of the company. All of a sudden you are living the dream and the opportunity of fame and great fortune. Players know that at the start of the week and the more you go there the harder it is. For guys who need to make a living and have a family to feed, you have to go back. I hope never to go back because it's not something I'd cherish.

"Once you get on Tour you feel for the guy who's hitting 80 yards offline. You think that once his exemption runs out there is no way he can make a career on Tour, but players like Henrik Stenson have had that happen to them and now he's one of the best players in Europe. You never know. He stuck at it and kept trying, getting pummeled, learning from it and moving on. That's how you have to do it sometimes, especially if you believe you are good enough, you have to keep going. Who knows, you might eventually get there and be a great success."

Unfortunately for Nick, he has had to return to the School and not with any success. He now works for Sky Sports as well as playing occasional events on the Challenge and Main Tours.

2002

The Q School final moved to Emporda and Pals in Catalunya for the next two years, but bad weather marked the move. The local wind – the Tramontana – blew hard while so much rain fell that it filled the bunkers, yet the challenging conditions brought out the best in what was to prove a very strong field. No less than 13 of the 39 players who gained Tour Cards this year went on to be winners (in order of finish): Philip Archer, Phil Golding, Mads-Vibe Hastrup, Marcel Siem, Simon Khan, Paul Broadhurst, David Dixon, Charl Schwartzl, Robert-Jan Derksen, Richard Sterne, Jose Manuel Lara and Damien McGrane.

Meanwhile, the return to Q School of a player of the calibre of Paul Broadhurst is always hard to understand. It is the former champion having to barrel up with the rest of those in the last-chance saloon who is most at risk of embarrassment. His lifestyle is threatened more than almost anyone else; his confidence is paper thin otherwise he probably would not be here; and anything other than a good Tour Card is failure on a huge scale.

Paul was successful this year, but had missed out the year before and knows how hard Q School is for the thirty and fortysomethings. "I take a bit of interest (in Q School) because of friends like Peter Baker who you hope is going to make a comeback like me. But it's not that easy and as time goes by you can get a bit frustrated with your game and things don't always go very well. It's tough. Do I have any advice? Well, I wish I had the answer of how to get through. I do know that Q School is a tough place to be when you're not playing well."

2003

Playing well in the Walker Cup is no guarantee of a Q School triumph. Two years ago, Nick Dougherty used the momentum of a Walker Cup win to take a Tour Card, but teammate Richard McEvoy could not join him back then. This year, with two years of pro experience behind him, McEvoy wins the event. The quality of players behind McEvoy is as tough as ever; 35 Cards were handed out including to South Africa's Louis Oosthuizen.

McEvoy had lived on the fringes of the Main Tour since 2001 and this was already his third Q School visit. Like hundreds of excellent players he had bounced between the Main Tour and the Challenge Tour.

"I suppose winning Q School means I should know how to do this, but it is still a very strange event. If you make the cut after two rounds in a normal tournament and someone says 'you have to make the top 30 now", you could probably do that no problem. But here, it plays on your mind and that's why the scores are higher than what they should be. Some people overdo it before the fifth and sixth rounds, maybe that's the secret," says Richard.

The total prize money for the Q School tournaments rose to £109,000, the first time the amount had breached the £100,000 barrier, while another notable Card winner was Ben Banks, son of Genesis keyboard player Tony.

2004

San Roque returned as the host of Q School this year with the Old and New Courses providing some of the most dramatic settings for the final rounds, while total prize for the entire School rose to £135,000. Another Swede, Peter Gustafsson, wins with 38 others close behind including Francesco Molinari, Stuart Manley, Gonzalo Fernandez-Castano, Richard Finch, Pelle Edberg, Sam Little and Gregory Bourdy.

The story of the week, though, belongs to Neil Cheetham of Sheffield, England, who eagles the very last hole to scrape in for a Tour Card right on the mark. It is a remarkable achievement and his form holds into his very first Tour event in South Africa a month later where he is only denied the title after a two-man playoff. Strangely, however, Neil's prize of €82,000 is more than he will earn in the whole of the rest of the season and he fails to retain his hard-won Card.

2005

As First Stage venue numbers rise from five to six, Q School Tour Cards once again become harder to win as the European Tour administrators decide to cut the number of available Cards from those finishing 35th and ties to 30th. It sounds like a small change, but the careers of six or more players a year will suffer. Only 32 Cards are given away this year with Swedes Johan Edfors and Jarmo Sandelin among the standout names along with Tom Whitehouse (the winner) and Robert Rock who finishes 2nd. Meanwhile, total prize money across the three stages of the School increases again, this time to £183,000.

In terms of end-of-season near-misses, David Drysdale of Scotland could be a contender for the most heart-wrenching ever. After finishing a single place short of retaining his Card via the Order of Merit (he ended up 117th which was €586 short of 116th and safety), Drysdale then made it all the way through the six rounds of Final Stage only to miss out again, this time by a single shot.

2006

The story of this particular Q School is of two men at opposite ends of their career. The four-time US PGA winner and the only native American Indian on any golf Tour, Notah Begay (one of Tiger Woods' best friends at Stanford University), is a welcome addition to the European Tour along with 18-year-old amateur Oliver Fisher from England.

The two men both win Tour Cards amid dreadful conditions. Rain forces two days of cancellations at San Roque's Final Stage and the six-day tournament is eventually completed over eight days, an unwanted record for Q School. Spain's Carlos Rodiles and Alexandre Rocha of Brazil finish joint winners, but all those who survive the last day deluge of rain and an especially nerve-jangling 90-minute delay are good value for their Cards.

2007

This School is fully chronicled in Part One of this book, the overall winner this year is Austria's Martin Wiegele with names-for-the-future like Pablo Larrazabal and Paul Waring also achieving Tour Cards. The Final Stage tournament would be the last (for the moment, anyway) at San Roque.

2008

The record 969 players take part including Jesus Maria Arruti of Spain who was setting another mark – his 20th appearance at the School. A total of 42 different countries are represented while Scotland stages a Q School event for the first time at Dundonald in Ayrshire. Final Stage moves to PGA Catalunya in northern Spain with rounds played over the Red and Green courses (later known as Tour and Stadium). Sweden's Oskar Henningsson emerges as the winner while the likes of England's Danny Willett and Chris Wood also come through. Another noteworthy name plays in First Stage: Rory McIlroy, but the superstar-in-waiting finishes runner-up at the Dunhill Links Championship before his scheduled Second Stage appearance and his winnings from Scotland are enough to hoist him into the top 115 players on the Order of Merit, so his Q School journey ends prematurely.

2009

Another new country stages a First Stage tournament – Denmark – as the number of countries represented in the overall field of 915 players jumps to 48. The winner of Final Stage is Simon Khan who had not been to the School since 2001. The boost of winning this event is proven when he goes on to win the BMW PGA Championship at Wentworth just six months later. Also gaining a card is Stephen Gallagher who will make the Ryder Cup team in 2014.

2010

This is another year or firsts: Austria stages its inaugural Q School tournament while as many as 21 players out of the 34 Tour Card winners at Final Stage are Q School rookies. The overall winner, however, is journeyman Simon Wakefield of England who is joined by Scottish brothers Lloyd and Elliot Saltman, France's Victor Dubuisson (a Ryder Cupper within four seasons) and South African George Coetzee who will soon go on to be a multiple Tour winner. A record number of 21 rookies gain their Cards year.

2011

Winning Q School is one thing, but using it as a career springboard is another. South Africa's Branden Grace makes his fourth appearance at the School and gains his Card for only the second time, yet goes on to win four times in the next European Tour season and finish 6th in the Race To Dubai. Meanwhile, overall winner of Final Stage in Catalunya this year is David Dixon of England who has fellow countrymen Sam Hutsby, Andy Sullivan and Richard Bland filling the next three places. Unlike Grace, Dixon does not retain his card in 2012 and will once again return to the School.

2012

The number of Tour Cards is reduced to 25 plus ties from 30 as officials again put extra emphasis on the Challenge Tour. England's John Parry wins overall, but Scotland's Garry Orr is the star of Final Stage; he breaks two Q School records: firstly, he becomes the oldest ever Tour Card winner at 45 years and 202 days and, secondly, it is 20 years since his last Tour Card via the School. Among those missing the day four cut are American stars of the future Brooks Koepka and Peter Uihlein who resort to Challenge Tour to get Cards.

2013

A record four Americans are among the 27 Q School graduates this year: John Hahn, Connor Arendell, Brinson Paolini and Jason Knutson. Nine of those gaining Cards become rookies on next year's European Tour and one of those – Marco Crespi of Italy – will also go on to win an event in his maiden season on Tour, while Belgium's Thomas Pieters (tied 20th) will be a European Tour champion within two years. Among those missing out is former Ryder Cup player Oliver Wilson who finishes 35th and two shots out of the Tour Card places. Yet, as evidence of how strong the Q School competition has become over the years, Wilson is still good enough to win the prestigious Alfred Dunhill Links Championship the following season.

2014

A Q School full of the usual spectacular stories is won by Finland's Mikko Korhonen who leads 27 golfers (out of the 924 in total who originally entered) to Tour Cards for next season. But the first Finn to win Final Stage is not the best story at PGA Catalunya, that honour is reserved for American John Hahn who is returning to the School for the second time. Hahn, from Cincinnati, Ohio, shoots an incredible 58 on the fourth day after looking likely to miss the four-round cut. The 12-under-par record round took Hahn from tied 104th into the top 15, yet the vagaries of Q School did not finish there. The 25-year-old then stumbled over the last two rounds, first with a 78 on day five and then a 72 over his final 18, finishing tied 50th and missing his Card.

Meanwhile, Italy's Renato Paratore becomes the third youngest ever Q School graduate at 17 years and 341 days and the youngest since 1982, over 30 years ago when there were far more places available. Also successful is England's Matthew Fitzpatrick, the 2013 US Amateur champion, who drops outside the top 25 after 12 holes of his final round, but then proves his class with a series of birdies that leaves him in 11th place. Fellow countryman Tom Murray, son of former European Tour winner Andrew, wins a Card as well as Matt Ford of Kent. Ford had failed at all of his nine previous Q School attempts during the week and even applied for a job as a postal worker this year because he thought his time would never come, yet it does this year at the age of 36. He finishes 4th and goes on to dramatically retain his card at the very end of the 2015 season thanks to a thrilling last round in Hong Kong at the Tour's final event of the year. Those missing out at Final Stage in 2014 include previous Tour winners Peter Hedblom, Lee Slattery and Johan Edfors. Then there is France's Sebastian Gros who was sailing merrily towards his first ever Tour Card until bogeys at each of the last three holes including a three-footer on the 18th that lips out. He falls short by a single shot and breaks down in tears when he tries to explain his round to the Sky Sports cameras.

2015

This year, the statistics throughout the whole tournament were revealing: a total of 953 players took part and 43 of them went all the way from First

Stage to Final Stage where golfers from 26 countries vied for Tour Cards and 32 former European Tour champions lined up with their total of 58 titles.

There were no fanfares at Final Stage to mark the 40th anniversary of the School, but the dramas were still of the highest order. It began when two early leaders slumped: Italy's Filippo Bergamaschi barely made the cut and Lukas Nemecz of Austria shot a horrid 80 on day four but just sneaked in. On the positive side, Ryan Fox of New Zealand managed a 64 to play the last two rounds. After 72 holes, well-known names such as Nick Dougherty and Johan Edfors left for the airport along with recent Walker Cup stars Jimmy Mullen and Ashley Chesters, but perhaps the saddest story of the first four days was ex-Ryder Cupper Soren Hansen who dropped five shots in his final five holes to miss the cut. His €9 million of prize money in the bank meant nothing at the School.

Then on the sixth and last day, the stories came rolling in. Potential stars of the future like Ireland's Paul Dunne (who came through a six-man Second Stage playoff) and Marcus Kinhult of Sweden played steady rounds for their Cards. The Swede's support group of six family and friends promptly broke down in collective tears after his final putt.

Meanwhile, Stuart Manley of Wales burst through with a best round of the day 66 for tied 13th and 10 Englishmen were successful led by Ross McGowan who had shot the round of the week himself the day before, a 64 on the tough Stadium course. Another man in tears was Englishman Matthew Southgate, someone with enough normal-life troubles let along golfing ones at the School. He put his own testicular cancer survival and his niece's leukaemia behind him to finish 6th, and it was all he could do to speak during the post-round interview: "What's going on at home is very tough, but to be able to put a smile on my families face, you just can't buy that. I hope the next time I play here (at PGA Catalunya) is at the Ryder Cup, if they get it." A third Englishman Chris Hanson almost slipped up, but even a 78 wasn't too many – he received the very last Card.

But the disasters were many and varied. Experienced Irishman Damien McGrane slid inexorably to a 6 over last day score when par would have provided him with a Card for next year, but the worst meltdown was poor second-year pro Dimi Papadatos of Australia. The 24-year-old triple bogeyed the last hole to miss his first ever Card by a shot, a collapse that rivaled any from the past 40 years. But one man's despair is another man's joy because the Aussie's troubles took the mark for Tour Cards from 8 under down to 7 and that meant ex-Ryder Cupper Edoardo Molinari and early tournament leader Nemecz were suddenly inside the crucial top 25.

Aptly, the three joint winners at the 40th School included a 40-year-old – Ulrich Van Den Berg of South Africa. He shared the silver salver with Daniel Im of the USA and Spaniard Adrian Otaegui.

The Future of the European Tour Q School

In its 40 years of existence, the European Tour Q School has changed everything from its name to its final venue, from the number of entries to the number of Tour Cards handed out in the climactic Final Stage. And the man who is taking the School forward into its next decade believes there are more changes still to come.

Mike Stewart took over the job as Tournament Director in 2001 and is certainly thankful that one element of the School has not altered – it allows direct entry to the European Tour.

"It's healthy for the Tour and brilliant for the fans to see new players come bursting through from the School. One minute the player is battling away on some small regional events and then he catches fire at the School, makes the Tour and suddenly has won an event or enough cash to keep his Tour Card for a few seasons," says Mike.

Examples of that situation are many. In the 2014 Q School, 27 golfers won Tour Cards and 12 of them retained them while graduates like Matt Fitzpatrick, Anirban Lahiri and Rikard Karlberg actually won tournaments. That was the most success by Q Schoolers in a decade, but there have been plenty of other individual stories that have pleased Mike in the recent past: Nicolas Colsaerts going from 2008 Q Schooler to Ryder Cup winner four years later; Branden Grace winning four times after his Q School success in 2011; or Simon Khan winning the 2009 School and grabbing the prestigious PGA Championship at Wentworth just over six months later.

Mike wants this kind of progression for the pros on the fringes of the Tour, something that the PGA Tour in America has changed recently. The US Q School tournament (the first ever to be launched) still exists, but Tour Cards are now given to the Web.com Tour (the equivalent to Europe's Challenge Tour), not the main US PGA Tour where the superstars battle for millions of dollars.

"There are certainly no current plans to change our Q School to be like the US Tour, but I suppose it's impossible to predict too far into the future as the European Tour continues to evolve."

One reason for some kind of alteration is the growing ties between the European and Asian Tours. There is a possibility that the Schools of the two Tours will come together with perhaps a Grand Final that features the best of both Q School qualifiers. But such possibilities are conjecture as the fifth decade of the European version begins.

"At the moment," says Mike, "I can see our Q School growing in terms of players and even events." If the entries number more than 1,000 then the eight First Stage tournaments could easily become nine or more. Certainly the successful career starts made by young Americans like Brooks Koepka and Peter Uihlein via European Tour membership has brought over more of their fellow countrymen. And the number of Asian golfers at the School grows each year.

More tournaments and collaboration with the Asian Tour could take Final Stage to a new country, somewhere between both continents. However, that decision is not just about greater cooperation. "At the end of the day, we need good weather conditions, especially in November for the golfers aiming for a Tour Card," says Mike. "All the courses we operate – for First, Second and Final Stage – are as well set-up as they can be for the time of year and the number of preparation days that we're allowed. We're very happy with the system at the moment, but it never remains the same."

So there may be more golfers and tournaments and probably a changing number of Tour Cards in the next 10 years, but the European Tour wants something to always remain the same: Q School must be one of the toughest tests in golf.

Appendix

List of 40 Q School Winners 1976-2015

Year	Winner(s)	Venue(s)
1976	David A Russell	Foxhills & Walton Heath
1977	Sandy Lyle	Foxhills
1978	Stephen Evans & Glenn Ralph	Foxhills & Downshire
1979	Charles Cox & Keith Williams	Don Pedro & Quinta do Lago
1980	Paul Carrigill & Manuel Montes	Don Pedro & Quinta do Lago
1981	Gordon Brand Jr & Robin Mann	Don Pedro & Quinta do Lago
1982	Jose Rivero & Grant Turner	La Manga
1983	D Ray, A Oldcorn & F Regard	La Manga
1984	Robert Wrenn Jr	La Manga
1985	Jose Maria Olazabal	La Manga
1986	Wayne Smith	La Manga
1987	Mike Smith	La Manga
1988	Jesper Parnevik	La Manga
1989	Heinz-Peter Thul	La Manga
1990	David Silva	Le Grande Motte & Golf Massane
1991	Andrew Hare	Le Grande Motte & Golf Massane
1992	Retief Goosen	Le Grande Motte & Golf Massane

Year	Winner(s)	Venue(s)
1993	Brian Nelson	Le Grande Motte & Golf Massane
1994	David Carter	Golf Massane
1995	Steve Webster	San Roque & Guadalmina
1996	Niclas Fasth	San Roque & Sotogrande
1997	Chris Van der Velde	San Roque & Guadalmina
1998	Ross Drummond	San Roque & Sotogrande
1999	Alastair Forsyth	San Roque & Sotogrande
2000	Desmond Botes	San Roque & Sotogrande
2001	Johan Skold	San Roque & Sotogrande
2002	Per Nyman	Emporda & Golf Platja de Pals
2003	Richard McEvoy	Emporda & Golf Platja de Pals
2004	Peter Gustafsson	San Roque
2005	Tom Whitehouse	San Roque
2006	Carlos Rodiles & Alexandre Rocha	San Roque
2007	Martin Wiegele	San Roque
2008	Oscar Henningsson	PGA Catalunya
2009	Simon Khan	PGA Catalunya
2010	Simon Wakefield	PGA Catalunya
2011	David Dixon	PGA Catalunya
2012	John Parry	PGA Catalunya
2013	Carlos del Moral	PGA Catalunya
2014	Mikko Korhonen	PGA Catalunya
2015	U Van Den Berg, D Im & A Otaegui	PGA Catalunya

Acknowledgements

This book was around 10 years in the making and many, many people have played their part in bringing it to fruition, so right from the start, let me acknowledge all those of you who were interviewed by me, who passed on information or who helped me in any way since the days when this project was known as Golf On The Edge. I cannot list everyone, but this book is only possible because of you all - thank you.

In addition, very special thanks go to nine people: my very own Q School Class of 2007 (Sion Bebb, James Conteh, Phil Golding, Euan Little, Andy Raitt, Martyn Thompson and Guy Woodman) who were unfailingly honest and generous with their time and their thoughts; Chris Wood, now a splendid European Tour champion, who allowed me a unique inside look at his Q School journey; and finally Q School tournament directors John Paramor, Andy Stubbs and, particularly, Mike Stewart whose support and enthusiasm has been so special.

In addition, a few others have followed me (or pushed me forward!) during the last decade: everyone at the European Tour, especially the press department and Q School tournament staff; my buddies at Hampstead Golf Club; my agent Jonathan Hayden, photographer Richard Kendal and designer Bill Hazlegrove (all good friends); and, of course, my wife Kate – darling, this book exists because of you.

Lightning Source UK Ltd.
Milton Keynes UK
UKOW06f2026061215

264200UK00001B/9/P